Contents

Preface

Nepal's constitution drafting process (2008 to 2015) was meant to institutionalize a new political system that would adequately represent and recognize all sections of Nepali society, including those that have historically been excluded by the state. But this was not to be. Instead, powerful political parties manipulated the process and finally produced an exclusionary constitution. The Interim Constitution of 2007 had introduced a wide range of provisions for progressive transformation, including federalism, citizenship, inclusion and secularism. The drafters of the constitution watered down all of these provisions in 2015. As a result, the country stood psychologically divided on September 20, 2015, Nepal's constitution Promulgation Day. The people of Kathmandu and the hill and mountain regions were happy that the constitution had been promulgated and celebrated the day by lighting lamps. In contrast, the Madhesis and Tharus in the Terai region observed a Black Day to mourn the deaths of their community members who had been killed by the state security forces while protesting certain provisions of the constitution.

As a witness and close follower of constitutional politics, I decided to unveil the closed door disputes and political negotiations in a book. I have put in my best efforts to provide a comprehensive record of the entire process so that the members of the present generation and the next can learn about the flawed process followed by the Second

Constituent Assembly (CA) to draft Nepal's constitution. The book is a political analysis of key events, issues and peoples during the crucial period of constitutional writing. Those interested in learning about the political strategies employed to undermine the legitimate rights of marginalized communities, should have much to gain from this book.

This book narrates how even a constitution passed by almost 90 per cent of people's elected representatives can be full of flaws. It also demonstrates how mandates of popular movements to affect changes may result in dilution through manipulative and ambiguous constitutional phraseology.

Often, the fresh mandate of a political movement helps institutionalize the agendas of change. The promulgation of the constitution by the Second CA proves this. The First CA, although progressive in favour of marginalized communities, failed to draft a constitution. Dr Baburam Bhattarai's government, of which half the cabinet ministers were from the Madhesi parties, failed to meet the constitutionally stipulated deadline of 28 May 2012 to promulgate the constitution. Prime Minister Baburam Bhattarai made the announcement at midnight on a Sunday that the assembly's term had expired automatically. The Supreme Court had previously ordered that the term of the constituent assembly could not be further extended as had been done in the past. As time passed, the mandate of the movement seemed to fade and this ultimately worked against the interests of the marginalized communities. The process and content of the new constitution failed to protect the interests of marginalized communities, including Madhesis, Tharus, Muslims, Janajatis and women.

Had the constitution been framed through the recommendations of the First CA, Madhesis and Janajatis would have been granted equal rights to compensate for the long discrimination perpetuated by the ruling class against them. Rather, three years after the dissolution of the First CA, the new constitution was framed to protect the interests of the ruling community in Nepal.

The Nepali Congress (NC) and Communist Party of Nepal (Unified Marxist-Leninist) (CPN-UML) remained the key players of the game that was rigged to dissolve the First CA. They believed that they would perform well in elections for a Second CA, as the parties with a strong presence in the First CA (especially the Communist Party of Nepal-Maoist Centre and the Madhesi parties) would be blamed for failing to draft a constitution. The Maoist and Madhesi forces, who participated in the government during the First CA, were not successful in undertaking substantive development projects. Hence, the NC and CPN-UML chose a development agenda to fight against the newly-emerged political forces. Their prognosis proved to be somewhat accurate and they emerged as the first and the second largest parties in the Second CA. Even the royalist and pro-Hindu Kamal Thapa-led Rastriya Prajatantra Party-Nepal, which could not win a single seat under the first-past-the-post[1] voting system, won as many as two dozen seats under proportional representation. It was a kind of revival of the old political forces which were intent on perpetuating the interests of the ruling class.

During the Second CA, Madhesi forces boycotted the constitution-making process and took to the streets. Their main concern was that the major forces—NC, CPN-UML and CPN-MC—had violated the provisions of the Interim Constitution. Madhesi forces launched a movement against the major parties which backtracked from the progressive provisions of the Interim Constitution, especially Article 138 (3) which states, "The final settlement on the matters related to the restructuring of the State and the form of federal system of governance shall be as determined by the Constituent Assembly."

Federalism remains the most important issue in the constitution of Nepal. The major forces of the country want to undermine federalism because of their fear of losing their grip over the Nepali state. Moreover, the Nepalese bureaucracy, business communities, Army and media fear the loss of their existing dominant role in the State affairs once the country is organized under a federal structure.

Resistance to a federal structure that enables Madhesis and Janajatis to practice local autonomy has geopolitical aspects as well. Nepal is sandwiched between two giant neighbours—China in the north and India in the south—making geopolitical influence an important factor in the process of federalism. China believes that India would have greater influence over Nepal if the Madhes region remains strong in federal Nepal. With India making its strong presence in Madhes, China would not be able to neutralize Indian influence. On the other hand, India believes that it should not remain confined to the Madhes, but it should have its influence over all the regions of the country.

Nepal's new constitution has adopted certain regressive provisions relating to secularism, citizenship, inclusion and representation and federalism. This is clear backtracking from the progressive provisions of the Interim Constitution.

Compared to the secularism enshrined in the Interim Constitution, the new constitution dilutes the provisions of secularism under the pretext of upholding the Sanatan Dharma, an alternative name for the Hindu religion. As such, the constitution has actually upheld the idea of a Hindu State.

Likewise, the Interim Constitution had stipulated that citizenship would be given on the basis of the nationality of either the father or mother. But the new constitution has changed that. A child wanting to obtain citizenship by descent must prove that both his/her parents are Nepali citizens.

Article 138 of the Interim Constitution envisioned autonomous provinces but the new constitution gives more power to the centre than the provinces.

Another reason why the constitution proved regressive for marginalized communities was because CPN-MC Chair Pushpa Kamal Dahal, whose party had once launched an armed conflict for the equality and empowerment of marginalized communities, abandoned the cause and joined hands with the NC and the CPN-UML to sign the 16-Point Agreement of June 2015, in which the signatories agreed to 'fast-track' the constitution's promulgation. In addition, NC President Sushil Koirala and CPN-UML Chair K.P. Sharma Oli both represent the conservative factions of their parties. None of the Second-tier leaders of the NC and the CPN-UML could convince these old leaders of the significance of protecting the agendas of change that the marginalized communities championed.

I believe the root cause of the Madhes movement was the violation of the Interim Constitution by the major forces. While there were some concerns with the content, the movement was more against the arbitrary process used in the Second CA and the way Madhesis CA members were thrown out of the CA by force using marshals (security persons employed inside the Parliament).

Instead of attempting to understand the aspirations of the Madhesi people, the CPN-UML and the then-Prime Minister Oli perpetuated a campaign against Madhesi leaders. Madhesis are fighting for equality and dignity. They want an end to linguistic, cultural and other types of discriminations against them. In the Second CA, the behaviour of the major three parties infuriated the Madhesi and Janajati forces. They appealed to the speaker to suspend the proceedings to protect their interests. Strict adherence to due processes was critical to ensure that the constitution protected the interests of all citizens. The process that was adopted in the Second CA to promulgate the constitution was totally flawed.

There are major barriers to the constitution's implementation. For example, the election provisions in Articles 84 and 86 of the constitution are almost unimplementable. Contradictory language has been used to dilute the principle of proportional inclusion, which, unless amended, will impede the change agenda. It is widely acknowledged by election experts that it will be extremely difficult for the election commission to hold elections without suitable amendments.

The Madhesi forces stood against the use of ambiguous language in the constitution that could push the country into a constitutional crisis. Neither Kathmandu nor the ruling class understood the contribution and farsightedness of the people living in the Terai. Of late, they have started to realize this weakness in the constitution. Sooner or later, they will realize that the Madhesi forces were right in demanding the cancellation of the 16-Point roadmap to formulate the constitution through the fast-track process.

To sum up, this book deals mainly with three different aspects of the constitution: 1) conspiracies behind the constitution drafting process; 2) contradictory provisions in the preamble, and the provisions relating to citizenship, federalism, inclusion, judiciary and electoral system and 3) factors influencing the constitution such as human rights, Nepal–India relations and Madhes politics among others. The book also includes chapters on the January 23 Amendment to the constitution, which was not sufficient to address the demands of the agitating parties, and suggestions on the way out of the constitutional crisis in Nepal.

Dipendra Jha

[1] FPTP: first-past-the-post, is a basic system of simple majoritarian formulae of Parliamentary general elections whereas PR proportional representation systems focus on the inclusion of minority voices.

Introduction

A meeting of the Constituent Assembly (CA) held on September 14, 2015 endorsed 57 articles of the Revised Bill of the constitution within a few hours. In another few hours of discussion, the CA cleared 176 additional articles on September 15, 2015. On September 15, 2015,NC lawmaker Pradip Giri objected to this fast-track process and sought time to speak in the Parliament but Speaker Subas Chandra Nembang did not allow him to speak. If we count the total hours of discussion, we reach to the conclusion that the CA passed over 230 articles in less than twelve hours. I believe that it was not a democratic process but a case of forced acceptance and forced rejection. A carrot and stick approach was used to drop the amendment proposal. This was a breach of Article 70 of the Interim Constitution, which stated that all the articles and annexures are required to be discussed and endorsed by two-thirds of the CA members present in the assembly.

This raises a fundamental issue of the legitimacy of the constitution. Claude Klein and András Sajó argued that the process that does not follow pre-existing rules of procedure is called a creation *ex nihilo*. The constitution was crafted completely by a handful of leaders of the big three parties—the Nepali Congress, the CPN-UML and the CPN-MC behind closed doors in collusion with some political elites and technocrats and was presented in the CA for a ritual and forced endorsement. The United

States Institute of Peace (USIP) after doing research on twenty-five countries' constitution making processes wrote that 'Constitution making is a deliberative process, and especially when integrating the public participation model, needs to be given adequate time, it is a mistake to attempt to short-circuit this process.'

The Nepali state system has been designed in such a way that it automatically co-opts those who advocate changes and makes them part of the power centre when the ruling class realizes that such persons cannot change the system. The Nepali ruling class has a high accommodative capacity to co-opt rebellion in their system. The new generation came with the commitment to make changes; they however ultimately became part of the ruling elites. The best example of it was the CPN-MC leaders who fought a guerilla war for more than ten years to bring about revolutionary changes in the country but ultimately surrendered and became the new ruling elites earning a lot of money and becoming part of the power centre. The ruling elites know the tactics that 'incorporation, rather than exclusion is the best form of control' (White, 1996).

The 16-Point Agreement with the CPN-MC, NC and CPN-UML paved the way for them to adopt the fast track process of constitution-making. In the name of "fast track" process, legal and constitutional principles were violated i.e. the leaders (Madhesi and Tharu leaders in CPN-MC, CPN-UML and NC) were forced to abide by the party decision. They suspended some of the rules and procedures, curtailing the right of the people to have a voice on the content and fairness of the constitution. The protest in Terai districts continued and security forces were heavily mobilized in those districts to quell the protests. Even the Nepal Army was mobilized by misinterpreting the Local Administration Act. Finally, on September 20, when the constitution was declared, most of the Terai districts were suffering under curfew and prohibitory orders. More than fifty people were killed before and after the constitution promulgation in confrontation with the security forces when protesting against the constitution.

Such a situation was accepted as normal by the state and the people around it. There are other examples of such fatalism in Nepalese history. When there was a devastating earthquake, people suffered a lot, but they did not protest against the State because they were resigned to their fate. Dor Bahadur Bista wrote "Nepalis are fatalist by nature and believe more in fate and Karma." C.K. Lal often says that Nepal will remain in status quo for the next fifteen years meaning it will not witness any new cycle of conflict nor will it make any progressive change. R.R. Nelson called this situation one of it 'Low Level Equilibrium in which the situation remains at stable equilibrium level of per capita income, both rate of investment and saving are low.' Michel Foucault opines 'regimes of power often set a mechanism through which certain discourse comes to inscribe, describe and normalize social meaning and action'.

I was surprised to see the real face of the Nepali activists who were competing to take selfies with the Foreign Minister Kamal Thapa at the stairs of the Universal Periodic Review (UPR) hall in Geneva. And the reason? He opposed India, rejected Madhesi dissatisfaction with the constitution and justified the killing of Madhesis in Terai during the Madhes movement. I realized that there was no opposition to the power centre and ruling elites in Nepal because most activists who were supposed to oppose rights violations are actually from the same ethnic group as the state elites. At the stairs of the UPR hall, the Nepali human rights activists were in a hurry to take selfies with the DPM

Thapa who was accused of suppressing the democratic movement in 2006 by the Rayamajhi Commission. To understand this character of Nepal's civil society, Foucault's lens of linguistic politics is important as he claims that the language of dialogue in civil society is 'controlled, selected, organized and redistributed' by a handful of producers whose primary goal is to acquire power.

I realized that Nepali civil society champions the fight for democracy but when it comes to changing discriminatory structures they can be as conservative as the rulers and sometimes even more conservative. When it comes to sharing power with other communities, they have failed to display any liberal and democratic character. Our system is democratic but the ruling class is not. This is what we felt during the Madhes movement when people were killed on the street; even the moderate Khas-Arya people maintained silence at this crucial time. This is the problem with moderates and higher middle class opinion makers of the ruling community. Their public position on Madhes seems moderate but in reality they can be as conservative as the political leaders of their community. If inclusive democracy has to function in Nepal, the issues of social inclusion have to be addressed and the ruling class must be open to accommodating the aspirations of the marginalized communities.

This constitution is stained with blood. It does not matter how many amendments you carry out now; it will remain a controversial document. The parties are tackling the demands of Madhesi and Janajati forces for a constitutional amendment in a highly grudging manner. This will further fuel the sense of alienation and anger in Madhes. Madhesis are angry that the security agencies acted with such brute force to crush the Madhes movement. 80 per cent of the victims who were shot at by the police were hit by bullets above the knee, mostly in the chest and head, a blatant violation of national and international law. Major political parties of the country must understand that if they do not address the genuine demands of the moderate Madhesi forces, in the near future the time will come when they will have to negotiate with more radical forces such as C.K. Raut and his followers.

There can never be warm feelings towards this constitution among the larger sections of Madhesis, Tharus and other Janajatis as it was promulgated after brutally suppressing a democratic movement in the Madhes that resulted in death of scores of innocent Madhesis. So the legitimacy of the constitution will always be in doubt. A power deal to make someone the Prime Minister was the main reason why the political parties rushed to promulgate the constitution.

CPN-MC must rechampion the cause of marginalized communities in order to address their grievances. Although the leaders of the NC and the UML say that the constitution was endorsed by an overwhelming majority of 90 per cent of the CA members, the reality is that many lawmakers including those from the NC, CPN-MC and Madhesi parties have strong reservations regarding many of its provisions. Many of them were forced to vote for the constitution by the top political leaders. Not only that, the constitution violates promises made by the NC and the UML in their manifestos that they would guarantee autonomy and inclusion. A close comparison of NC and UML's election manifestos with the constitution reveals this.

This book provides a detailed analysis of issues that marginalized communities wanted to be addressed in the new constitution. These include provisions relating to state restructuring, political representation, affirmative action, citizenship, language and secularism.

As far as state restructuring is concerned, the ruling parties structured the provinces in a way that divided the Madhes in five parts, contrary to the desires of Madhesi and Janajati forces. Tharus' clusters were also split as their areas were mixed with the hill provinces.

On this issue we can learn a lot from India's experience. After independence, India created mainly language-based provinces but soon it also accommodated people's ethnic aspirations.

Nehru who was a proponent of unitary system accepted the Telugu demand for Andhra (1953) and this led to the formation of States Reorganization Commission. Indian scholar Shakti Sinha in his paper 'Federalism and Development Cooperation: An Indian Perspective' that he presented in Kathmandu at a workshop in November, 2016 stated:

> The stage was set for the creation of linguistic states, and later on grounds of ethnicity (tribal states of North East), accession to India (Sikkim), colonial history (Goa), and regional backwardness (Uttarakhand, Jharkhand, Chhattisgarh and the latest, Telengana). India which only had fewer than a dozen states (part A states) at independence now has 29 states and 7 federally run territories. The Indian State 'has proved to be fairly responsive to the demands for relatively autonomous Statehood. This massive rearrangement of the sub-national governance arrangements, far from adding to centripetal pressures actually ended up creating a robust federal union, since linguistic reorganization created 'cohesive cultural and political units...effectively cooperating through a broad spectrum of federal bodies.

As far as the citizenship issue is concerned, the new constitution denies women the right of transmitting Nepali nationality to their children. The issue of affirmative action was a central one for the marginalized communities but since the new constitution increased the clusters (groups) eligible for reservation (from seven in the Interim Constitution to fifteen in the new constitution) the new constitution will certainly fail to ensure affirmative action for the marginalized communities. Even the historically dominant groups have been allowed reservations. Reservation for all means reservation for none.

As far as representation in the Parliament is concerned, the new constitution reduced the percentage of PR representation from 58 per cent to 40 per cent. It also gives eight representatives to all the provinces in the upper house of the Parliament. As far as language issue is concerned, the marginalized communities wanted the dominant language of the province to be the language of the province, but the new constitution states that Nepali will remain the language of communication. The marginalized communities particularly the Madhesi forces wanted the central government to adopt a multilingual policy allowing other languages such as English and Hindi to be the official languages of the country but the constitution makes Nepali the sole official language. Janajatis have fought long for ensuring secularism and the constitution stipulates that the country would be secular but it also provides special protection to the Sanatan traditions. This means that the provision of secularism has been severely undermined. These are the core issues that this book addresses. I hope that the following chapters will clearly demonstrate how hard marginalized communities fought for their rights, and how their concerns were completely ignored in the Second CA, in which two major Parliamentary parties—the NC and the UML—had almost a two-third majority.

1

Understanding Nepal

More Than Just the Country of Mount Everest

In February 2014, I was in the United States of America to attend the International Visitors' Leadership Program (IVLP) when I met a social leader who had once visited Nepal and was planning another visit soon.

Curious, I asked him what he knew about Nepal. He responded that Nepal is a Himalayan country, well-known for Mount Everest and Gurkhas.

Not fully satisfied, I asked what else he knew about the country. He added that Nepal suffered from a decade-long civil war which led to the abolition of the monarchy and Nepal has newly become a republic.

His response is similar to many from outside Nepal, whom I have met on different occasions. They are familiar with a half-reality about the country. This is because the rulers of the country in the past promoted the identity of Gurkhas, Mount Everest and the Himalayas. The promotion of such a limited identity has led to a deep-rooted culture of discrimination and impunity.

Nepal is not merely the country of Mount Everest. It is not just a Himalayan country. There are many aspects of which the world is still unaware. It is also a country of lush, productive plains called the 'Madhes' or Terai (Tarai), which is home to approximately half of the country's population.

Nepal is a nation with multi-ethnic, multi-lingual, multi-religious and multi-cultural characteristics. Geographically, Nepal is divided into three basic regions: mountains (Himalayan), hills (middle land) and plains (Terai or Madhes). Unlike the mountain and hill regions, the Terai, a swathe of low-lying land situated in southern Nepal, is not well-known to visitors, tourists and the outside world.

It would not be wrong to say that even many Nepalis living in the hills and mountains have little knowledge about Terai and the people residing there. People in hill areas believe that people living in Terai are Indians, not Nepalis, simply because a majority do not speak the Nepali language, they do not wear Daura Suruwal and Dhaka Topi (male) and Phariya Cholo (female), which people having hill origin claim as their national dress, and Madhesi do not look like the people in the hills and mountains. In the streets of Kathmandu people of the hill areas use the derogatory terms such as 'Bhaiya', 'Dhoti', 'Marsiya' and 'Indian' when speaking to the street vendors from Terai. This discriminatory treatment by their own fellow citizens makes them feel like they are not Nepalis. "Like We Are Not Nepalis" was the common utterance of the interviewees when a team of Human Rights Watch was in the Terai monitoring protests while the police crackdown was under-way, killing three dozen people in the Madhes movement. The rights body later used the utterance as the title of its report on Protest and Police Crackdown in the Terai Region of Nepal, which was published in October 2015.

Around 50 per cent of Nepal's population reside in the Terai. This region has a predominance of three major groups: Janajati (indigenous communities with their own language and traditional culture not within the Hindu caste structure), also known as the Tharu people, Madhesis (plains-based communities with cultural, linguistic, and kinship ties with India), and Pahadis of various ethnic/caste groups (migrants from the hills).

The terms Madhesis and Pahadis have metamorphosed from geographical descriptors into stereotypical ethnic connotations. The residents of southern plain, whose population is around 35 per cent speak Maithili, Hindi, Bhojpuri and Awadhi. Traditionally, they have been using 'Hindi' as their lingua franca to communicate with speakers of other languages in Terai. the majority of speakers in Terai understand Hindi more than Nepali language.

Country of Deeprooted Discrimination

Nepal is a country with great caste and ethnic diversity. Despite diversity, one community (members of Pahadi (Hill-Origin) upper-castes) has ruled the Nepali state for centuries, creating a sense of alienation among various other groups, including those living in the Terai. Both Madhesis and Tharus have long faced discrimination from Nepali state authorities. Such discrimination is apparent from their lack of representation in the judiciary, army, and other public sectors. These communities have comparatively low access to education, healthcare, and other governmental benefits. In spite of a decade-long civil war from 1996 to 2006 waged by Maoists partly to wrest power from these traditionally dominant groups, political power in the capital, Kathmandu, continues in large part to be exercised by members of upper-caste hill Bahun-Chhetri.

The nationally dominant hill Bahun-Chhetri ethnic groups have historically marginalized Madhesi, Tharus, Janjatis, Dalits and Muslims. The more manageable geography of the Terai has resulted in it having comparatively better infrastructure than the hill and mountain regions. Even though there has been an inclusion quota implemented in order to create an inclusive state, these laws have failed to trickle down to the marginalized communities.

Government investment and development lag behind in the Terai. Notwithstanding this the region is essential to the life of the nation, as it is the only route for goods and people to and from India. When these trade routes are cut off, the whole country suffers.

The term "Madhesi" is often used to include all non-hill people who reside in the Terai such as Muslims, caste Hindus and indigenous groups. However, as identity politics increasingly dominates Nepal's political scene, some groups residing in the Terai are demanding to be seen as separate from the "Madhesis". As a broad grouping, the Madhesis have been discriminated against and marginalized by the Nepal State. For example, in the Terai, with the exception of one or two districts, all chief district officers, police superintendents, district judges, government lawyers, the heads of the land revenue offices and tax offices, local development officers are from the hill community.

Country with Reluctance to Change

Like the landlocked geographical structure of Nepal, the mindset of its people seems to be locked too. They can fight and die but cannot easily accept change. Consequently, political movements continue to take place generally every ten year or so. Despite these movements, structures and systems remain the same in practice.

People accept the status of poverty and development as something written in their fate and, as such, they are reluctant to change these realities. Instead, unskilled and partially educated people are migrating to Gulf countries to change their fate whereas the educated sons and daughters of top bureaucrats, politicians, judges, army officials, and media tycoons move to the United States and Europe. Their fathers and mothers remain in Nepal with old-fashioned ways of thinking and a deep commitment to keeping the old structure intact.

Country of Brain Drain

Brain drain is another problem hampering further development in the country. With the system remaining unchanged, there is frustration among youth who are compelled to leave the country due to lack of employment opportunities. Everyday, nearly 1,500 youths (18–35) leave the country for foreign employment, particularly in the Gulf countries. Remittances, which contribute around 30 per cent of total Nepal's Gross Domestic Product (GDP), are gained at the cost of approximately four dead bodies each day.

A Brief Political History of Nepal

Nepal has a strong legacy of a feudalistic polity and a system of governance that has marginalized a large portion of the population on the basis of socially constructed notions of caste, class, gender, ethnicity and geography. Till 2006, a feudal monarchy ruled over the country for more than 200 years, including some years of dictatorship by hereditary Rana Prime Ministers.

The first People's Movement of 1990 introduced a multiparty Parliamentary system of governance by overthrowing the absolutist partyless panchayat system. Ironically, the minority of high-ranking male Brahmins who remained dominant in all sectors of the state abused and misused the twelve years of representative democracy. The dominant political parties manipulated the elections with a motive to control the state systems. Massive corruption, lack of transparency, the rural-urban gap and inefficient implementation of Kathmandu-centric economic policy benefitted a thin-layer of middle-class elites that created frustration among the poor, landless, farmers, labourers and slum-dwellers.

First, the people's movement failed to transform discriminatory socio-economic structures as per the expectations of the people. The political struggles in the past did not produce the expected social and economic outcomes, partly because the political struggle remained far from a larger movement for social change.

The political elites inherited the hegemonic nature of the state created by the autocratic Rana and royal regimes as a long legacy of domination of the lower classes using various means of soft power as language and culture.

Incorporating the people's frustration with the emerging political hegemony, the Maoists party declared a 'People's War' on February 13, 1996, that lasted for more than ten years. The majority of the poor were persuaded by the Maoist slogans for social transformation and emancipation from the cycles of exploitation. In their language, it was called a radical change in a feudalistic system of governance and social structures.

In the western region, the Maoists' armed movement spread throughout the countryside and within a short period of time, they tapped into the landless, youth, Dalits, women, and ethnically and geographically excluded groups to fight against those who were regarded as feudal groups and exploiters. However, while a proximate cause of the armed conflict might have been an interest in acquiring political power, the foundation that legitimized the violence was primarily influenced by the scarcity of basic needs and identity crises.

A state of emergency was declared in the year 2000 and the unified command force led by the Royal Nepal Army was mobilized to crush the armed movement. The so-called democratic government used suppressive methods to deal with direct violence that took place in various parts of the country whilst ignoring violence that was generated by the system and structures. Following the royal massacre in 2001, the deceased King Birendra's brother Gyanendra acceded to the throne.

In October 2002, King Gyanendra dismissed the elected government led by Nepali Congress leader Sher Bahadur Deuba and grabbed executive power in violation of the 1990 constitution. With an illegitimate royal takeover, there began a continuous power struggle among three political forces: the King backed by the Royal Nepal Army, the political parties, and the Maoists. Killings and destruction by both Maoists and security forces were commonplace whereas neither the Royal Government nor the political parties initiated any fundamental structural change of the state and society.

Two attempts were made to resolve the conflict through negotiation and dialogue following a seven-month-long ceasefire in 2003 and another three-month-long ceasefire in 2005. However, these attempts were used by both sides as a strategic opportunity to prepare for another round of war. This pattern continued until 2005, when seven political parties called the Seven-Party Alliance (SPA) and the Maoists signed the 12-Point Agreement in New Delhi, India. This agreement is widely seen as the fundamental turning point in Nepalese politics as it boosted the People's Movement, and led to the end of royal regime in April 2006.

The International Crisis Group described this achievement, stating: "Gyanendra accepted popular sovereignty, reinstated the Parliament and invited the mainstream seven-party alliance to implement its roadmap including election of a constituent assembly to rewrite the constitution in line with the parties' five month old agreement with the Maoists". The SPA and the Maoists signed the Comprehensive Peace Agreement (CPA) on November 8, 2006, ending the ten-year armed conflict that claimed over 13,000 lives and led to thousands of displacements.

The CPA was signed with the objectives of ending historic structural discrimination, addressing root causes of the conflict, creating democratic space for all marginalized communities, restructuring State organs and reforming security sectors. In April 2008, the former rebels CPN-MC Maoists won the majority of seats in the constituent assembly election.

However, the post-conflict situation in Nepal remains fragile. Many underlying causes of the conflict have been ignored by the elites in charge of implementing the peace process who have remained steadfastly focused on power-sharing deals.

Reference

[1] "Like We Are Not Nepali—Human Rights Watch," 2015, 7 August 2016 <https://www.hrw.org/report/2015/10/16/we-are-not-nepali/protest-and-police-crackdown-terai-region-nepal>

[2] Rizal, Dhurba, *The Royal Semi-authoritarian Democracy of Bhutan*. Lexington Books, 2015.

[3] Panday, D.R., "Social Movement, Civil Society and Regime Change in Nepal," 2011. <https://nepalstudycenter.unm.edu/MissPdfFiles/Social%20Movement_Dec25_06ver3pdf.pdf>

2

Death of a Dream
End of the First Assembly

Journalist Prashant Jha has said in his book *Battles of the New Republic* that the dissolution of the First Constituent Assembly was the death of a dream as far as a federal, inclusive and republican constitution was concerned. I realize in hindsight that Madhesi civil society members, and I as a lawyer who has always championed the cause of marginalized communities, made a critical mistake in not making efforts to save the First CA. Had the First CA promulgated the constitution with the 11 Province Model, other provisions of the constitution regarding inclusion, proportional representation, citizenship and judiciary would have been far better.

I still recall May 26, 2012, a day before the dissolution of the First Constituent Assembly, when political parties were debating whether or not to extend the tenure of the CA further. Upon the invitation from the UDMF, we (myself, Tula Narayan, Vijay Kant Karna and some other Madhesi civil society members) gathered in the evening at Masala Cottage, Baneshwor to discuss the constitutional issue.

The three major political parties had agreed on the 11-Province federal structure. Madhesi leaders—Mahantha Thakur, Upendra Yadav and Bijay Kumar Gachhedar—had reached an understanding with the three major parties that they would allow them to move ahead with the constitution-making process, by adopting the 11-Province Model. At the same time, it was understood that the Madhesi leaders would express their reservations regarding the federal map.

In accordance with the understanding, the Madhesi leaders Mahantha Thakur and Bijay Kumar Gachhedar informed the press about their disagreement with the 11-Province Model. They also informed that they would not obstruct the major parties' decision to promulgate the constitution. The proposed 11-Province model divided Madhes into four provinces.

However, Madhesi leaders could not stick to the understanding they had made with the key political parties as protest against the 11-Province Model escalated in the country, particularly in the Madhes. The Madhesi demonstrators protested against the remarks of the Madhesi leaders, who had taken part in the inter-party dialogues which had come up with the 11-Province Model under the influence of the key parties. Some protestors even burnt effigies of key Madhesi leaders.

We, the civil society members met Sadbhavana Party Chairperson Rajendra Mahato, who had returned from Terai that day and joined the meeting. We opposed the 11-Province Model. And so did he when he met the leaders of the major political parties.

In the meeting with the UDMF leaders, we suggested that they either go in for the federal structure as per the State Restructuring Commission's report, which had proposed two provinces in Madhes or seek the dissolution of the CA given the condition that the major parties did not agree on two provinces in Madhes.

During the time of the Bhattarai-led government, an agreement was reached to introduce an inclusion bill in the Parliament within fifteen days. The bill was supposed to include the bulk entry of Madhesi youths into the Nepal Army. It also included a provision to guarantee citizenship by descent to the children of citizens by birth.

The then defense minister Sharad Singh Bhandari prepared a policy paper for the bulk entry of 3000 Madhesi youths into the Nepal Army and their pre-recruitment training throughout the Terai. Speaking about the policy at The Reporters' Club, he said: "Where there is discrimination, there is possibility of secession." Without presenting the main content, the media presented the policy in a different way. This statement dragged him into a controversy, and later CPN-UML and NC parties demanded his resignation.

Neither the UDMF nor his own party chairperson Bijay Kumar Bijay Gachhedar defended him.

At that time, we did not realize that they (the NC and CPN-UML) were trying to hatch a conspiracy to dissolve the First CA which had the majority of almost two-thirds of change-seeking political forces—the Maoists and the Madhesi parties. The NC and UML parties had conspired not to allow the First CA to work well and effectively.

Understanding for the Election of Second Assembly

At around 4 pm on March 14, 2013, Madhesi Janadhikar Forum-Democratic leader Jitendra Dev called me and asked:

"Has the Supreme Court given any verdict barring those without citizenship to be registered as voters?"

He also asked me to come to the International Convention Center (ICC) immediately thereon to discuss the issue. At the ICC, I saw top Madhesi leaders—Mahantha Thakur, Rajendra Mahato, Mahedra Ray Yadav and Hridayesh Tripathi—and the top leaders of the major parties.

On July 15, 2013, the Supreme Court (SC) issued a stay order directing "not to register names in the voter list of those without a citizenship card."

In my meeting with the leaders, I told them that they might not be able to reach an agreement if they did not try to settle the question by invoking the 'remove difficulty clause' of the Interim Constitution. I argued that the Supreme Court's orders would not prevent them from reaching an understanding because they were going to amend the constitution and the Supreme Court's job was just to interpret the constitution. The Supreme Court has been mandated to interpret the constitution and it is for the CA to determine the contents of the constitution.

The Supreme Court had rendered Section 11 of the Voters' Registration Act, 2007 defunct. This section had stated that the voters could register their names in the voters' list on the basis of their citizenship. It further provided that if they were unable to demonstrate citizenship, they could also register as voters by producing any of their identity cards.

I suggested to the leaders that they could revive the above section of the act, to resolve the problem. Then CPN-UML leader, K.P. Sharma Oli, came to the office of Jitendra Dev and furiously asked:

"What laws have you read? Tell me if an Act can become a part of the constitution?"

I replied:

"Yes sir, it is possible."

I told Oli that the constitution of the Kingdom of Nepal mentioned that the provisions relating to the constitution would be as per the Citizenship Act, 2020. He looked convinced by my argument. Then he told Mahantha Thakur to convince Bhim Rawal of these provisions, who was working on his laptop, but Rawal continued to oppose it.

In the meantime, Rajendra Mahato, who appeared to be in a furious mood, intervened, and asked Oli why other party leaders should convince Rawal. The UDMF leaders left the room angry, warning that the UDMF would not help the government to hold the CA elections.

As we were preparing to leave the hall, CPN-MC leader Barshaman Pun and Nepali Congress leader Minendra Rijal approached us to sympathize with our demands. Even Maoist leader Pun told us that he supported our demands.

Then, CPN-MC Chair Pushpa Kamal Dahal also said there was no harm in incorporating the provisions as demanded by the Madhesi parties. Dahal later convinced UML leader Jhalanath Khanal and then an understanding was reached to register voters even without the citizenship certificates.

Around 20 per cent population in Madhes is still without citizenship. These people have not been able to obtain their citizenship certificates for various reasons although they are genuine citizens. If they were disenfranchised, the Madhesi parties might suffer a humiliating defeat in the elections. This is the argument I used to convince them to employ the special provision for those without citizenship.

I also added that the elite voters of Madhes were with the NC and the CPN-UML while others were with the Madhesi parties. If the requirement of citizenship for registering voters was not removed, the Madhesi parties would lose votes. I also argued that the voters in last general election without citizenship made the President and the Prime Minister since the representatives in the CA representing people without citizenship certificate voted for the top posts. Hence, it would be wrong for them to deny people without citizenship certificates the right to vote. With these arguments, Madhesi parties were happy. They assured me that they would make no changes to whatever

I would draft for the special provision for those without citizenship to exercise their rights to vote. I made a draft, and advocate Surendra Mahato endorsed it.

Given below is the original text from the 11-point Agreement signed between UDMF and major political parties on March 14, 2013.

> *4. Voters' List*
>
> *4.2. For the purpose of the next election to the Constituent Assembly (CA), a special campaign will be launched in coordination with the Home Ministry, EC and other bodies to:*
>
> *a) update the voters' list based on the citizenship certificate and to provide citizenship certificates to the Nepali citizens who have the right to get it;*
>
> *b) to update the voters' list of those having their names missed despite the provision (a) as per the clause 11 of the Voter Registration Act, 2063 BS based on the voter's registration of the Act 2064 and thereafter.*
>
> *While doing so, the biometric voters' list will be prepared by the Election Commission based on the voters' roll for the 2008 CA elections.*
>
> *10. On Citizenship*
>
> *The children of Nepali citizens who have acquired citizenship by birth shall be provided certificates of Nepali citizenship by descent. As it is immediately necessary for the election purpose, such citizenship shall be provided by removing the difficulty in the constitution.*

Although the parties made an agreement that those, who did not have citizenship certificates, could vote in the election, there was very little time to make the people aware of the agreement. I suggested to the leaders to ask the Election Commission (EC) to publicize the information so that those who do not have their citizenship could register their names on the voters' list. The EC had previously advertised in the media outlets about the compulsory requirement of citizenship for the registration of voters' names in the voters list. It was just a day before the deadline of registration when the EC launched this advertisement.

After the constitution was amended through a Presidential Decree, the EC made changes in the Election Laws, which added bureaucratic hassles. As per the amended legal provisions, those without citizenship certificates who wanted to register their names in the voters list required recommendations from their village development committee or municipality offices. Local government bodies declined to make recommendations just to avoid risks. Consequently, only 50 to 60 people without their citizenship certificates were eligible to vote during the Second CA elections.

Second CA Election Campaign

I, along with Prashant Jha, visited most of the Terai districts during the Second CA elections. Ironically, we found that the voters and leaders thought that Parliamentary elections were being conducted. They were talking about water, roads, electricity and other development issues, not about finishing the job of drafting a new constitution.

Madhesi parties also failed to convince voters why it was important for them to vote for Madhesi parties. During the election, there was clear polarization among the voters of Pahadi Khas-Arya and others. The NC and UML had spread a rumour that the Madhesi and Maoist parties were promoting casteism and division of the country in the name of identity and empowerment of marginalized communities. As a result, Khas-Arya voted primarily for the NC and CPN-UML parties.

Leaders of Madhesi parties did not achieve anything for their own constituencies, even though they were in the government for almost four years. The Sadbhavana

Party split into two; the Madhesi Janadhikar Forum-Nepal Party divided itself thrice just for ministerships. Instead of demonstrating commitment toward the issues, they were mainly concerned about consolidating power. The mainstream media portrayed Madhesi leaders as indulging in alleged corruption at a time when the preparations for the Second CA elections were underway. This adversely affected the results of Madhesi parties in the Second CA elections.

It is not that the voters did not vote for Madhesi parties but that their votes were divided among five or six parties, including Madhesi parties as well as CPN-MC (Maoist Centre), CPN-UML and NC. Consequently, Nepali Congress and the CPN-UML won many seats. It was shocking for the Maoist and Madhesi parties to see the election results and these parties were reluctant to join the CA.

Preconditions to Join the Second CA

Two things were put forth as preconditions for joining the Second CA—formation of a Parliamentary committee to probe allegations in the CA, and a four-point agreement to accept the issues agreed upon during the First CA. As per the agreement, only the disagreed upon issues from the First CA would be discussed in the Second CA. The political parties agreed to send the issues to the constitution Drafting Committee and disputed issues to Baburam Bhattarai-led Political Dialogue and Consensus Committee (PDCC).

The NC and CPN-UML parties were busy from the beginning to promulgate the constitution. The massive earthquake that devastated Nepal in April 2015 changed everything. The NC, CPN-UML and the CPN-MC, which shifted its alliance, made a 16-Point Agreement that departed from what the parties had agreed upon earlier. It was a clear departure from all the previous agreements. The 16-Point deal was a challenge to the sovereignty of the CA because it said there would be 165 first-past-the-post seats and a fixed 45-member Upper House. The agreement referred to eight provinces without a description of their boundaries.

I was shocked to see the agreement that stated whatever was agreed upon in the First CA would not be a part of the Second CA. The thematic committee's report had recommended the CA to adopt the 14-Province Model. The judicial committee had also agreed to incorporate the provisions of a constitutional court, proportional inclusion in the judiciary, and the establishment of a Judicial Council both at the central and the provincial levels. Likewise, the Fundamental Rights Committee of the First CA had suggested limited clusters similar to the Interim Constitution for reservation. Many progressive agendas were agreed upon in the First CA. Some thematic committees had agreed to ensure cultural and economic rights of the marginalized community. Had the constitution been promulgated by the First CA, it could have been an excellent charter.

Reference

[1] http://nepalitimes.com/news.php?id=17209#.V-dQNFcZDdk

3

Petition in Supreme Court Against 16-Point Deal

16-Point Deal

On June 8, 2015, four major political parties—Nepali Congress, CPN-UML, the then CPN-MC Maoist and Madhesi Janadhikar Forum-Democratic—signed a 16-Point Deal, that stipulated that the names and boundaries of federal provinces would be decided after the promulgation of the constitution.

In fact, the 16-Point Deal was a trick to dilute federalism as ensured in Article 138 of the Interim Constitution, which was added as a result of the Madhes movement. I call this article the 'blood Article' since it was inserted in the Interim Constitution only after 57 Madhesis lost their lives protesting for federalism.

Article 138 (3) of the Interim Constitution states:

> The final settlement on the matters related to the restructuring of the State and the form of federal system of governance shall be as determined by the constituent assembly.

Unofficial Translation of the 16-Point Agreement Signed by the Leaders of the Four Parties on June 8, 2015

1. The Federal Democratic Republic of Nepal will have eight provinces based on five criteria of identity and four criteria of capability.
2. Two-thirds majority of provincial assemblies will be required to decide the boundaries of the provinces.
3. The Nepal Government will form a federal commission to recommend on demarcation of federal provinces. The commission will have a tenure of six months. The Legislature-Parliament will take a final decision on the demarcation with a two-thirds majority after the recommendation of the commission.

Parliament and Electoral System

4. There will be a bicameral Parliament comprising Federal legislature Parliament and the Upper House. Provincial Parliaments will be unicameral.
5. Mixed electoral system will be adopted for Parliamentary election. There will be 275 members in the Parliament. There will be 165 constituencies based on geography and population. A total of 165 lower house members will be elected through first-past-the-post (FPTP) system. The rest—110 will be elected through the proportional representation system.

6 The Upper House will have 45 members—40 of the members will be elected equally from each federal province. The remaining five will be nominated by the President on the recommendation of the council of ministers.

Forms of Government

7. To run the state affairs, a federal democratic republic multiparty Parliamentary system of governance will be adopted. The leader of the party having a clear majority or having support of other parties in the Parliament will become the executive Prime Minister.

8. There will be a constitutional President in Nepal. An electoral college of the federal legislature Parliament and provincial assemblies will elect the President.

   (The UCPN (Maoist) has its differences on the parliamentary system of governance and the constitutional President. Despite this, the party agrees to taking forward the constitution writing process.)

9. After the promulgation of the new Constitution, the election of the President, Vice President, Prime Minister, Speaker and Deputy Speaker will be held by the transformed Legislature-Parliament as per the Interim Constitution 2007.

10. Until the next election of the House of Representatives, the transformed Legislature-Parliament will hold the election of the Prime Minister, vote of confidence, no confidence motion and cabinet formation as per the Interim Constitution 2007. The impeachment of the President, vice President, Prime Minister, speaker, deputy speaker will be in accordance with the Interim Constitution 2007.

Judicial System

11. An independent, impartial and efficient judicial system will be formed as per the concept of independent judiciary.

12. The Supreme Court will be the court of record. It will be authorized to make final interpretation of the constitution.

13. A constitutional court will be formed in order to settle disputes on the jurisdictions between the provinces and the centre, between provinces, between provinces and local bodies, and election-related disputes of the house of representatives, National Assembly and provincial assemblies. The constitutional court shall have the final say on these issues. The court will be chaired by the Chief Justice of the Supreme Court and will comprise two senior-most judges, and two legal experts who are qualified for the post of Supreme Court justice. The tenure of the constitutional court will be 10 years from the promulgation of the new constitution.

14. The provision on the formation of the judicial council will be as determined by the Interim Constitution 2007.
15. The constitution writing process will be taken forward based on the spirit of this fundamental agreement on federalism, forms of government, electoral system, and judicial system.

Local Body Election

16. The election of local bodies will be held as soon as possible to strengthen the representation and participation of the people.

Sushil Koirala, Prime Minister and President Nepali Congress

K.P. Sharma Oli, Chairman, CPN-UML

Pushpa Kamal Dahal, Chairman, UCPN (Maoist)

Bijay Kumar Gachhedar, Chairman, Madhesi Janadhikar Forum-Democratic

The third point of the 16-Point Deal states that provincial boundaries will be endorsed by the transformed Parliament based on the the technical committee's report. It is clear that nowhere in the world does Parliament make new clauses for the constitution. Parliament just amends the constitution but it does not introduce articles of the constitution.

The constituent assembly had the sole authority to introduce new articles in the constitution related to federalism. Once the new constitution is promulgated, the CA would be automatically transformed into the Parliament. Accordingly, postponing the decision of federal boundaries in the post-constitution promulgation period for the Parliament was not legal.

Moreover, the 16-Point Deal also attempted to contradict most of the issues that had already been decided by the First CA, including forms of governance, the judicial system and the electoral system. These were later adopted by the Second CA through the Record and Study Committee.

Moving the Supreme Court against 16-Point Deal

Around a week had elapsed since the four parties agreed on promulgating the constitution through the 16-Point Deal. Rakesh Mishra, who had returned to Kathmandu from Biratnagar, and Tula Narayan Shah, one of my close friends, gathered for a social evening at Timor, a restaurant located at Summit Height.

During our talk, Tula Narayan argued that the 16-Point Agreement did not carry any political ideology. It was solely an alliance of Khas-Arya to continue their grip over state power. He illustrated his argument, stating that those backing the 16-Point Deal—CPN-MC Maoist leader Shakti Basnet, CPN-UML leaders Top Bahadur Raymajhi and Bhim Rawal, and NC leaders Bhishnu Paudel, Ramesh Lekhak and Minendra Rijal—belong to the the same social caste.

Then he asked: "Why wasn't Prabhu Shah from CPN-MC (Maoist) included in the Deal? Why wasn't Bimalendra Nidhi from NC consulted? Even though UML party does have Madhesi leaders, they were not consulted either."

That evening, Tula Narayan clearly interpreted the motive behind the 16-Point Deal. The Deal was not struck among the signatories of the major political parties, but among elite classes, mainly Bahun Chhetri of hills region.

To respond to Tula Narayan's analysis, I simply accepted his arguments. But Rakesh, who is the smartest among us, said:

"Dipendra, you're a lawyer. Can't the 16-Point Agreement be challenged at the Supreme Court?"

I responded affirmatively on the basis that the issue was constitutional.

It was 8 pm when we started drafting the petition. I suggested to Tula Narayan not to be a petitioner, but to rather have his wife Rita Shah take the matter to the Supreme Court. Rita had her own identity as a woman activist. I put her name and the name of Vijay Kant Karna as the petitioners. I also added the name of Rakshram Harijan, who has been assisting me in legal work at my law firm—Terai Justice Centre.

On June 12, 2015, we approached the Supreme Court with the writ petition against the 16-Point Political Deal. But the Court Registrar refused to register it, citing that it was a political issue and could not be challenged in the court.

Subsequently, I prepared another writ to challenge the rejection. The case was heard by the single bench of Justice Cholendra Shamsher Rana. Justice Rana asked me why I was challenging the Deal since it was not a constitutional issue, but a political understanding. To respond, I informed the Bench that the Baburam Bhattarai-led committee had accepted the 16-Point Agreement, and he had put his signature on that document. Then, I produced a copy of that Deal before Justice Rana. I had received the copy from NC leader Amresh Singh. Finally, Justice Rana ordered the writ petition to be registered.

The first hearing was scheduled on June 18, 2015. After I entered the court premises on the first hearing date, I was shocked and upset to find out that the writ petition was not on the cause list. That day I had gone to the court to plead with thirty reference books.

To my surprise, Assistant Registrar told me:

"We have lost your file."

I could not sense from his response what the motive was behind losing the file on the hearing day. That was the first time in my career that such an important file had been lost on the hearing day. It was disappointing, and I soon met with the Chief Justice to complain about it.

I later learned that after my complaint, the Chief Justice asked the assistant registrar about the loss (although I am not aware if he found the response reasonable). When I asked junior Supreme Court staff about the matter, I was informed that the file had been handed over to the assistant registrar. I questioned him on the loss and indicated that I expected the matter to be proceeded with the following day. Indeed, the file was miraculously found and I was to learn what a difference a day makes.

On the day the file was lost, the case was to be heard by Justice Gopal Parajuli's bench. The next day, it was scheduled for Justice Girish Chandra Lal's bench. My pleading contained the following text:

> The 16-Point Deal was the breach of the Interim Constitution Article 138 (a) and 182. The Parliament is authorized just for the amendment of the constitution Article; but not for introducing Articles in the constitution. The constitutional provisions clearly state that the name of federal boundaries shall be determined by the CA.

I was the sole pleader of the case. Some of my lawyer friends attended the hearing and I asked them to support my arguments.

Usually I study the mood of the bench while pleading. It helps me to be strategic with my arguments. When I started pleading, I observed the mood of Justice Lal, which made me expect a positive response. After attentively listening to my 30-minute argument, he started writing the order. I was told that the order would be passed after lunch break.

During the lunch hour at the Supreme Court canteen, a few senior lawyers stated they expected a stay order as the bench of Girish Chandra Lal always gives orders as per the constitutional line. Such an outcome was beyond my expectation. Rather, I expected merely a show cause notice and the scheduling of a hearing date for both sides to present arguments. The senior lawyers were right. A stay order was issued directing the CA to promulgate the constitution with the determination of federal boundaries and power sharing provisions between federal and provincial Parliaments as per Articles 138 and 82 of the Interim Constitution. The spirit of the order was that the new constitution without federalism could not be promulgated simply because neither the Parliament nor any commission after the constitution promulgation was authorized to determine the federal boundaries. The court upheld my argument that pursuant to the Interim Constitution, the CA had the sole authority to do so, and the Parliament could only amend the constitution.

With the Supreme Court's stay order from the bench of Justice Lal, a political tactic to postpone federalism was successfully foiled, and the new constitution promulgated on September 20, 2015 was a Federal Constitution.

The judgement by Justice Girish Chandra Lal is reproduced below:

Bench of Justice Girish Chandra Lal

An Order

Case: A writ of Certiorari and Mandamus

Vijay Kant Karna, a resident of Pokhariya ward no.1, recently staying in Kirtipur et al.........1 Applicant

Versus

The Office of Prime Minister and Council of Ministers Singhdurbar, et al.................1 Opponent

In this writ the bench after perusing the case file and hearing the arguments presented by applicants' lawyers advocate Dipendra Jha, Sunil Ranjan Singh, Dhirendra Kumar Shah, Raman Kumar Karna, Rajesh Ahiraj, Sunil Kumar Patel and Gaurisankar Mahato, orders the staff to present the case to the bench after the notices are legally served along with the copies of this case, to the defendants No 4,5,6,7 and after they furnish their written replies themselves or through the office of the Attorney General within 15 days from the day this order is issued on how they contest this case and why an order as demanded by the petitioners should not be issued.

Among the major demands of this writ are Parliament and electoral system, governance system, judicial system, citizenship and Madhesi Commission and the court will reach a conclusion after the defendants will submit their written replies on these issues and the court conducts a hearing on that.

As far as the issue of some political parties signing a 16-Point agreement in violation of the Interim Constitution is concerned, the preamble of the Interim Constitution states that the Interim Constitution, 2007, drafted on the basis of political consensus, is being promulgated to institutionalize the gains attained through revolution and movement till the time a new Constitution is not framed through the constituent assembly.

Article 1(1) of the Interim Constitution stipulates that this Constitution is the fundamental law of the land and Article 2 of the constitution states that it will be the duty of every individual to uphold this Constitution. This Constitution has provisioned that there will be Constituent Assembly, Legislature

Parliament, Executive, Judiciary and political parties and there can be no denying that the state and state established organs should abide by the constitutional law and prevalent laws.

As far as the federalism issues are concerned, Article 138 (1) of the Interim Constitution maintains that progressive reconstructing of the state shall be done with inclusive, democratic federal system of governance by doing away with centralised and unitary state so as to end discrimination based on class, caste, language, gender, culture, religion and region.

Article 138 (1a) stipulates Nepal will be restructured in a forward looking manner with inclusive, democratic and federal system of governance in order to end discrimination based on class, caste, language, gender, culture, religion and region by ending the centralised and unitary system. Sub-Article 1 (a) stipulates that recognizing the desire of the indigenous peoples and of the people of backward and other area including *Madhesi* people towards autonomous provinces Nepal shall be a federal democratic republican state. Provinces shall be autonomous and vested with full authority. The boundaries, number, names and structures, as well as full details of the lists of autonomous provinces and the center and allocation of means, resources and powers shall be determined by the constituent assembly.

Article 138 (2) stipulates that in order to restructure the state as stated in Articles 138 (1) and 138 (1a), there shall be constituted a high level commission to make suggestions on the restructuring of the State. The composition, function, duty, power and condition of service of such commission shall be as determined by the Government of Nepal.

Article 138 (3) of the Interim Constitution states, "The final settlement on the matters related to the restructuring of the State and the form of federal system of governance shall be as determined by the constituent assembly." When this thing is analysed in the context of Article 82 of the Interim Constitution since Article 82 of the Interim Constitution stipulates that the business of the constituent assembly shall end on the day of the commencement of the constitution passed by the constituent assembly, it is clear that the dissolution of the CA before it restructures the provinces in a forward-looking manner including settling of the issues such as delineation of the Pradeshes, fixing their number, names and structure will be against the constitutional provisions.

If attempts are made to frame the new Constitution by bypassing the existing Constitutional provisions, the new Constitution could be controversial, country's peace and order could be threatened and doubts about another conflict could be created.

In that case the state can suffer irreparable loss. Therefore the court issues an interim order till another order telling the defendants not to do anything against Articles 1, 82 and 138 of the Interim Constitution.

Justice Girish Chandra Lal
Signature
Date: June 19, 2015.

Consequences of the Supreme Court's Interim Order

One day after the issue of the stay order, I heard a lawyer in the Supreme Court canteen saying that everybody involved in the hearing was Madhesi: the petitioners, the justice, the Chief Justice, and the lawyer defending the case. The lawyer added that, in fact, Justice Lal had praised me just two weeks before the court decision for my higher education in the UK. It was clear to me that this lawyer was trying to prove a conflict of interest in the court decision. This categorization became a widespread rumour, and journalist Rishi Dhamala questioned me directly about it.

In response, I noted that Madhesis had never objected to any of the court orders issued by a Pahadi justice in response to Pahadi petitioners. However, if this was perceived as a problem, then the Supreme Court regulations could be changed such that a writ filed by a Madhesi should not heard by a Madhesi Justice and a Pahadi justice cannot hear a writ filed by a Pahadi petitioner.

In my view, the remarks of the lawyer and the journalist were racist, and I faced the consequences after the Supreme Court's interim order. I experienced a series of activities as a campaign to defame my character. Once, my signature was forged and placed in a statement of an armed outfit from Terai, stating that I was a legal advisor. The media debunked it. In another instance, the partners of THRD Alliance, a Terai-based human rights organization founded by me, were accused of corruption in the organization, and a jumbo team visited the office for inspection, which not only proved the allegation false but also resulted in praise of the organization's work. Then, a photoshopped image with the jacket of THRD Alliance carrying a gun was made public. It also turned out to be false.

These systematic attacks were attempts to weaken my efforts to help marginalized communities to fight the battle for justice. In the best interests of THRD Alliance, these personal attacks were one of the reasons I resigned from the organization to work solely as an independent lawyer.

The reaction to my constitutional challenge reminds me of journalist Kishor Nepal, who defined poverty as "the symptom of society in which anyone who wants to do something differently is attacked by others from the same society. That is why society remains the same, as no one dares to change."

Major Parties stands Against Supreme Court's Order

In response to the Supreme Court's interim order against the implementation of the 16-Point Agreement, the signatory parties held an urgent meeting at Baluwatar that same afternoon. NC Vice-President Ramchandra Paudel, CPN-UML Acting Chair Bam Dev Gautam, Chair of CPN-MC Pushpa Kamal Dahal and Chair of Madhesi Janadhikar Forum-Democratic (MJF-D) Bijay Kumar Gachhedar jointly issued a statement against the court order at around 4 pm on June 19, 2016.

The joint statement (translated into English) is summarized below:

At a time when the constitution drafting process is entering a crucial juncture as a result of long discussion and political agreement which has injected a feeling of exuberance and confidence among the public about promulgation of the constitution, the Supreme Court order passed by a single bench has drawn our serious attention. The SC's order stands against the sovereign right of the people to frame their Constitution through the CA, principle of separation of power and the prerogatives of the CA given by the Interim Constitution of Nepal, 2007. The CA is an independent and capable body as far as the making of the constitution is concerned, and its decision in this matter will be final. It is the sovereign right of the CA to decide what kind of Constitution it wants to make and when. Nobody can challenge this fact in any manner. We want to reiterate that we will continue with the constitution making process so as to complete the draft of the constitution and promulgate it in a short period.

संयुक्त वक्तव्य

लामो समयको छलफल र राजनीतिक सहमति पश्चात् संविधानसभाबाट संविधान निर्माणको कार्य संविधान मस्यौदाको अत्यन्त महत्वपूर्ण चरणमा प्रवेश गरिरहेको र यसबाट संविधान निर्माण हुने कुरामा जनतामा उत्साह र विश्वास बढिरहेको समयमा सर्वोच्च अदालतको एकल इजलाशबाट संविधान निर्माणको प्रक्रियाका बारेमा गरिएको आदेश प्रति हाम्रो गम्भीर रुपले ध्यान आकर्षित भएको छ। यो संविधानसभाबाट संविधान बनाउने जनताको सार्वभौम अधिकार, शक्ति पृथकिकरणको सिद्धान्त तथा नेपालको अन्तरिम संविधान, २०६३ मा व्यवस्थित संविधानसभाको विशेषाधिकार विपरीत छ। संविधान निर्माणको सम्बन्धमा संविधानसभा स्वतन्त्र र सक्षम छ तथा संविधानसभाको निर्णय नै अन्तिम हुने तथ्य स्वयं सिद्ध छ । कस्तो संविधान कसरी बनाउने भन्ने विषय संविधानसभाको सार्वभौम अधिकारको विषय हो । यो तथ्यलाई कसैले कुनै किसिमले चुनौति दिन मिल्दैन र सक्दैन । संविधान निर्माणको प्रक्रिया संविधानसभा स्वयंले निर्धारण गर्ने विषय हुंदा कहीं कतै प्रश्न उठाउन सकिन्न । संविधान निर्माणको सन्दर्भमा देशका प्रमुख राजनीतिक दलहरुले गरेको १६ बुँदे राजनीतिक सहमति अत्यन्त महत्वपूर्ण रहेको र सोही आधारमा संविधान निर्माणको प्रक्रिया निरन्तर अगाडि बढ्ने कुरामा प्रष्ट गर्दै सबैलाई हामी आश्वस्त गर्न चाहन्छौं । अतः विद्यमान राजनीतिक संक्रमणकाललाई यथाशीघ्र समाप्त गरी संविधान निर्माणको जारी प्रक्रियालाई निरन्तरता दिदै छोटो अवधिमा नै संविधान निर्माण गरी घोषणा गरिने कुरामा पुनः जोड दिन चाहन्छौं ।

रामचन्द्र पौडेल,उपसभापति, नेपाली कांग्रेस

वामदेव गौतम, का.वा.अध्यक्ष, नेकपा (एमाले)

पुष्पकमल दाहाल 'प्रचण्ड', अध्यक्ष, एनेकपा (माओवादी)

विजयकुमार गच्छदार, अध्यक्ष, मधेशी जनाधिकार फोरम (लोकतान्त्रिक)

The then-PM, and President of NC, Sushil Koirala, were to sign on the joint statement. I heard that the then Attorney General, Babauram Kunwar, strongly opposed PM Koirala's signature on the statement. As a result, NC Vice President Ramchandra Paudel signed instead.

The signatory parties defended the 16-Point Deal citing that they would not respect the Supreme Court order. This is the first time in the history of Nepal that the ruling parties made a public statement that they would defy the Supreme Court order, a statement that I believe, brought the rule of law and democratic system into question.

This statement triggered the third Madhes movement. Where the interim order boosted confidence among Madhesis that the judiciary was capable of dispensing justice to all—including Madhesis—the political statement proved that justice was not the goal of the elite politicians.

There was, however, some light in the political abyss. NC leader Bimalendra Nidhi had strongly opposed this statement signed by his senior party leader and he was very much critical about the 16-Point Deal as well. In his interview with Kantipur TV program 'Fireside', he strongly defended the Supreme Court order. This stand of NC leader Nidhi in defence of the stay order for federalism brought us together to work on constitutional issues until the new constitution was promulgated. Even after the promulgation of the constitution, he sought my technical support basically in the contents of the bills tabled by him in the Parliament for the amendment of the new constitution.

The Supreme Court's stay order finally ensured federalism in the constitution. With federalism remaining intact with the court's order, the country is today officially recognized as the Federal Democratic Republic of Nepal. This was a major breakthrough in my litigation career.

4

Conspiracy Behind 'Fast Track' Process

The motive behind adopting the fast track process of Constitution-making was a power deal among NC, CPN-UML and CPN-MC. They had mutually agreed on promulgating the constitution under the NC leadership, then handing over the Premiership to UML Chair KP Oli, the post of the President to Sushil Koirala and the post of Speaker and powerful ministries such as Home to CPN-MC (Maoist). This power Deal negatively affected the constitutional clauses, specifically in Part 33, Transitional Provisions. Let us look at some of the examples.

The constitution of Nepal 2015, Article 298 (2) states:

> *(2) The Prime Minister shall, on the basis of political understanding, be elected no later than seven days after the date of the commencement of the constitution where the Legislative-Parliament is not in recess at the time of commencement of this Constitution, and after the date on which the session is summoned in accordance with clause (6) of Article 296 commences where the Legislative-Parliament is in recess, and a Council of Ministers shall be formed under his or her chairpersonship.*

The above two articles, which smartly incorporated the strict deadline of selecting someone Prime Minister, clearly shows the greed for power and manipulation.

People in the Terai began expressing their dissatisfaction when the preliminary draft of the constitution was brought through a "fast track" process for suggestions and feedback in mid-August 2015. As per CA Rules, the lawmakers had to be given seven days' time to peruse the draft before any other proceedings could start on the draft of the constitution and Sadbhavana Party lawmaker Laxman Lal Karna raised this issue in the CA following which the CA amended the CA Regulation replacing the seven days' time to three days' time, meaning now lawmakers only had three days' time to give their feedback on the draft.

The fast track method was ostensibly adopted to respond to the post-earthquake period. Rule 93(3) of the constituent assembly Rules of Procedure 2014 stipulated that CA members would be given a week's time to study the first draft of the constitution. However, this clause was amended and decreased to three days. This timeframe was not sufficient for public feedback and suggestions. It was clearly in the breach of rule of law principles and democratic values.

When the Nepal Law Society invited me to share my observations on the first draft in a programme attended by approximately 100 CA members in Hotel Annapurna, almost 80 per cent of the total participant CA members complained that they did not have a copy of it, and that the time allocated for the feedback was very short. If a CA member was not provided with sufficient time to read the charter properly, one can draw the conclusion that the ruling parties wanted to promulgate the constitution as early as possible. The real reason for the haste, however, was for the ruling parties to distribute the power and resources of the reconstruction process.

On July 20, 2015 the two-day national campaign of collecting public feedback on draft constitution began across the country. Though the CA schedule mentioned that two weeks had been allocated for public consultation on the draft, the people were given only two days to give their feedback. Amnesty International said the two weeks' period of public consultation was not enough while the short duration set for compiling the public comments on the draft has further complicated the constitution writing process."[1]

In addition, the CPN-MC (Maoist) leaders were in a hurry to get immunity from war-era human rights abuses and corruption charges. CPN-UML having complete monopoly over human rights industries in Nepal proved to be a credible partner for the CPN-MC that could guarantee blanket amnesty. Seizing upon this reality, the CPN-MC shifted the pole from social justice to the ruling elites. The 16-Point Deal simply intended to postpone the federalism issue. The CPN-MC buried all agendas of change and equality that it had raised to rally the support of the marginalized community during its decade long guerrilla war.

Fortunately, as described above, the Supreme Court issued a stay order saying that postponing federalism in the new constitution was against Article 138 of the Interim Constitution, which I believe is a product of the Madhes movement.

Undeclared Whip

On September 9, 2015, United Democratic Madhesi Front (UDMF), an alliance of four key Madhes-centred political parties, questioned the legitimacy of the constitution-making process in the constituent assembly and boycotted the CA process. Although the ruling CPN-UML claims that the

1. http://kathmandupost.ekantipur.com/printedition/news/2015-07-22/allot-more-time-to-collect-feedbacks.html

2015 Constitution was endorsed by almost 90 per cent of the CA members, the punitive whip that the CPN-UML and the Nepali Congress imposed on their CA members, questioned the fairness of the constitution-making process.

It is relevant to remember Professor Krishna Prasad Khanal's views in this context. He said that the constitution can be sustainable only if the four political forces—NC, CPN-UML, CPN-MC-Maoist and UDMF—and three social groups—the Khas-Arya community, Adivasi Janajatis and the Madhesi community—agreed on major issues of the constitution. According to him, if any of these political forces or the social groups felt isolated from the constitution-making process, then the legitimacy of such a constitution will remain challenged.

Whips are normally not issued in the CA. The theory behind 'no whip in a CA' is the belief that a CA is different from a Parliament where decisions are made on the basis of majority votes. There is also a belief that every CA member carries the independent voice of the citizens whom they represent. A CA is also supposed to protect the interests of groups who have not sent representatives to the CA. These norms and obligations require a CA to frame the constitution by forging maximum consensus.

The leaders of the major political parties such as UML, NC and CPN-MC repeatedly told their party CA members not to go against the party lines or else they would face action.

Unlike the CPN-UML, the NC had allowed its CA members to register amendment proposals to the First draft of the constitution in the CA. However, the party eventually forced its CA members to withdraw their amendment proposals.

NC CA member Gagan Thapa, who had registered two amendment proposals—one along with other CA members of the NC and another separately—later stood up in the CA and said that he withdrew his proposals as per the party's decision. This was a clear breach of the CA norms as the party put pressure on its lawmakers to prevent them from raising the issues even though they were in the interests of the people.

CA members Arzu Rana Deuba and Mahalaxmi Upadhyay (Dina) of NC had registered a joint amendment proposal (Registration No 25) wherein they sought two amendments. First, that the word 'secularism' was sought to be replaced with the phrase 'religious freedom,' and second, that citizenship should be granted either in the father or mother's name. These two CA members also demanded that sons-in-law and daughters-in-law should be given equal legal status and proportional inclusion of women should be guaranteed in all state organs.

NC leader Prakash Sharan Mahat registered an amendment proposal seeking mention in the preamble of religious freedom and protection of traditional religion and cultural practices by the state. Mahat's proposal also demanded the mention of pluralist multiparty Parliamentary representative democracy in the preamble. Similar was the amendment proposal registered by CA members Ramesh Lekhak and Minendra Rijal of NC to mention pluralist multiparty Parliamentary representative democracy in the preamble.

CA members Gagan Thapa, Jivan Pariyar and some other leaders of NC registered another amendment proposal of the constitution (Registration Number 23) demanding to have proportional representation in all state bodies—federal, local, province level legislature and executive. They also demanded proportional inclusion of Dalits and other communities in all state organs including in public service commission jobs, judiciary, security agencies, constitutional appointments and ambassadors.

All these NC CA members subsequently withdrew the amendment proposals at the 'request' of the party leadership with the hope that these amendments would take place soon as per the promises made by their top leaders. This demonstrates the low level of democratic practices in the NC—the country's oldest democratic force.

CA members Lalbabu Raut and Shivajee Yadav of Federal Socialist Forum-Nepal, Akbal Ahmed Shah, and Bijay Kumar Singh of Terai Madhes Democratic Party and Narsingh Chaudhary of Sadbhavana Party also registered an amendment proposal demanding inclusion of secularism, Madhes movement in the preamble, and, in addition to Nepali, recognition of Hindi and English as official languages. It also demanded demarcation of first-past-the-post seats be on the basis of population, inclusion of 'or' provision in the citizenship clause, guarantee of proportional inclusion in state organs, and guarantee of state restructuring on the basis of the report of the former State Restructuring Commission.

Unified CPN-Maoist, which is now called CPN-Maoist Center registered a 13-page note of dissents demanding: 1) the addition of the word 'or' in the citizenship clause, 2) a directly elected President, 3) reappointment of the office bearers of all constitutional bodies including the judiciary, 4) the authority of transitional justice mechanisms to probe into the incidents of rights violation that occurred during the Maoist insurgency, 5) a federal court structure; and, 6) 35 FPTP seats reserved for women.

The majority rejected these amendment proposals.

During this same period, I met the then Speaker Subash Nembang and handed over my 40-Point suggestions for amendment to the constitution. In my meeting, I tried to convince him why these amendments were needed. He assured me that he would try to convince top leaders including then Prime Minister, K.P. Sharma Oli, to receive my amendment suggestions favourably. Yet, at the end of the day, none of them were incorporated into the constitution.

Even though feedback and suggestions were collected from the public, they were also not incorporated into the constitution. CA members registered amendment proposals all of which were ignored by those crafting the final constitutional document.

Had the public feedback and amendment proposals been accepted, the country would not have been forced into an impasse. Major political party leaders lost the opportunity because of the lust for power by a few technocrat lawyers and leaders.

A strong party whip and lack of independence of the CA members is one of the major factors behind accepting some of the conservative clauses of the constitution. NC leader Gagan Thapa, who is well known to be vocal and relatively rational with his argumentative skills, also failed to push for amendments this time. Consequently, the country incurred a huge economic loss, social polarization and backtracking from a progressive path. The undeclared whip resulted in the failure to accommodate the voices of the marginalized communities particularly Madhesis, indigenous nationalities, Dalits and women and gave rise to conflicts in the country.

The new constitution made by the people's representatives for the first time in Nepal's history had a chance to bring the marginalized communities on par with the rest of the communities especially the ruling hill elites but the statute failed to address the issue of social justice.

Madhesis protested for more than five months, blocking the Indian border entry points for three and a half months, to pressurize the government to meet their demands. Instead of addressing their demands, the government injected sentiments of ultra-nationalism among the people, portrayed the protests of Madhesis as an Indian-sponsored movement and accused India of interfering in domestic affairs.

The country's new constitution should have been a more progressive document than the Interim Constitution. But in reality, it has failed to ensure the rights that had already been ensured under the Interim Constitution. What agitating Madhesi parties demand is the retention of the provisions of the Interim Constitution as far as the issues of proportionate inclusion, delineation of electoral constituency and citizenship are concerned.

32-Points Suggestions for the Amendment

Immediately after promulgation of the constitution, I asked NC leader Amresh Singh to send me a copy of the official document. I reviewed the charter throughout that night and early in the morning I posted a list of 32 suggested amendments on my Facebook page.

A week after the constitution's promulgation, I travelled to Biratnagar. There I was surprised to hear a young Muslim leader arguing that this constitution is discriminatory because it cheated people in 32 different places. I listened to his argument at a local chowk in the city about the problems in the constitution while taking my name as the reference of the 32-Point note in his hand. According to the young leader, he had bought the note from a nearby photocopier shop for 20 rupees. I subsequently learned that more than 100,000 copies were circulated to help the people understand about the defects of the constitution.

Although I went to the shop to verify, I did not reveal my identity as the author of the note to either the young Muslim leader or the shopkeeper.

After ten days, Vijay Kant Karna, my friend who was a petitioner in the case against the 16-Point Deal at Supreme

Court and Laxman Lal Karna came to my office to see and discuss the list of 32 suggested amendments. After that meeting, four more points were added.

Later, an English translation of the 36-Points was circulated to the international community. The 36-Points were later reduced to 11 points by the agitating UDMF. One evening at around 8 pm, Hridayesh Tripathi, who was a member of the negotiating team for the UDMF, told me that he had a meeting with NC leader, Mahesh Acharya, who was a member of the negotiating team for the government. Mahesh had sought the document during the negotiation for the amendment.

The 11-Point demands of the United Democratic Madhesi Front (UDMF) were as follows:

1. There should be delineation of autonomous provinces, including two autonomous provinces in Terai/Madhes region from Mechi to Mahakali, based on historical background and identity in accordance with the Interim Constitution 2007 Article 138, 1 (a), past agreements with marginalized communities including Madhesi, Indigenous and Janjatis and reports prepared by the Committee on State Restructuring and Distribution of Powers formed through the First Constituent Assembly in 2008 and High Level State Commission on State Restructuring. The autonomous provinces with high power have to be guaranteed.
2. Under fundamental rights chapter, ensure a separate article with a clear provision of proportionate inclusion for the marginalized communities.
3. Guarantee proportionate inclusion in all the state organs, levels, agencies and service commissions in all state organs at all level, including federal and provincial structures as well as service commissions.

4. Determination of population-based constituencies for the election of House of Representatives and mixed electoral system as provisioned in the Interim Constitution. Formation of national assembly through single transferable electoral system from the votes of elected representatives of provincial assembly on the basis of population and compulsory representation from each province.
5. For the marital citizenship, there should be a clear provision in the constitution itself, not in federal law, and their representation in the constitutional bodies has to be either through nomination or as per the provision of the Interim Constitution.
6. Restructuring of judiciary in accordance with fundamental norms of the federal state, and appointments in the Supreme Court, high courts and local courts in accordance with proportionate inclusion. Appointments of judges in the high courts and local courts on the basis of provincial laws.
7. Execution of multilingual policies in all federal, provincial and local bodies.
8. Formation of Inclusion Commission with representatives from all the communities and all other commissions with their clear jurisdictions. Also, ensure the provision of representation from each province in the natural resources and financial commissions.
9. Formation of local bodies and special structures as per the provincial laws.
10. Democratization of the Nepal army, giving it a national shape, and guarantee of proportionate inclusion in all security agencies including Nepal army.
11. Nepal should be defined as a multi-national state and not as a monolithic national state.

Suggested Amendments to the constitution of Nepal, 2015

Preamble, Definition, Citizenship and Fundamental Rights:

1. Include the phrase 'Madhesh Andolan' or 'Madhesh Uprising' in the preamble.
2. Article 4: 'Secularism' is included in the definition of the state, but the explanatory note defines it as "the preservation of ancient religious culture, including religious and cultural freedom."
3. Article 11: Provision of citizenship through father 'OR' mother is mentioned, but in Articles 11(6) and 11(7) it does not accept the independent existence of women passing nationality to their children. It therefore renders women as Second-class citizens. The child of a Nepali woman married to a foreigner will only get 'naturalized' citizenship (as opposed to 'by descent'). In order to pass citizenship by descent, the father must be a Nepali citizen.
4. Article 289(1): The Article prevents the naturalized citizens from holding prominent positions like the President, Vice-President, Prime Minister, Deputy Prime Minister, Chief Justice, Speaker of the Lower House, Chairman of the Upper House, Chairman of the Province, Chief Minister of the Province, Speaker of the Provincial Parliament, and the security heads. This implies that foreign women married to Nepali men will not be able to hold these positions.
5. Article 289(2): Except for the aforementioned positions, in order for naturalized citizens to hold other Constitutional positions, they will have to have resided in Nepal for at least five years.
6. Article 38: Proportional inclusion of women has been ensured; same provision needs to be ensured for Madhesis, Dalits, Janjatis, Muslims and Tharus.
7. Article 40: Proportional inclusion of Dalits has been ensured; but in the Article pertaining to Dalits, it says the inclusion will be ensured according to 'existing laws' needs to be removed.

8. Article 42: On the question of social justice it says, "Participation in the state apparatus will be ensured on the basis of 'theory of inclusion'." The word 'proportional' has to be retained as in Article 21 of the Interim Constitution.

State Structure and the Devolution of State Power

9. Annex 4 Article 56(3) provides for seven federal provinces.; Under this, the whole of the Madhes is divided into six different provinces. Jhapa, Morang and Sunsari districts should be included in Province 2; seven Terai districts from Nawalparasi to Kailali should be included in the Tharuhat/Avadh Province.
10. Since Article 56(2) ensures a three-tiered state structure consisting of a Center, Provinces, and Local Units, the provision for Districts should be removed from Article 56(4).

Parliament, Electoral System, and the Government Structure

11. In Article 84(1)(a), the election constituencies for 165 members of lower house directly elected through First-past-the-post (FPTP) should be determined on the basis of voting population. Right now, it is determined on the basis of population and geography. Special provision could be adopted for remote districts like Manang, and the districts in Karnali.
12. In Article 84(1)(b), the provision for the Proportional Representation (PR) in the lower house should remain the same as provided under the Interim Constitution, Article 66(3) (b).
13. In Article 84(1)(b), under PR in the lower house, there's a provision for the representation of eight groups—Women, Dalits, Janajatis, Khasa-Aryas (Read: Bahun-Chhetris), Madhesis, Tharus, Muslims, and Underprivileged. The clause relating to the 'Khas-Arya' group and the corresponding explanatory note should be removed.
14. According to Article 86(2), of the 59 MPs to be elected through PR, there's a provision for eight MPs each from

the seven federal provinces it is commendable that at least three have to be women; at least one has to be a person living with disability; and at least one has to be Dalit. But it has to be revised in order to reflect the size of the population—it is recommended that there be at least ONE MP from each state, and the rest be proportional to the population in each province.

15. There is a provision of mixed electoral system for the federation (Center) and the Provinces, but not for the Local Units. (The provision for proportional representation should be retained at the local level also).
16. It has been decided that the Commission for the Determination of Electoral Constituencies will reassess the constituencies every twenty years. This has to be done every ten years. [Article 286(1)(2)]
17. It is a commendable, and a positive achievement, that the executive branch (cabinet) at the central level (Federation)—Article 76(9)—and the provincial level (Provinces)—Article 168(9)—will be formed on the basis of the theory of inclusion.
18. Under the current statute, there is no provision for the executive branch (cabinet) at the central level (Federation) (Article 82(2)), and the provincial level (Provinces) (Article 174(2) to be taken to the court in instances of the breach of their codes of conduct. This needs to be amended and there should be a provision for any breach of the codes of conduct to be taken to the civilian court(s).

Judiciary, Constitutional Commission

19. Part 11—Judiciary: Since this Constitution already determines the federal structure of the state having been delineated between the center (Federation), Provinces, and the Local Units, the phase "district courts" has to be removed, and replaced with "local courts".
20. There is no provision for inclusionary practice while nominating judges in the courts; this has to be amended ensuring an inclusive nomination of the judges. [Articles 129(1), 139(3)]

21. There is a provision that the determination of the number of judges, their appointment, recommendation for their promotions, and their transfers will be done on the basis of the 'existing federal laws'. The authority for the determination of the numbers, and appointment of judges should be carried out on the basis of provincial laws.
22. Since Provincial Court has been designated as the court of records (Article 139), it should also have the jurisdiction to review the cases and decide every case other than that pertaining to cases deserving life sentences.
23. The statute ensures separate Constitutional commissions for Women (Article 252), Dalits (Article 255), inclusion (Article 258), Janajatis (Article 261), Madhesis (Article 262), Tharus (Article 263), and Muslims (Article 264). It also adds that these commissions can be reviewed every ten years (Article 265). The provision for review should be omitted and these commissions should be made permanent.
24. Chief Minister from each province should also be included as a member of the National Security Council. [Article 266]
25. Article 267 guarantees admission of Women, Dalits, Marginalized Janajatis, Khas-Arya, Madhesis, Tharus, Muslims, and people from underpriviledged backgrounds in Nepal Army according to theory of equity and inclusion; but this fails to take into account the collective admission of Madhesis according to the spirit of 8-Point agreement between the UDMF and Nepal government.
26. It is commendable that the recruitment of all sections of the citizenry into the civil service will be based on the theory of proportional inclusion.
27. Article 283, which ensures inclusion in Constitutional bodies is commendable. It also ensures inclusion in nominations of ambassadors (Article 282); this is definitely positive.

5

Citizenship Politics in Nepal

Past Constitutional Provisions on Citizenship

The right to citizenship in Nepal has long been unequal and discriminatory. Nepal's third constitution, *The constitution of the Kingdom of Nepal 1958*, did not have citizenship provisions. Instead, the 1952 Citizenship Act defined a Nepali citizen as any of the following: one born in Nepal; one permanently settled in Nepal; one whose parents were born in Nepal; or, a woman married to a Nepali. This law allowed anyone who lived in Nepal for at least five years to acquire naturalized citizenship.

Citizenship was first enshrined in the constitution in 1962. These new provisions reflected the narrow nationalism that King Mahendra envisioned, and his resentment against a burgeoning democratic movement that was especially strong in the southern belt of Nepal, including Biratnagar, Janakpur, Rajbiraj and Jhapa. King Mahendra tried to suppress any democratic uprising by creating Constitutional and legal barriers to citizenship in the Terai.

Article 8(2)(d) of the 1962 Constitution required people who were not of 'Nepali origin' to spend twelve years in Nepal to qualify for naturalized citizenship, while those of 'Nepali origin' could get citizenship after only five years of residency. This provision left the term 'Nepali origin' unexplained for discretionary interpretation by the administrative executives. It is to be noted that speaking and writing in Nepali was a precondition under those legal provisions, which effectively discriminated against non-Nepali-speaking Madhesis. Many Madhesis and Tharus in the Terai, as well as other ethnic communities from the mountains and hills, faced difficulties in acquiring Nepali citizenship simply because they could not speak and write the Nepali language.

Although the 1962 Constitution recognized citizenship by birth, the provision was dropped the following year out of concern that 'a large number of Indians acquired Nepalese citizenship', which was perceived as a threat to the demographic composition and identity of the country. Rights activists criticized this provision for being against the spirit of national and international laws. It has particularly infringed the rights to equality, equal protection and protection against discrimination.

In 1995, a high-level Citizenship Committee formed under the chairmanship of the then Member of Parliament, Dhanpati Upadhyay estimated that 340, 000 people of Nepal were stateless or without citizenship certificates, and most of them were Madhesis. The committee put forth a number of recommendations for legal and procedural reforms.

Following the end of the decade-long Maoist insurgency and the signing of the Comprehensive Peace Accord, the 2006 Interim Constitution included a provision whereby all those who were born in Nepal before April 13, 1990 and who had domiciled in Nepal would be retroactively granted citizenship by birth. Citizenship under this provision was limited to a one-time opportunity, and persons above 16 years of age were eligible to apply for citizenship.

In 2008, a total of 170,042 persons acquired their citizenship certificates by birth. However, any of their offspring who were under 16 years of age remained deprived of citizenship, on the ground that their parents were not Nepali citizens at the time of their birth. Moreover, many people who were eligible to acquire citizenship by birth under this provision were ignorant of the limited period of time in which they could apply.

On January 8, 2012, Home Minister Bijay Kumar Gachchhadar instructed local administrations across the country to issue 'citizenship by descent' to those born before one of their parents had acquired Nepali nationality. However, this order was disobeyed by the Chief District Officer (CDO) of Jhapa, Geha Nath Bhandari.

This incident of disobedience by the CDO is evidence that it does not matter what position you hold, even after getting elected the hill elites do not allow you to extend assistance to marginalized communities such as the Madhesi and the Tharu. To maintain a position of power, you have to follow the orders of hill elites or be ready to be thrown out of power. Because the hill elites have only one implied policy which is being implemented strictly, "Ki ta hamra ki na ramra, (if not mine it is bad). In Nepal, you cannot be good by keeping views other than those of the hill elites.

New Constitutional Provisions

Discriminatory citizenship provisions in the country have a long history of patriarchal, discriminatory and hill-oriented constitutional provisions on citizenship. Section 10 of the 1952 Nepal Citizenship Act contained a bizarre provision stating that sons born in Tibet from a Nepali husband, who lives in Tibet, and a Tibetan wife were to be Nepali citizens, whereas daughters would be Tibetan nationals. Nothing substantial has changed since 1952 as far as patriarchal values are concerned. The same pattern continues today, and political parties have introduced even more regressive clauses into the new constitution.

The citizenship provisions under Part Two of the new constitution are regressive when compared with those of the Interim Constitution and its predecessor, the 1990 Constitution of the Kingdom of Nepal. For example, today citizenship by descent shall be conferred on the basis of either mother or father, as per the Interim Constitution. However, the provision of 'father or mother' has been written in such a language that it gives the sense of 'father *and* mother', meaning both parents must be Nepali citizens.

Likewise, Article 11(5) of the new constitution states that a child born to a Nepali mother inside Nepal and permanently domiciled in Nepal will get citizenship by descent even if the father is unknown. However, the citizenship of this person will be converted into naturalized citizenship under Federal Law if their father is found to be a foreign citizen. Naturalized citizens are not entitled to the full rights afforded to citizens by descent. For example, naturalized citizens are not eligible to hold various high level positions in public office. This provision was not found in the last six Constitutions of Nepal. This provision made women like Sita Devi Yadav, recently elected as treasurer of Nepali Congress, unqualified to be the Chief Ministeror the speaker of the province, the President or the Prime Minister. However, she was a signatory to this constitution making her a second-class citizen. Isn't it a strange citizenship provision in Nepal which is unlike anywhere else in the world?

Historically, there are three ways to confer citizenship across the world: blood, soil and marriage. However, conferring citizenship through blood (descent) has been combined with soil (birth) in Nepal, and naturalized citizens have been treated as second-class citizens, as per the constitutional provisions of citizenship. This will have a direct impact on matrimonial bonds and family ties of the Madhesi community across the Nepal–India border. These citizenship provisions are discriminatory from the perspective of gender, ethnicity and national origin. As per the new constitution, citizenship can be acquired only on grounds of descent and matrimonial naturalization, but not on grounds of birth which is against Article 7 of Child Rights Convention and Article 15 of Universal Declaration of Human Rights..

The Interim Constitution included a provision with the aim of granting naturalized citizenship to children of mixed marriages (where one of the parents is Nepali); however the Ministry of Home Affairs did not grant a single naturalized citizenship certificate in the five years following the Interim Constitution. In addition, acquiring naturalized citizenship requires overcoming many complex and time-consuming administrative hurdles, such as preparing and collecting many required documents. These conditions are particularly difficult for the marginalized and disadvantaged communities, as they are putting them at a higher risk of being stateless.

Administrative Hurdles for Madhesis

Madhesis, who are still perceived as migrants from India, face a host of challenges in acquiring Nepali citizenship. Madhesis comprise a diverse community of Hindus, Muslims, Dalits and indigenous people having different livelihood occupations and migratory and settlement history in the Terai region. Madhesis generally speak non-Nepali mother tongues, which is a problem since Nepali is considered the official national language. Since Madhesis are clearly distinguishable from Pahadi people by their complexion, surnames, dress and language, they face many procedural and administrative barriers in getting citizenship certificates.

Most of the Chief District Officers (CDOs) responsible for the distribution of citizenship certificates belong to the Pahadi community. Lack of diversity and inclusiveness in administrative bodies may lead to problems for Madhesis in obtaining citizenship, especially with the fear of being seen as Indians. Before 2007, it was mandatory for those men applying for citizenship to include a photo wearing a Dhaka-Topi (Nepali cap), and those who did not wear Dhaka Topi were not qualified as 'Nepalis' and denied citizenship.

It was, and still may be, difficult for illiterate Madhesis to have discussions about their certificates with the Nepali-speaking CDOs and administrative officers. In the absence of local knowledge and language, on some occasions the authorities misunderstood and mistreated citizenship applicants. This situation has also led to the rise of more middlemen in the local administration for mediation between local Madhesis and Government authorities, resulting in corruption in the citizenship process.

For many applicants, preparing all the documents necessary for their citizenship certificate is a challenge. Further delays in the citizenship-granting process are caused by police inquiries on applications. This has led to corrupt practices, as applicants may bribe police and authorities in order to get the work done more expediently.

Ultimately, due to burdensome administrative procedures, many rural, illiterate and poor Madhesis do not apply for the citizenship until they are required to submit a photocopy of their citizenship document particularly at the time of availing state opportunities, services or while seeking bank loans or securing admission of their children in schools and universities.

Judicial Hindrances

When one faces injustice or one's rights are violated, an independent judiciary is expected to provide a remedy. But what if one section of the community feels the judiciary is "biased"? This is the case with Madhesis after the Supreme Court delivered a number of verdicts related to citizenship. Madhesis feel that justice has been denied. UK's Lord Chief Justice Hewart had opined long ago that justice should not only be done, but should manifestly and undoubtedly be seen to be done.

For instance, in 1997, the government formed a Citizenship Monitoring and Work Evaluation Committee, which distributed a total of 34,090 citizenship certificates. The Supreme Court, however, declared that the distributed citizenship certificates were null and void, citing that the distribution process for those citizenship cards had violated the constitutional and legal provisions related to citizenship distribution in Nepal.[1] The Supreme Court did not deny that the recipients of those certificates should be entitled to citizenship, but instead found fault with the process of distribution and its legality.

Even after 2007, when Madhesis achieved representation in politics and power in the state, the judiciary remained in favour of the 'status quo' on citizenship matters. The Supreme Court's stay order against the government of Nepal, which directed the government not to implement the Home Ministry's circular to provide Nepali Citizenship Certificates to the children of all those who have received citizenship by birth, left those youths stateless. Later, the court vacated a stay order on the election provisions of Nepal, which blocked voters

1. *In Search of Justice*, updated version, 2013, p. 18, published by THRD Alliance.

without citizenship from registering their names on the voters' list.

In 2012, Advocate Shri Prasad Pandit and Advocate Pravinta Basti filed a writ petition in the Supreme Court seeking a stay order against a Home Ministry circular, which ordered District Administration Offices (DAOs) across the country to issue citizenship certificates to those born before one of their parents had acquired Nepali citizenship. The Home Ministry opposed the petition, even after the urging by me and advocate Sunil Ranjan Singh. So we filed a third party intervention, seeking the court's intervention to prevent statelessness amongst children who have been denied citizenship certificates, and thereby the fundamental rights including the right to equality, employment and property. On February 16, 2012, the Supreme Court issued an interim order granting a stay on the Home Ministry's decision and a stay notification was issued to the District Administration Offices. The judgment states that granting citizenship by descent to persons other than those defined in the Interim Constitution is not a matter of executive decision. But "Such things should be fixed by amending Article 8(2) of the Interim Constitution, which is under the jurisdiction of Parliament, and until the final decision is made such notifications shall not be carried out." The stay remained in effect for more than a year. The Home Ministry did not attempt to vacate the stay. The Supreme Court did not address the arbitrary deprivation of citizenship. The issue of the children of citizens by birth was later addressed by the political parties when they invoked removal of difficulties clause of the constitution to amend the constitution in 2013. As per this amendment, children of citizens by birth were granted citizenship of descent.

Media Projection and Hangover of Traditional Nationalism

When the major political forces—the CPN-MC, the Nepali Congress, the CPN-UML and the United Democratic Madhesi Front (UDMF)—were slowly working towards a deal in March, 2012, there were forces attempting to scuttle constitutional amendments on citizenship. They did not succeed because the UDMF took a hard but reasonable stance on the issue.

Two writ petitions were filed in the Supreme Court in 2013 against the government's decision to distribute citizenship as per the constitutional amendments. However, the court refused to issue a stay order. When this second attempt also failed, media outlets successfully spread a rumour that many Indians were acquiring citizenship in various Terai districts including Banke, Kapilvastu, Siraha and Parsa. The CDOs used this biased media campaign to complicate the citizenship distribution process by demanding additional documents from applicants.

As discussed, the 1962 Constitution and the Citizenship Act, 1964 did not define what the term "Nepali origin" meant. It was deliberately left to the officials responsible for distributing citizenship certificates in different districts to interpret the term. So the Nepali media tried to promote the traditional definition of "Nepali origin", which excluded many people of the Terai.

The constitution of the Kingdom of Nepal, 1990, was the first law of the land to substantially curtail the powers of the Shah monarchy. It did not, however, depart from the Shah monarchs' chauvinist approach. In the book *Constitutional Nationalism and Legal Exclusion in Nepal,* Mara Malagodi claims that this constitution incorporated even harsher provisions to discourage Madhesis from acquiring citizenship. The 1990 Constitution not only repealed the provision of citizenship by birth, but also made foreigners qualify for naturalization. Restrictive clauses such as "Nepali origin" and "ability to speak and write Nepali" were prerequisites for acquiring naturalized citizenship. The UN Resident and Humanitarian Coordinator Field Bulletin titled "Citizenship in Nepal: Historical evolution and the current situation in a typical Terai District, Banke", August, 2011, citing David N Geller, argued that there was a perception that people of "Nepali origin" are deemed to be "more or less 'Pahadi'. Madhesis are perceived as Indians".

It seems that while Kathmandu needs the fertile land of the Terai, its grains, fish, rivers, roads, forests and bricks, it does not want the people who live there! The new constitution carries this legacy of "hill male nationalism". This sentiment is amplified by mainstream media, which is still not prepared to ensure easy distribution of citizenship to Madhesis and women. So there is a long way to go to create an equitable Nepal from gender and ethnicity perspectives.

Do Citizenship Provisions in the constitution Affect Madhesis Alone?

The citizenship provisions affect all people, not merely Madhesis. Nepali women, for example, are significantly affected by the provisions. The state has not done enough to ensure equal rights for Nepali women. Such a reluctance on the part of the state is evident from the fact that citizenship provisions relating to women in the new constitution are discriminatory. The two following examples highlight this fact:

First, many Nepali women leave the country for foreign employment. If a child is born abroad to a Nepali mother as a result of rape, or if a child is born abroad to a Nepali mother and a foreigner father, the Nepali mother is forced to return and reside in Nepal along with the child in order to maintain her child's citizenship.

Clause 5 of Article 11 of the new constitution states that a child born to a Nepali mother inside Nepal and permanently domiciled in Nepal will get citizenship by descent even if the father is unknown.

But this clause is silent about the fate of Nepali mother's foreign-born child, whose father is unknown.

Similarly, children of a Nepali mother and foreign father could get citizenship by descent only when the husband of the Nepali woman is granted Nepali citizenship and they can provide proof that the child was born on Nepali soil. This may be impossible to prove in some cases in the Terai, where it is common for women to seek medical treatment services across the Nepal-India border during labour and delivery. In this case, a Nepali woman whose husband is a foreign national goes to border towns of India such as Barginiya, Bhithamod, Raxaul and Sunauli, to deliver her baby, then her child will be given naturalized citizenship. For this child to get citizenship by descent, it must be born in Nepal.

Secondly, many Nepali parents send their daughters abroad for their studies, including to the UK, USA, Canada and Germany. However if they get married there, they could be impacted again by the citizenship provisions.

Sub-Article 6 of Article 11 of the new constitution states that a foreigner woman married to a Nepali man can acquire naturalized citizenship in accordance with the Federal Law. However, children of Nepali women married to foreign men are only entitled to naturalized citizenship, and only if they have lived in Nepal and have not acquired citizenship of a foreign country. As previously mentioned, naturalized citizens are not entitled to all the rights to which the citizens by descent are entitled.

If their grandchildren wished to return to ancestral home to live with their grandparents, they would be eligible for the naturalized citizenship. Accordingly they would come back to become second-class citizens in this country. Consequently, their grandchildren might ask some day what sort of a discriminatory constitution have their grandparents promulgated. The State should not punish its daughters. The provisions for providing citizenship to the foreigner wife of a Nepali man, and the foreigner husband of a Nepali woman, are not equal. This clause is silent in the case of a foreign woman married to a Nepali man.

International Interests/Concerns

At the Universal Periodic Review (UPR) in Geneva in November 2015, the international community expressed its concerns over gender discrimination in the citizenship articles of Nepal's new constitution. Even the National Human Rights Commission, which is a constitutional body, commented in its speech to the UPR that citizenship provisions in the new constitution discriminated against women. The US Embassy in Nepal still has a message on Twitter saying the Nepali citizenship clauses favour men while discriminating against women. American Ambassador to Nepal Alaina B. Tepliz, in an article in the Kathmandu post, wrote:[1]

> In 27 countries, including Nepal, women do not have the same rights as men to confer nationality to their children. In Nepal, a provision in the constitution prevents Nepali women married to foreigners from transmitting citizenship to their children. This is unfair to women, and also creates the risk of Statelessness for their children. As the government prepares legislation to amend or replace the current

> citizenship law, we urge officials and legislators to ensure the law allows all Nepali parents to transmit citizenship to their children on an equal basis.

Similarly, Amnesty International wrote an 11-page open letter to Prime Minister K.P. Sharma Oli seeking urgent attention to a number of concerns regarding the new constitution, including citizenship Articles 11(3)&(5). In the UPR session, around thirty countries made similar arguments in favour of amending discriminatory citizenship provisions in Nepal's new constitution.

However, the ruling parties justify the discriminatory citizenship provisions by saying that strict citizenship provisions are needed to stem the influx of people from neighbouring countries, particularly from India with which Nepal shares an open border. Nepali media outlets have successfully spread fear in the hill areas that Indian immigrants are acquiring Nepali nationality.

The Way Forward

Citizenship provisions in the constitution should be flexible. A strong state mechanism could be created to implement and monitor those provisions.

A citizenship provision should include all Nepali citizens by granting them citizenship certificates and preventing foreign nationals from acquiring Nepali citizenship. For instance, citizenship by descent has to be conferred on the basis of either mother or father. Furthermore, gender equality within the citizenship laws must be addressed. Provisions that discriminate against women, such as the existing citizenship through marriage provisions, should be removed from the new constitution. In the case of non-resident Nepalese, identity cards could be provided to help them do business in Nepal and while ensuring easy access to their motherland.

In the end, the power of issuing citizenship should be vested in the state. The responsibility of distributing citizenship certificates should be removed from security agencies, and instead granted to local bodies such as municipalities or village development committees (VDCs). A permanent Citizenship Commission should be established at the central level to monitor, improve and control the citizenship functions of local agencies.

Many argue that there should be a robust system in Nepal to prevent forgery and abuse in the distribution of citizenship certificates. After revelations of fraud in obtaining Nepali citizenship, the government has become very strict in granting certificates. Introducing punitive measures to prevent abuses can keep citizenship fraud in check. Such a provision would disincentivize fraud and send a clear signal to wrongdoers. However, the paramount requirement in any amendment is that these laws and provisions should ensure the rights of children and guarantee their right to citizenship, and encourage genuine citizens to acquire citizenship.

Chinese Communist Revolutionary leaders Mao and Lenin believed in a global village and according to them, all struggle is basically class struggle, which should be borderless. I think Lenin would have been upset to see the Nepali version of his ideology as implemented by my country's communist leaders, who have maintained a rigid stance on the citizenship issue in Nepal. The CPN-UML, the second largest party in the Parliament mainly opposes citizenship on the basis of mother's nationality. It was the main party that introduced a clause in the new constitution that bars naturalized citizens and citizens by birth from becoming President, Prime Minister, speaker and chiefs of security agencies, among other Constitutional posts.

On June 1, 2016, I had the chance to talk to the Nepali Congress leader Sher Bahadur Deuba at his residence in Budhanilkantha after he was elected as the party President. The NC was a key opposition party in the coalition government led by the UML. Amendments of the constitutional provisions that discriminate against women was, among others, one of the proposals I discussed with NC President Deuba. His response was that the NC had no problem with amending the citizenship clauses as proposed. He claimed that it was the Madhesi leaders who were reluctant to provide citizenship rights to foreign sons-in-law.

This general impression held by the progressive hill community, that Madhesi parties are advocating equality in the constitution but are not open to give equal citizenship rights to their daughters, is not founded on facts and is quite contrary to the views of the Madhesi community. This impression is promoted by the UML and some of its leaders like Bhim Rawal, who believe that only pure Gorkhali first class hill-males should rule this country. Rawal's article in Kantipur, among others, disclosed the fact that the ambiguous, contradictory, confusing and discriminatory language which has been incorporated in the new constitution was deliberate and was done under his leadership. In one of his articles published in Kantipur, he defended his position that liberal citizenship provisions would create threats to national sovereignty in Nepal. This stance on the citizenship issue was backed by NC and CPN-MC (Maoist Center) lawmakers as well. The position of these leaders demonstrates an intention to discriminate against women and Madhesis while providing citizenship to themselves.

Major national political parties such as NC, the CPN-UML and Maoists view that an increased Madhes population would force them to increase election constituencies, which will ultimately limit their political space.

The constitutional articles have been written with the fearful psychology that a large number of Indians will cross the border, obtain citizenship and rule over the country. This ignores the reality that India, including the Indian States of Uttar Pradesh and Bihar, have made significant economic progress in recent years, and that few Indians would intend to relocate to Nepal. The data does not support the fear of migration from India increasing the population of the Madhesh. Rather, the data shows that the highest levels of migration were from Sikkim, Bhutan, West Bengal and Darjeeling to Jhapa and Kathmandu. The granting of citizenship to these migrants never came into the debate or the media because their origin within their countries is hill, and Nepali nationality is considered equal to hill origin.

In April 2013, the Forum for Women, Law and Development, published a study on the estimation of people without citizenship certificates in Nepal. The study showed that, as of July 16, 2011, 23.65% of the population aged 16 and above or 4,346,046 individuals lacked citizenship certificates.

On the one hand, the Nepal-India open border is identified by Hill people as a concern that unnecessarily heightens fears among the Pahadi (Hill) people that Indians acquire Nepali citizenship certificates. The NC, UML and Maoists see the increase of population in Terai as a threat to their existence and this is the only reason why they are adamant not to ensure representation by population. This is the only reason why they do not agree to create population based local bodies and population based first-past-the-post constituencies.

Pahadi people love to migrate from the hill regions to Terai but they like to keep more constituencies in hill areas. This is ironic and is giving rise to a sense of alienation among large sections of the population in Terai. Actually, the movement against the constitution was fuelled in Madhes by the highly regressive provisions in the first draft of the constitution which were later changed in the final draft. However, the provisions contained are I think too hard for any constitutional expert to give a clear and concise interpretation of the citizenship chapter. The reason they are so confusing is that the constitutional provisions on citizenship were completely drafted under a fearful psychology and through a hollow nationalist lens.

The 22-Point Agreement signed between the government of Nepal and the Madhesi Janadhikar Forum-Nepal on August 30, 2007, was intended to "end all aspects of discrimination against Madhesi" so as to create an environment for an inclusive Nepal where the mainstreaming of Madhesis could be truly reflected. It proposed to solve problems related to citizenship by redeploying the Citizenship Distribution Teams to the villages in order to create an easy and accessible distribution of the citizenship certificates. In recognition of the continued deprivation of citizenship and in furtherance of the government's obligations under the Comprehensive Peace Agreement, the August 30, 2007 Agreement and subsequent agreements, including the Four-Point Agreement signed on August 28, 2011, the Home Ministry drafted a circular to address the issue of the stateless children, specifically the denial of citizenship to already born children of parents who acquired citizenship by birth in 2007 and 2008.

However, Dr. Baburam Bhattarai's Government did not do much to enforce the Four-Point Agreement that had an important provision on citizenship as well. Past records show that whenever Madhesi parties joined the government, the citizenship issue remained an integral part of all the agreements but the deals they have made, are yet to be implemented in the true sense. Bureaucrats, lawyers, civil society and media, as the protectors of hill nationalism, do not allow Madhes-based parties to work on the issue of citizenship independently.

Reference

[1] http://kathmandupost.ekantipur.com/news/2016-03-29/womens-day-every-day.htm

6

Constitution

Preamble, Definition, Fundamental Rights and Directive Principles

Title of the constitution Itself Fails to Reflect Political Change

The latest constitution of Nepal passed by the Second Constituent Assembly that came into effect on 20 September 2015 is named 'The constitution of Nepal, 2015' which fails to reflect the political changes that have taken place in the country.

In the constitution's Preamble under Article 4(1), Nepal is officially defined as a Federal Democratic Republic. The text of Article 4(1) is as follows:

Nepal is an independent, indivisible, sovereign, secular, inclusive, democratic, socialism-oriented, federal democratic republican State.

The framers of the constitution, particularly those representing the Nepali Congress and the CPN-UML have never fully accepted the idea of Nepal as a federal state. This lack of commitment is evidenced by its omission in the title of the constitution. It is important to note that the term 'republican' is similarly missing from the constitution's title.

The title of the constitution of Nepal during the monarchy system was 'The Constitution of the Kingdom of Nepal, 1990'. Had the existing name been replaced with 'Constitution of the Federal Democratic Republic of Nepal', the people could have felt greater ownership of the constitution.

While a short name may be 'sweet' and easier, if it results in the loss of authenticity it cannot be justified. From my perspective, the dishonesty of the major political parties on the constitution starts right from the title of the constitution itself.

Term 'Committed to Socialism' is Confusing

Although the fifth paragraph of the preamble starts with the term "being committed to socialism...", the new constitution has failed to fully adopt the characteristics of liberal democracy and the characteristics of socialism in the true sense from the ideological perspective. The constitution has expressed customary commitments towards press freedom, independence of judiciary, human rights, and civil liberties, among others.

But, it is not clear if the drafters of the constitution are really committed to socialism. Or if the insertion of the term 'being committed to socialism' was intended to appease the public by suggesting that the goal of the people's war has been achieved given the constitution expresses a commitment to socialism. If the constitution of Nepal is meant to ensure commitment to socialism, then it is certainly not clear what kind of socialism it is committed to, as there was never any debate on the insertion of socialism in the constituent assembly and thus there is no record of the drafters' intentions.

The term socialism is not used in preamble alone. The term "socialism oriented" is also found in Article 4, which defines the state's characteristics. The preamble of the constitution is like a mixture of morning tea with evening alcohol, which results in the loss of its authentic flavor.

No Recognition of 'Madhes Movement' in Constitution

The preamble is a mirror of the constitution. The Second paragraph of the preamble accepted the glorification of various movements in the past such as the people's movements and the armed conflict. Surprisingly, the constitution does not acknowledge the Madhes movements that led to the inclusion of federalism, to the characteristics of the new Nepali State and the loss of Madhesi lives. The constitution has undermined the three big Madhes movements that took place in the country since 2007. This was a missed opportunity for the major parties to ensure broad-based ownership of the constitution by the Madhesi and Tharu people. Had the Madhes movement been recognized in the constitution, it could have increased the acceptance of the constitution in the Madhes.

Similarly, the preamble also rejects citizens' rights to self-determination. The constitution fails to recognize Nepal as a country of multiple-nationalities. Article 3 of the constitution states:

> All the Nepalese people, with multiethnic, multilingual, multireligious, multicultural characteristics and in geographical diversities, and having common aspirations and being united by a bond of allegiance to national independence, territorial integrity, national interest and prosperity of Nepal, collectively constitute the nation.

The above article of the constitution negates the concept of multiple nationalities. We have heard UML leaders say that recognition of multiple nationalities in the constitution could become grounds for secession in the future. The UML had discussed this issue in its party gathering in Chitwan in 2015 opposing the idea of multinationalism.

Although Madhesi and Janajati parties had demanded more than one language of official communication the major parties negated their demands. A schedule of languages was therefore not incorporated in the constitution. Rather the constitution adopts one language policy at the centre. Major parties agreed to mention in the constitution that the Language Commission would give its report about how to promote languages of the country within a year. This period has been increased to five years.

Likewise, Article 7 (1) states that "Nepali language in Devnagari script shall be the official language of Nepal. The provinces can determine other languages in addition to Nepali as State language."

There are mainly three major nationalities in Nepal: Khas-Arya, Janajatis (indigenous nationalities) and Madhesi-Tharu. NC leader Pradeep Giri often acknowledges the composition of multiple-nationalities. There are also other sub-categories but basically, each of the three large groups has its own culture, language, history and psychology. Nepal is not a country of one nationality. However, the last line of Article 3 of the new constitution attempts to obscure this reality.

In fact, there is nothing to fear about multinationalism within a single country. Many modern countries have used this term in their constitutions to accommodate diversity and provide a strong tool to maintain national integrity, including Pakistan, United Kingdom, United States, Nigeria, Turkey, Bosnia and Herzegovina, Montenegro, Brazil, Russia, India, South Africa, Ethiopia, Madagascar, Spain, Canada, and China. Likewise, in India, most states are based on linguistic identity including Tamil Nadu (Tamil), Andhra Pradesh (Telugu), Odisha (Odia), West Bengal

(Bengali), Maharashtra (Marathi), Punjab (Punjabi), Haryana (Haryanvi), and Kerala (Malayalam).

Some of the Northeastern states of India including Nagaland and Mizoram are based on ethnic federalism.

But Nepali leaders involved in the constitution writing failed to see this term from a liberal perspective, and this is in direct opposition to Madhesi and Janajati forces, including the Terai Madhes Democratic Party (TMDP) and Federal Socialist Forum, Nepal, which strongly defend Nepal as a country of multiple nationalities.

The constitution attempts to impose one dominating nationality upon others rather than accepting the country as a country of different nationalities. The countries, which recognize multiple nationalities in their constitutions, have less chances of division when compared to those countries identifying one nationality. Our constitution drafters lacked farsightedness. They failed to understand the recent trends of multi-nationalities. Various human rights treaties to which Nepal is a signatory have also acknowledged multinationalism in a single country.

Consequently, the failure to acknowledge the Madhes movements in the preamble and substantive articles of the constitution has led to disappointment among a large section of the country's population in Madhes. The 'Madhes movement' carries a big psychological message for the Madhesi people. Amendments to the constitution without mentioning 'Madhes movement' undermines the values and sacrifices that the Madhesis made during the movements. This omission has caused Madhesi leaders and youth to feel humiliated and disrespected.

7
Federalism in Nepal

When the elections to the First Constituent Assembly were held in 2008, there was no dispute among the political parties about the change agenda to end the centralized and unitary structure of the state. However, disputes on federalism, particularly on the federal boundaries, emerged almost immediately following the First CA elections. In the making of the constitution, disputes among political parties over the number and boundaries of federal provinces created major hurdles. This led to dissolution of the First Constituent Assembly, and delayed the mandate to promulgate the constitution in time.

During the Second CA, federalism within a Seven-Province structure passed by an almost 90 per cent majority, and was outlined in the constitution of Nepal promulgated on September 20, 2015. The Seven-Province federal structure was ultimately agreed upon following the rejection of approximately half a dozen different federal models that had been proposed during the First and Second Constituent Assemblies, but which failed to reach a broad consensus among the political parties.

At the time of writing, Madhes-based parties, largely representing the Madhesi and Tharu communities across the Terai region, remain opposed to the current federal set-up.

Origin of Federalism in Nepal

The political agenda of federalism in Nepal dates back to 1950s when the Terai Congress, a regional party, advocated the creation of a Terai Autonomous Region in a federal set-up. However, it was not until the restoration of democracy in 1990 when federalism came to the forefront of the political agenda.

Following the 1990 People's Movement I, three political parties out of the forty-four registered with the Election Commission mentioned federalism in their manifestos as part of their political agenda: Nepal Rastriya Jana Party, Sadbhavana Party and Nepal Rastriya Janamukti Morcha. However, each of these parties had different bases for advocating federalism. The Nepal Rastriya Jana Party was in favour of federalism based on ethnicity, while the Sadbhavana Party wanted an autonomous Terai region. Nepal Rastriya Janamukti Morcha, on the other hand, wanted administrative federalism.

Before the launch of the Maoist Insurgency on February 4, 1996, Baburam Bhattarai of the United People's Front Nepal, which was the predecessor of the CPN-Maoist party [now CPN-Maoist (Centre)], submitted the party's 40-Point demand to the government led by Sher Bahadur Deuba. Although federalism was not specifically mentioned in the 40-Point demand, some issues, including self-governance for regions with ethnic dominance and equality for all languages in Nepal, and regional autonomy for backward areas to end discrimination between the hills and the Terai, indicated federalism.

During the decade-long Maoist insurgency, Maoist leaders continued raising the issue of federalism. In April 2003, when the former Maoists entered into negotiations with the government for the second time, it had proposed that the essence of the new constitution should be to guarantee ethnic and regional autonomy for suppressed caste/ethnic groups, Madhesis and ignored regions, with the right to self-determination (Sharma & Pokhrel, 2004: 158).

Interestingly, the Comprehensive Peace Accord signed between Maoists and the government on November 21, and other related deals to end the centralized and unitary structure of the state, did not spell out the term 'federalism',and the reason for excluding the term 'federalism' is yet unknown. What is clear is that one of key proponents of federalism, the Sadbhavana Party led by Anandi Devi, which was a member of the Seven-Party Alliance for some reason, failed to incorporate federalism in the Interim Constitution of Nepal, 2007. Within a week, some activists of Madhesi Janadhikar Forum-Nepal led by Upendra Yadav burnt a copy of the Interim Constitution in Kathmandu. The arrest of the MJFN members triggered widespread protests across the region. After three weeks of the movement, political parties were forced to amend the Interim Constitution to insert federalism. This was one of the major demands of the Madhesh Movement.

In April 2007, the Interim Constitution was duly amended for the First time to ensure federalism in the country. Below are the inserted provisions relating to federalism:

> Article 138 (1A)
>
> Nepal will be restructured in a forward looking manner with inclusive, democratic and federal system of governance in order to end discrimination based on class, caste, language, gender, culture, religion and region by ending the centralised and unitary system.
>
> Sub-Article 1
>
> Recognizing the desire of the indigenous peoples and of the people of backward and other areas including Madhesi

> people towards autonomous provinces Nepal shall be a federal democratic republican State. Provinces shall be autonomous and vested with full authority. The boundaries, number, names and structures, as well as full details of the lists of autonomous provinces and the centre and allocation of means, resources and powers shall be determined by the constituent assembly.
>
> Article 138 (2)
>
> In order to restructure the state as States in Article 138 (1) and 138 (1a), there shall be constituted a high level commission to make suggestions on the restructuring of the state. The composition, function, duty, power and condition of service of such commission shall be as determined by the government of Nepal.
>
> Article 138 (3)
>
> The final settlement on the matters" related to the restructuring of the state and the form of federal system of governance shall be as determined by the constituent assembly.

As evidenced by these provisions, the Interim Constitution did not require or define a specific federal structure, rather it gave the First Constituent Assembly (CA) the mandate to define it. The first meeting of the First CA held on May 28, 2008, officially declared Nepal as the Federal Democratic Republic of Nepal.

With federalism enshrined in the Interim Constitution, almost all political parties, including the NC and CPN-UML, expressly endorsed various forms of federalism as the common agenda. Even fringe parties with only one or two representatives in the CA adopted federalism as part of their political agenda. Only the Rastriya Jana Morcha, led by Chitra Bahadur KC in the CA, expressly opposed federalism. This party, with only four members in the CA, argued federalism was a system rejected worldwide and was not appropriate for a small and underdeveloped country like Nepal.

Rejection of Federal Models

Before the current Seven-Province federal model was incorporated in the constitution of Nepal 2015, disputes among political parties over the number and boundaries of federal provinces led to the rejection of four different federal models. These models are set out below.

14-Province Model

The State Restructuring and Devolution of State Power Committee of the First CA, in its report published on January 20, 2010, recommended carving out 14 provinces. The NC and the CPN-UML rejected this model as it recommended too many provinces. Instead, these two parties strongly demanded the formation of the state Restructuring Commission (SRC), as provisioned in the Interim Constitution.

The United Democratic Madhesi Front (UDMF), however, stood against the formation of the SRC, arguing that the SRC should have been formed before the CA thematic committee started its work.

11-Province Model Diffused

On November 22, 2011, the NC, CPN-UML, the CPN-MC and the UDMF forged a consensus to form the SRC. Initially, there were eight members: Sabitri Gurung, Ramesh Dhungel, Bhogendra Jha, Sarbajit Khadka, Krishna Hachhethu, Malla K Sundar, Stella Tamang and Surendra Mahato.

As per the Terms of Reference (ToR) assigned to the SRC, the commission was given the task to study the majority and dissenting opinions in the report of Restructuring of the state and Distribution of State Power Committee to identify the contentious issues and recommend compromise or common ground solutions. The ToR also stated that the commission would look into federating units on the basis of identity and economic viability.

Since the government did not assign a Chair to the SRC, the members mutually decided to rotate the leadership in every meeting. It was later decided that Madan Pariyar be appointed the full-time Chair of the Commission. With his appointment, the SRC had nine members. The commission's task was, first, to reach a consensus, and, if this was not possible, second, to settle issues on the basis of majority. Identity was reaffirmed as the major consideration in the formation of the federal units.

One of the SRC members, Surendra Mahato recalls: "We were of the view within the Commission that geography could be a factor in identity as far as naming of the provinces are concerned. But eventually we all agreed that ethnic identity would be the main basis of federating state boundaries. While doing so, this will also not stop us from recognizing the river civilization."

SRC member Mahato further recollects a journalist noting that this was the only commission without a majority of the Khas-Arya group. The journalist doubted if this commission could protect the interests of Khas-Arya who did not want identity-based federalism. This led to my understanding that Khas-Arya group had a notion from the very beginning that there should not be identity based federalism, he adds.

During the work of the SRC, voting was required on some issues in which everyone except the chair participated. The chair informed the members that he would vote only at the time of finalizing the report.This was also one of the reasons for the SRC's failure to produce a consensus report.

Three members of the SRC—Ramesh Dhungel, Sabitri Gurung and Sarba Raj Khadka—did not agree on the issue of people's identity. They showed their reluctance to submit the report in a timely manner. They even wrote a letter to the SRC Chair, seeking extension of the deadline and redefining of the work proceedings of the commission. They demanded that the commission start its work from the scratch. After the SRC meeting failed to pass the extension proposal, the three members walked out of the meeting hall and decided to boycott subsequent meetings. They did not attend any further SRC meetings.

The majority of SRC members, who were in favour of timely submission of the report, wanted to avoid criticism that the CA's work was impeded by their failure to complete the SRC report in time.

The SRC members had agreed that they would not speak before media about anything related to the contents of the report. Some members, however, passed on the information to the public and media before the final report. The federal map was printed in the media before the report was submitted to the government. Nobody knows who leaked it, but it seems the intent was to make the report controversial and the national media, intentionally or unintentionally, became complicit in the plot.

The Khas-Arya group, generally the Nepali Congress and CPN-UML, and the mainstream media outlets, which are under the influence of Khas-Arya group, did not want to federate the country. Rather, they favoured the continuity of an administrative division of the country into five development regions.

The SRC majority report reduced the number of federal units from 14 to 11. They followed the CA's criteria of creating a federal unit for those communities whose population was at least one per cent or more. They also followed the CA's suggestion to create an autonomous area for Sherpas, notwithstanding the fact that Sherpas do not comprise even one per cent of the population. The West Jadan province suggested by the CA did not have one per cent population of the intended ethnic group—Lamas. As Dalits are part of many other groups and geographically dispersed across the country, the SRC report suggested a non-territorial province for them.

The SRC minority report by Ramesh Dhungel proposed six provinces in favour of a north-south division. This division, however, was not in conformity with the SRC's Terms of Reference.

The 11-Province model would have given Nepal's diverse population an opportunity to take pride in their identity. This model reflected the federal models of India, Pakistan and Ethiopia, where most or all provinces were created on the basis of identity.

Only after the major parties rejected the 11-Province model recommended by the majority of the SRC, did it become clear that the government had sought the formation of SRC merely to diffuse the CA's Restructuring of the state and Distribution of State Power Committee Report which suggested creating 14-Provinces mainly on the basis of identity. The government favoured the 6-Province model submitted by the minority of the SRC as the one that best suited their interests.

On May 15, 2012, the NC, CPN-UML and CPN-MC-Maoist (Centre) came up with another 11-Province model. This federal model proposed to divide the Madhes into five provinces, and was unofficially endorsed by Bijay Kumar Gachhedar and Mahantha Thakur of United Democratic Madhesi Front (UDMF). Unofficial endorsement meant that while they would not support the proposal publicly, neither would they create any obstruction against the proposal.

In response to their silence on the 11-Province model, demonstrators burnt effigies of these Madhesi leaders at Baneshwor in Kathmandu as well as in different parts of the Madhes. SP Chair Rajendra Mahato subsequently voiced dissent to the 11-Province model, which ultimately forced Madhesi leaders Gachhedar and Thakur to publicly oppose the deal.

Likewise, Janajati forces within and outside of the Maoist party opposed the 11-Province model and forced the party to backtrack from the deal.

The failure to reach a deal on federalism among the political parties ultimately led to the dissolution of the First CA on May 28, 2012 without promulgating the constitution.

Eight-Province Model in 16-Point Agreement

The combined strength of the NC and the CPN-UML in the Second CA was almost a two-third majority, and from the beginning of their mandate began to strategically dilute federalism. On April 25, 2015, a devastating earthquake struck Nepal, giving the major parties an excuse to fast track the constitution writing process in a manner favouring this strategy.

On June 8, 2015, the NC, CPN-UML, CPN-MC-Maoist (Centre), and Bijay Kumar Gachhedar-led MJF-D signed the 16-Point Agreement. The agreement stated that there would be eight provinces, although it lacked specific names and boundaries of the provinces. As per the agreement, a commission would be formed, with the mandate to submit a report on the federal structure within six months. This commission's report would be accepted or rejected by a two-thirds majority in the House.

However, as a result of the litigation following a writ petition filed under my stewardship, the Supreme Court issued a stay order for the implementation of the 16-Point Agreement.

Six-Province Federal Model

Following the SC's interim order, major political parties, which had earlier signed the 16-Point Deal, were compelled to incorporate federalism in the constitution in the June 30 draft. Just before the midnight in August 8, 2015, after several closed-door negotiations, the major political parties agreed on six federal provinces in Nepal.

The six-province federalism model triggered protests in mid-western and far-western regions, of Terai including Surkhet and Karnali areas.

Local demonstrators in Surkhet demanded the mid-western region be kept intact and Surkhet district be developed as the capital of the new province. As per the six-province model, some districts of the mid-western region were included in Province Number 6, comprising most of the far-western districts, while other mid-western districts were included in another province. Likewise, the locals of Karnali zone protested against the inclusion of the zone in the Far-West province in the six-province model. They also refused to be part of the province comprising Surkhet and other districts of the mid-western region. Demonstrators in Mugu, Kalikot, Jumla and Humla districts demanded that Karnali Zone be made a separate Karnali province.

The six-province model also triggered protests in Salyan and Rukum districts. The locals launched indefinite agitations demanding an undivided Rapti zone in the federal system. The locals in Rukum also protested against division of their district into two provinces (Nos. 5 and 6). Residents of Baglung also opposed the division of their district.

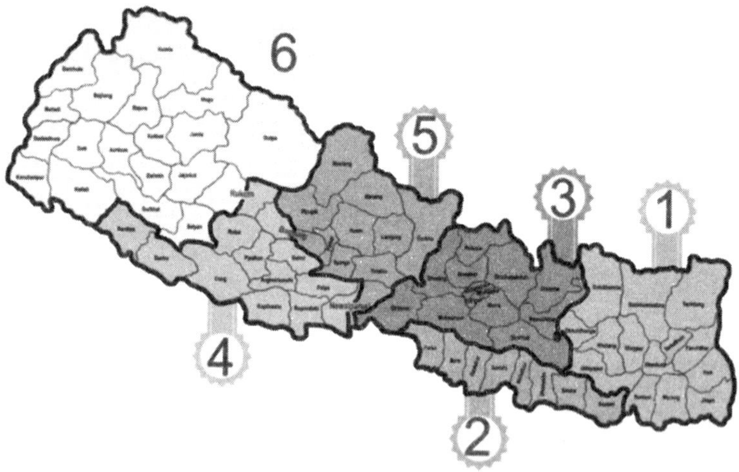

Map of six federal units that the major parties agreed for initially
Image Source: Nepali Times

Four demonstrators—three in Surkhet and one in Jumla—were killed during the protest against the six-province model when police opened fire to control the mob.

Seven-Province Federal Model

To address the demands of protesters in Surkhet and Karnali, major parties agreed to increase the number of federal provinces from six to seven. It is important to note that no scientific basis or principles of federalism were adopted to federalize either the six-province or the seven-province federal models.

Madhesi Dissatisfaction with the Current Federal Set-up

Madhesis have long been arguing that the north-south division of the country would make Madhesis a minority in all provinces, contrary to ensuring self-rule of the dominant nationalities, which is a basic principle of federalism.

Madhesi and Tharu communities were not satisfied with the six- and seven-province models as it failed to address their grievances. The dissatisfaction among Madhesis and Tharu people towards the seven-province federal model enshrined in the constitution triggered protests across Terai region. The State used security agencies to silence the voices of the marginalized communities. It seemed as though the ruling class did not take the reaction of the Madhes regarding the six/seven-province model seriously.

This federal model proposes to carve Madhes into five provinces mixing areas in the Madhes with hilly areas. One can understand why parties locked horns over Jhapa, Morang, Sunsari, Kailali and Kanchanpur districts. It can be assumed that these five districts of the Terai were put in hill provinces simply because there are large numbers of Pahadhi (Hill) people in these districts. Even though there was no dispute over Nawalparasi, Rupandehi and

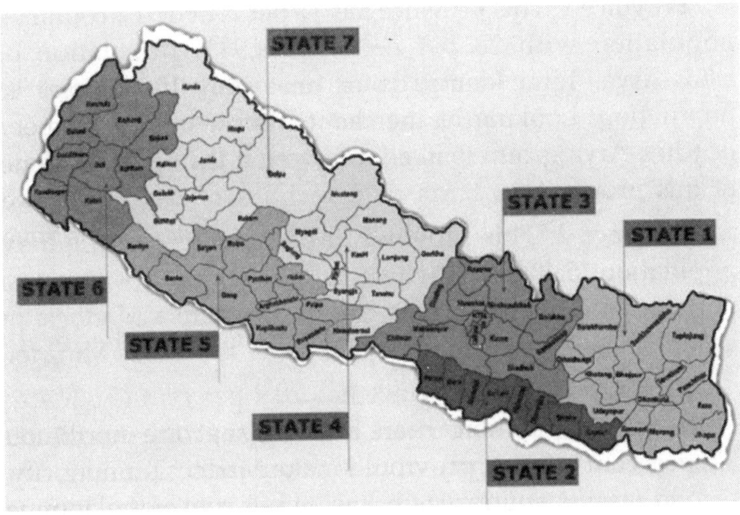

Map of Seven Province
Image Source: Kathmandu Post

Kapilvastu in the seven-province model, these Terai districts were also included in a hill province with Rukum, Rolpa and Pyuthan without any logic or public debate.

Gerrymandering with Federal Demarcation

The boundaries of the seven-province model set by the major political parties show that the provinces were gerrymandered to ensure that only members of Khas-Arya group could become chief ministers in six out of the seven provinces. The major parties adopted the policy of splitting and consolidating of other ethnic groups in these provinces to establish the domineering role of the Khas-Arya group. Likewise, the provincial boundaries ensure that political parties representing minority communities cannot aspire to become the Prime Minister of the country in the near future.

There are clear examples of the gerrymandering approach in the established federalism in the constitution of Nepal:

Province 1: This province has 17 per cent of the country's population with 28 per cent (4,534,943) population of Khas-Arya. Terai Janajati constitutes only 12 per cent of population. Looking at the demography, only a member of Khas-Arya group is likely to become the Chief Minister of this province.

Province 2: This province has 52 per cent of Madhesi population (5,404,145), which is 20.9 per cent of the total population. This is the only province where a Madhesi or a non-Khas-Arya member can become the Chief Minister.

Province 3: This province has 20.9 per cent (5,529,452) of the total population where Khas-Arya group constitutes 37 per cent of the province's population. Tamang, the second largest ethnic group has 20 per cent population in this province.

Province 4: This province has 2,413,907 population, which is 9.1 per cent of the country's population where Khas-Arya group constitutes 42 per cent, followed by Magar's 27 per cent population.

Province 5: This province has 4,540,222 population, which constitutes 17.1 per cent population of the country. This province has a dominance of 30 per cent of Khas-Arya group. The Magar community, with 16 per cent population, is the second largest ethnic group in this province.

Province 6: This province has 1,519,389 population which makes up 5.7 per cent of the country's population, consists of 62 per cent population of Khas-Arya. Hill Dalit group constitutes 23 per cent population in this province.

Province 7: This province has 2,552,517 populaiton which is 9.7 per cent of the country's population. Khas-Arya has 60 per cent population in this province. Tharu is the second largest ethnic group with 17 per cent population in this province.

Double Standards with Federal Demarcation

Article 56 of the constitution of Nepal gives the power to declare village councils and municipalities to the federal government and states that districts are to be defined as set out in Schedule 4. This means provinces do not have the power to restructure local bodies in the future. It also implies that, while demarcating the provinces after the promulgation of the constitution, districts cannot be split without amending the constitution. Madhesi and Janajati forces have been saying that district should not be a unit in the federal set-up but leaders of major parties have opposed the views of Madhesi and Janajati leaders. Notwithstanding their previous statements that districts should not be split, leaders of the major parties split Nawalparasi and Rukum districts to suit their interests. This was contrary to law.

Some federations give residual powers to the centre, some do it sub-nationally and some split such powers. The new constitution, however, gives this residuary powers to the center. This was a disputed issue in the CA and many lawmakers believed that the residuary powers should rest with the province. The concurrent lists of the centre and the provinces could curtail the powers of the provinces. The constitution also states that the provinces must coordinate with the centre while taking loans from a foreign country, which reduces the power of a province to that of a district development committee.

Speaker: A Man in a Hurry

During the First CA, Speaker Subas Chandra Nembang did not pay attention to a two-thirds majority vote. But, in the Second CA, he was a man in a hurry to push the promulgation of the constitution.

During the Second CA, Speaker Nembang unilaterally announced the formation of a Questionnaire Committee for the purpose of forcing a vote in the Parliament on contentious issues. The committee and its objectives were contrary to the terms of the 2006 Peace Agreement, which established consensus as the decision-making threshold. It raised questions over the speaker's neutrality and integrity.

The forced voting in the CA created fear among the fringe forces. The Madhes-based parties were pushed into a corner. The way the ruling parties acted vis-à-vis the Janajatis and Madhesis, it seemed that these groups either had to surrender or hit the streets to get their agendas incorporated into the constitution.

The CA members of the opposition parties protested the CA Speaker's decision to move the process ahead based on a majority of votes. They resorted to vandalism in the CA. The media outlets highlighted how on January 23, 2015, chairs were broken inside the CA instead of analyzing the dissatisfaction for a public debate. They portrayed CPN-MC CA member Umesh Yadav as a villain. No doubt the acts of vandalism should not be condoned, yet on the other hand, no journalists asked the CA Secretariat why, on that date, 650 Marshals were deployed inside the CA. The opposition parties perceived this deployment as evidence of the government's clear-intention to force the voting process following the formation of the Questionnaire Committee. The Marshals were lean young men with similar heights and hairstyles. They looked like trained soldiers and black commandos. However, no media source highlighted this fact. Most probably, the soldiers were hired and deployed in the CA without passing any laws or obtaining cabinet approval. As such, this move was against the established laws of the country. Ironically, no one was held responsible for this anti-constitutional deployment of soldiers in the Parliament.

During the First CA, the CPN-MC and the Madhesi parties were in an advantageous position and many of Madhesi and Janajati CA members had clearly signalled that they would defy the party whips and cross the floor on progressive agendas of the constitution. As the chair of the First CA, Speaker Nembang had smartly understood the dynamics, he had refused to move the constitution drafting process ahead in the name of consensus. Even on the last day before its dissolution, he refused to call a meeting of the CA despite frequent requests of Madhesi and Maoist leaders. To the media, he stated the reason, that there would have been a bloodbath if he had called the meeting. Yet in the Second CA , when the conservative forces of the NC and CPN-UML had a majority, the same Speaker was instrumental in moving the constitution-building process forward by majority vote, inviting violence and bloodshed.

Adoption of a Failed Hybrid Version of Federalism from the U.S.

The U.S. Constitution grants state governments key powers, including the right to determine how to choose delegates to the Electoral College. States also have a great deal of latitude to write their own constitutions and pass their own laws. All state governments have three branches (as in the national government), although the powers granted to the branches differ from state to state. In some states, for example, the governor has a great deal of power, whereas in others, his or her power is severely limited. States also use a variety of methods to choose judges.

The vast jurisdiction and control of the U.S. National Government has led some to conclude that state governments are of secondary importance. In 1941, for example, Supreme Court Justice Harlan Stone remarked that the Tenth Amendment (which reserves powers to the states) had no real meaning. State governments, however, are still vital political actors, and they have adapted to new roles and new circumstances. At the start of the twenty-first century, many states reasserted their strength and took on a larger role in homeland security, and economic and environmental policy.

The U.S. Constitution does not use the term federalism, nor does it provide extensive details about the federal system. Nevertheless, the framers helped created a federalist system in the United States, particularly in the ways the constitution allocates power.

A landmark U.S. Supreme Court case from 1819 concerned a state government's ability to tax a national bank. The court, relying on the necessary and proper clause, ruled that the national government had far more powers than the constitution enumerated in Article I, Section 8. The Supreme Court ruled that the necessary and proper clause allowed the national government to regulate air travel, combat industrial pollution, and foster the creation and growth of the Internet.

The U.S. Constitution also explicitly denies the national government certain powers. For example, Congress cannot tax exports or tell states how to choose electors for the Electoral College. The powers denied to the national government are called the prohibited powers. However, Nepal Constitution's Article 203 does not give power to the state governments to tax without the federal government' consent and federal laws set rules of levy tax where the state governments have no power to influence.

The U.S. courts have held that local governments are entirely under the authority of state governments and that a state can create and abolish local governments as it sees fit. But in Nepal, this power has been given to the center under Articles 56(4) and (5) and the central government has already formed a local body restructuring commission under Article 295.

The State Restructuring Commission (SRC) Report suggested that the provincial governments have jurisdiction and power to restructure local bodies. Even the three dissenting members of the SRC report agreed with the majority on this point. Indeed, the First CA State Restructuring Committee report also assured that the provincial government would restructure the local bodies. However, the new constitutional provision Article 295 is just the opposite of the SRC's reports and totally opposite of the U.S. practice to structure the local bodies of the states.

Federalism Practice in India

J.B. Kripalani, the President of the Indian National Congress at its Meerut session in November 1946 outlined the proposed constitution as follows:

> It will be a democratic constitution and will be federal in character. We may not, however, forget that, in the administrative as in the economic field, centralization more than is absolutely necessary is inimical to liberty. It is good, therefore, that the provinces in free India shall have the maximum autonomy consistent with external and internal security.

In India, no constitutional amendment is required for the purpose of altering the boundaries of states. An Act of the Parliament is sufficient. For example, the state of Andhra Pradesh was formed out of the state of Madras on linguistic grounds in 1953. After this, the states Reorganization Act, 1956 was enacted, followed by the constitution (Seventh Amendment) Act, 1956, both of which resulted in the formation of many states, e.g. Himachal Pradesh, Karnataka, Manipur, Meghalaya, Nagaland, Tripura, and Haryana. This is totally opposite of the situation in Nepal, where the constitution requires two-thirds of the federal Parliament along with a two-thirds majority of the state legislatures whose boundaries would be changed. This threshold seems almost impossible to meet, rendering the future altering of state boundaries unlikely.

States in India have been given rights to self-determination based on popular demand. The right to self-determination is not provided for in Nepal's Constitution, a right desired by the Madhes and Tharu people. In India, states such as Jharkhand and Chhattisgarh have received autonomy from their former larger states based on their cultural differences and incidences of historical deprivation. Uttarakhand was formed out of Uttar Pradesh for administrative convenience. In India, ethnic differences have always been considered the strongest case for political autonomy.

A similar method of giving special power of autonomy could have been given to the two states in Nepal's Terai:

Madhes Pradesh in central and eastern part and Tharuhat in the western part. This Indian example of federalism to treat special areas of domination of particularly ethnic communities and give them more power of autonomy to stop the threat of secession could have been adopted in Nepal. But it wasn't.

Failure of the KP Oli Government and 36 Dialogues with UDMF

Since the beginning, I have doubted that the K.P. Oli government had any intention to address the issue of provincial boundary revision. This government only invited the United Democratic Madhesi Front (UDMF) to the negotiation table because of national and international pressure, particularly from India. Minister of Foreign Affairs Kamal Thapa presented a four-point roadmap to address the Madhes problem, two of which were to be achieved through constitutional amendment. The four-point roadmap recommended revising provincial boundaries through a high level political mechanism.

The terms of reference suggested for the political mechanism were as follows:

1. Structure: A mechanism comprising the chairpersons of the Nepali Congress, the CPN-UML, CPN-MC-Maoist and the constituents of the United Democratic Madhesi Front (UDMF) should be formed.
2. Five districts (Jhapa, Morang, Sunsari, Kailali and Kanchanpur) should be declared as disputed districts.
3. Duration: the political mechanism should complete its work within ninety days.
4. The political mechanism should discuss the two-province model in the Madhes.

5. The decisions of the political mechanism should be binding on the parties and once work is completed, its decisions should be forwarded to the Parliament for amendments to the constitution.

However, just a day before his visit to India, and to show that he was committed to addressing the problem, Prime Minister K.P. Oli unilaterally proposed the name of Kamal Thapa as the Chair of the political mechanism. This was strategically targeted to discredit the mechanism, as Kamal Thapa was openly against the federal, republic and secular agendas. Appointing Kamal Thapa was a ploy to show support to the four-point roadmap knowing that the Madhesi parties would not join the political mechanism under the leadership of Kamal Thapa whose basic values contradicted the committee mandates he was to lead. Madhesi parties were also sure that dialogue with Prime Minister Oli would not reach any conclusions, as the PM himself was not committed to either federalism or proportional inclusion. So while there were thirty-six rounds of dialogues between the Oli government and the Madhesi Morcha, these dialogues were merely ritual and tactical. Both sides knew that there was no meeting point for them. As time passed, anti-Oli sentiments in the Terai grew. This sentiment increased as PM Oli made hateful remarks against agitating Madhesi communities, such as calling the human chain formed across the East-West highway in October 2015 a 'chain of flies' and equating the deaths of Madhesis protesting against the constitution to 'falling mangoes'. Of the over fifty people who died in the Madhes movement, seven were from Birgunj alone.

Without UML support, a constitutional amendment to revise province boundary is not possible. But it is also equally true that UML leadership was not ready to revise the federal boundary. So the NC and CPN-Maoist Centre believed a consolidation of power to remove KP Oli as Prime Minister was the only way to move the process forward. Success or failure of the constitutional amendment proposal is a different thing; first we need a leader who can initiate and pass the constitutional amendment proposal by the cabinet. The NC/CPN-MC (Centre) coalition government led by PM Pushpa Kamal Dahal registered a constitutional amendment bill in the Parliament as it had promised to amend the constitution to respond to Madhesi and other groups' demands. CPN-UML, the main opposition stalled the house proceedings to block the debate and the passage of the bill.

If the Dahal-led government fails to pass a constitutional amendment correcting the provincial boundaries, it will generate a deep sense of alienation among the Madhesis towards the state. The failure of a moderate force like the Madhesi Morcha will ultimately give way to extremist forces that could hijack the movement and become violent. Therefore, the government and the major political parties must cooperate to amend the constitution to correct the gerrymandering of provincial boundaries with two provinces in the Terai with special autonomy: one extending from Jhapa to Parsa and the other extending from Nawalparasi to some parts of Kailali before it is too late. Additionally, the provinces in the hills must ensure the identity of two dominant groups.

Conclusion

On state restructuring issues, it was the CPN-UML that dictated the terms. The NC accepted and the then CPN-MC-Maoist did not protest against the UML's stance. Indeed the Maoists' note of dissent on the constitution was window-dressing with no true will behind it.

There was an understanding among the three key political parties that NC leader Sushil Koirala would be appointed President.

When CPN-MC-Maoist and Madhesi forces were together championing the cause of Madhesis and Janajatis, the NC and UML feared losing their influence. However, later the CPN-MC-Maoist left the Madhesi and Janajati alliance and signed the 16-Point Agreement proposed by the NC and CPN-UML. The 16-Point Deal among these four parties proved to be the game changer.

The then CPN-Maoist leader Baburam Bhattarai had initially helped the issues of marginalized communities, including Madhesi and Janajati, by withholding the constitutional Political Dialogue and Consensus Committee (CPDCC)'s report. But in the end this tactic was not successful and he was forced to release the report.

Sadbhavana Party leader Laxman Lal Karna requested Bhattarai to give at least one night to peruse and pass the CPDCC report the following day. But Bhattarai did not listen to him. The discussion on the report was scheduled first at 5 pm, then at 7 pm, and finally at 9.30 pm. Karna argued that Bhattarai had not shown fairness that day. He appeared to have followed Dahal's line. When Dahal accepted the report, Bhattarai followed him.

8

Judiciary

The Most Contradictory Chapter in the constitution

Structure

A week before the deadline for public feedback on the First draft of the constitution, Dr. Baburam Bhattarai, the Chairperson of Constitutional Political Dialogue and Consensus Committee (CPDCC), invited Madhesi intellectuals, including me, to give feedbacks on the draft. I spoke on the provisions relating to judiciary, which I termed "the most conservative chapter" in the constitution. The constitutional provisions relating to the judiciary are not only contradictory but also regressive in some respects.

First, let us draw a distinction between Article 127(1) and Article 56(1) of the constitution:

Article 127(1) creates three levels of courts in Nepal: (a) District Court, (b) High Court and (c) Supreme Court.

Article 56(1) says that the Federal Democratic Republic of Nepal will have three layers of state structures: (a) Local, (b) Provincial and (c) Federal.

The term used for the first layer of courts mentioned in both of the articles is inconsistent. Article 127(1) uses 'district court' while Article 56(1) uses 'local'. They are contradictory. Why was the term 'local court' not used in this case?

The 'local' governmental bodies under Article 56(4), include village council, municipal council and district council. The main role of the district council is to act as a coordinating body but not to exercise administrative powers. However, the term 'district court' backs the same old district level structure, which has been in existence in Nepal since the panchayat era to exercise administrative powers. The constitution speaks of restructuring of the state, but preserving such a fraught term as 'district court' keeps the old administrative structure intact, which will propagate the existing discrimination, poor governance and the lack of opportunities at the local level. At a time when the concept of 'district' is proving to be a matter of controversy among the major political parties, the term 'District Court' itself is contentious.

The report of the Judicial Committee of the First CA, led by CA member Prabhu Shah, recommended the inclusion of a local/district-level court, without specifically mentioning the word 'district.' The same language was mentioned in the report of the Constitutional Committee for Studying Constitutional Archives, Disputes and Consensus of the Second CA. Major parties, however, deleted the term 'local' and kept the word 'district' in the draft constitution. Had the term 'local' been used, it would have had a broader and flexible meaning. It could also help change the judiciary into a truly federal structure at a time when it is functioning as a unitary structure.

Federal Supreme Court Changed to Supreme Court

The reports of the Judicial Committee of the First CA and the Constitutional Committee for Studying Constitutional Archives, Disputes and Consensus of the Second CA, suggested that the name of the Supreme Court be changed to 'Federal Supreme Court', but this was not incorporated when the constitution was promulgated.

If the term 'federal' was used in reference to two organs of the state (legislature and executive), why isn't the judiciary also federal? In the United States of America, for example, all three organs—legislature, executive and judiciary—are equally federal. The constitution of Nepal only explicitly states that legislature and executive are federal. It fails to clearly name a federal judiciary.

Earlier, the Judicial Committee of the First CA had agreed to have a Provincial Supreme Court, but in the Second CA the major parties dropped it. The Second CA also dropped the provisions relating to a Provincial Judicial Council and Constitutional Court, which had been recommended by the Judicial Committee of the First CA.

Omitted 'Proportional Inclusion' from Judiciary Chapter

To adopt the principle of proportional inclusion, the term 'proportional inclusion' has been incorporated into many state bodies. However, the term remains absent from the judiciary chapter of the constitution.

The First CA Judicial Committee and Second CA and the constitutional Committee for Studying Constitutional Records, Disputes and Consensus recommended that proportional inclusion be ensured in the judiciary, particularly with regard to the appointment of judges. But the Second CA did not incorporate the SC recommendation.

The preamble of the constitution states that Nepal will be proportionally inclusive. Article 42 of the constitution also states that all organs of the state would be proportionally inclusive. If the judiciary is not also required to be proportionally inclusive, it is contrary to the spirit of the fundamental rights outlined elsewhere in the constitution.

Failing to mandate proportional inclusion in the judiciary was a missed opportunity for the country to bring about judicial reform. As it stands, the constitution fails to properly represent the minority communities in this branch of government. The table below shows the data of judges in different courts. It clearly shows that there are very few judges representing minority communities.

Courts	*Total judges*	*Bahun/ Kshetri*	*Madhesi*	*Woman*	*Dalit*	*Muslim*	*Indigenous*
Supreme Court	21	15 (71.42%)	2 (9.52%)	3 (14.28%)	0	0	4 (19.4%)
Appellate Court (CJ)	16	12 (75%)	1 (6.25%)	1 (6.25%)	0	0	3 (18.75%)
Appellate Court	80	58 (72.5%)	7 (8.75%)	4 (5%)	1 (1.25%)	4 (5%)	10 (12.5%)
District Court	180	163 (90.55%)	3 (1.67%)	1 (0.55%)	0	1 (0.55%)	13 (7.22%)

Source: Judicial Council 2016

Past verdicts of the Supreme Court in the cases of language, costume, citizenship and inclusion have not been universally accepted by every community in the country. Ordinary citizens perceived these verdicts as forced upon them by another community that does not represent their interests.

Had proportional inclusion in the judiciary been ensured by the constitution, it would have ensured a more equitable reflection of the country's diversity. It would also help to dispel doubts about the judiciary being controlled by one community. It would increase the credibility of the courts.

The Beijing and Bangalore Declarations state that judicial diversity in the country's demographic composition is necessary to increase a court's credibility in the minds of the public.

This critique does not suggest that inefficient or weak candidates should be appointed as judges. A balance of competency and diversity can and should be maintained.

Further to a report submitted by lawmaker Sudarshan Nachiappan to the Indian Parliament in 2007, the equitable implementation and application of a law, no matter how good it is on paper, is not possible if the judiciary lacks diversity and inclusiveness. That same year, a Dalit was appointed Chief Justice of the Indian Supreme Court in accordance with the provisions of proportional inclusion that is enshrined in the Indian Constitution.

Provincial Judicial Councils

The Constitutional Dialogue and Political Consensus Committee of the Second CA formed a dispute resolution task force, which recommended that Nepal should have a centralized justice system and should establish a constitutional court. They proposed that for the central government, judicial appointments should be made by federal agencies, and for the provincial government, appointments should be made at the provincial level by Provincial Judicial Councils. These councils would also have the authority to take disciplinary and/or punitive action against judges.

Instead, the constitution implemented a centralized Judicial Council, which is a continuation of the unitary system and is not harmonious with a federal structure. Although Nepal is a federal country, these provisions also fail to reflect the principles of federalism.

For a truly federal judiciary, the appointment of the Chief Justice of provinces should be done in consultation with the governors and chief ministers of the respective provinces. The government should also consult the chief Justice while appointing the judges of the provinces. As it stands, the provincial government cannot appoint any employees. This means that the central government has the ultimate authority over the provincial high courts. Governors of the provinces should have the power to administer the oath of office to the chief judge and judges, as is the case in India.

Constitutional Court

Although the Dispute Resolution Subcommittee formed under CA member Laxman Lal Karna in the Second CA had widened the jurisdiction of the constitutional court, the new constitution made provision for only a constitutional bench at the Supreme Court.

The subcommittee proposed the formation of a separate constitutional court.

Its jurisdiction would include cases involving the distribution of powers between various political units at all levels, such as the center versus province, the centre versus local bodies, province-to-province, province versus local body, and local body versus local body. The Subcommittee also recommended that the constitutional court should decide cases involving constitutional disputes between the federal Parliament and the provincial assemblies. It would also have jurisdiction over: cases where a provincial act is in violation of federal act; the constitutionality of amendments to the constitution; jurisdiction between constitutional bodies, including disputes involving the President, vice President, Prime Minister, speaker, deputy speaker, chairman and deputy chairman of national assembly; issues of lawmakers' eligibility and validity of political parties; and advisory opinions to the President on constitutional questions.

Some leaders of the major political parties, however, did not favour giving rights to provinces and local bodies, and were against forming a constitutional court that they believed would ultimately serve the interests of other federal actors.

Some of the Supreme Court judges also did not want to have a separate constitutional court, fearing the loss of cases that would otherwise fall under their jurisdiction. It would also diminish the Supreme Court's status of being the final court of record. In meetings between the judges of the Supreme Court and top leaders, including CPDCC Chair Baburam Bhattarai and Prime Minister K.P. Sharma Oli, the judges formally opposed the formation of the constitutional court. Only one judge, Justice Girish Chandra Lal, was in favour of establishing a constitutional court. Madhesis and Janajatis believe that a constitutional court is necessary to decide upon disputes between provinces and the central government, and between different political units.

In summary, the constitutional provisions regarding judiciary are unitary in nature. This goes against the spirit of past movements and the federal principles espoused elsewhere in the constitution. The current legal process is cumbersome, and exacerbates problems of corruption in the judiciary and access to justice. Due to delays in the court system, many Nepali citizens would rather tolerate injustice than deal with the courts. Nepal's Chief Judges have said time and again that only around five per cent people have access to justice. Therefore, the country should have adopted a fully federal judicial system.

9

Role of India in Constitution Making

In the second week of December 2015, Professor Lok Raj Baral asked me to accompany him on a two-day trip to Delhi, India. I had earlier visited Bhithamod, Sursand, Sunauli and Siliguri, among other border towns of India, and I took the New Delhi visit as an important event. Many consider the city as a power center of the South Asia region, and this was my first ever formal visit to the capital of India.

While attending a seminar on 'Constitution Making in Nepal: Challenges and Opportunities' held in New Delhi from January 6 to 9, 2016, I met former Indian Ambassadors to Nepal, Jayant Prasad, Shiv Shankar Mukherjee, K.V. Rajan, and diplomat Sukh Deo Muni, an expert on Nepal–India relations. I was overwhelmed by their reflections on Nepal's constitution-making process, and the challenges and opportunities ahead.

During the same trip I also met Bharatiya Janata Party (BJP) lawmakers, who said that they had supported the secular provisions that were already enshrined in Nepal's Interim Constitution. This is what surprised me. The BJP leaders refuted the rumours about Indian interests in reinstating Nepal as a Hindu nation.

However, Indian National Congress leaders had a slightly different stance on the issues in Nepal, given that the government is led by their opposition, the BJP. Apparently, Indian National Congress leaders pushed the Nepali issue onto the Indian political agenda in order to oppose the Modi government. The Indian National Congress leaders blamed the Indian Government for pushing the agenda of Hinduism in Nepal.

The debate over India's policy involvement in Nepal led to a discussion in Rajya Sabha (India's Upper House) on December 7, 2015. 14 Rajya Sabha members blamed the Modi government for interfering in Nepal's domestic affairs, and for pushing Nepal towards Chinese influence. They also opined that Nepal's new constitution discriminates against Madhesis in Nepal.

Indian National Congress MP Karan Singh said that Nepal's new constitution rescinded rights guaranteed by the Interim Constitution. The Indian Government, he said, must persuade ruling parties in Nepal to carry the provisions from the Interim Constitution over to the new constitution.

During the Rajya Sabha debate, India's External Affairs Minister Sushma Swaraj clarified that the BJP Government is in favour of a "federal democratic republic of Nepal". She was also very critical of the constitution-making process in Nepal, arguing that the promulgation of the constitution lacked adequate debate and had backtracked from the more progressive provisions of the Interim Constitution.

I was glad that I was able to present the facts and myths about the constitution to the Indian leaders in Delhi, including members of the Indian National Congress. Later, all of them agreed that the constitution would not be justified if marginalized communities, including the Madhesi, Tharu and Janajatis, were sidelined from their involvement in the political arena.

In various statements, India called for the promulgation of the constitution in Nepal on a broad-based consensus. India made it clear that its main concerns were peace, prosperity and development in Nepal.

I also learned from meetings with officials of Indian Ministry of External Affairs (which is also referred to as the South Block) was also of the view that the problems with the new constitution were an internal issue and that Nepalis themselves should settle it.

Diplomat S.D. Muni commented on the way in which power-sharing played an important role in the making of the constitution. A power deal among key political parties, he said, triggered the promulgation of the constitution. I was impressed by his insight into how the process had taken place.

Also during these meetings, many Indian leaders and diplomats mentioned that the current dispute over federal boundaries could be settled if Jhapa in the east and Kanchanpur in the west were put under the hill provinces, and other districts such as Sunsari, Morang and Kailali were included in the Terai provinces.

"One Madhes, One Province" is not possible given the current context, as the Indian leaders argued. But instead, there could be two provinces in Madhes. They expressed frustration and concern at K.P. Sharma Oli's remarks that if Madhesis were given the provincial boundaries they demanded, they would merge with Uttar Pradesh and Bihar States in India.

India has played an active role in Nepal's modern political history. The Indian Government brought together the parties to sign a 12-Point Agreement in Delhi on November 25, 2005, which aimed to expedite the peace process in Nepal. India also helped bring Maoists into the mainstream politics by getting the two sides, the government and the Maoists, to sign a comprehensive peace accord in 2006.

India was the mediator for the 22-Point Pact signed between the government and the Madhesi Janadhikar Forum in 2007, after the movement took a violent turn, leaving dozens of people killed and displacing a number of hill people from the Terai. One year later, when the Interim Constitution failed to accommodate key provisions of the 22-Point pact, it triggered the second Madhes Movement of 2008, led by an alliance of Madhes based parties in the early days of the United Democratic Madhesi Front (UDMF). Subsequently, the UDMF signed an Eight-Point Agreement with the Nepal Government. India was again the facilitator to settle the issue with the Madhes-based forces.

India has made significant contributions to democratic movements in Nepal, including the settlement of the decade-long Maoist insurgency, and the more recent Madhes movements. Their efforts ultimately led to the formation of the constituent assembly, and the promulgation of the constitution.

India should continue to extend moral support to the forces which want to institutionalize a federal, democratic, secular and inclusive Constitution.

Indian Interventions During the Constitution's Promulgation

The 2015 Madhes movement against the draft and final constitution was going smoothly without Indian support. The movement was organic with what was an overwhelming participation by people staging demonstrations in the streets and at district headquarters.

After forty days of the movement, the Indian Government showed its concern following the promulgation of Nepal's Constitution that left Madhesis and Tharus politically underrepresented. India's solidarity with the movement, and opposition to the use of excessive force against the protesters, forced the government of Nepal to maintain restraint.

Consequently, India's serious concerns over the use of force led to a reduction in the number of killings of innocent people and demonstrators by the state. People in the Terai overwhelmingly welcomed this move to save their lives and thanked India for extending moral support to them.

India issued a series of statements outlining its formal concerns with the constitution-making process in Nepal. Indian Foreign Secretary S. Jaishankar visited Nepal in September 2015, proposing a postponement of the promulgation of constitution at least by a week, however this was rejected by the mainstream political parties. After returning to Delhi, he made a statement on his visit to Kathmandu.

Ministry of External Affairs
Government of India

Home Visits Media Center / Documents Overseas Indian Affairs E Citizen/Tenders Useful

Media Center

Home › Media Center / Documents › Speeches & Statements

Press Statement by the Foreign Secretary after visiting Nepal

September 19, 2015

I visited Kathmandu for two days as the special envoy of the Prime Minister of India. I was received by the Rt. Hon'ble President of Nepal Shri Ram Baran Yadav. I also called on the Rt. Hon'ble Prime Minister of Nepal Shri Sushil Koirala and met the key political leaders including Shri K.P. Sharma Oli, Prachanda ji, Shri Sher Bahadur Deuba and the leaders of the Madhesh based political parties.

India has been strongly supportive of constitution making in Nepal. We would like its completion to be an occasion for joy and satisfaction, not agitation and violence.

We hope that Nepal's political leaders will display the necessary flexibility and maturity at this crucial time to ensure a durable and resilient Constitution that has broad-based acceptance.

On the day of constitution promulgation (September 20, 2015), India noted the event with concern while many countries congratulated Nepal. Here is the statement:

Ministry of External Affairs
Government of India

Home | Visits | Media Center / Documents | Overseas Indian Affairs | E-Citizen/Tenders | Usefu

Media Center

Home › Media Center / Documents › Press Releases

Statement on the situation in Nepal

September 20, 2015

Throughout the process of Constitution making in Nepal, India has supported a federal, democratic, republican and inclusive Constitution. We note the promulgation in Nepal today of a Constitution.

We are concerned that the situation in several parts of the country bordering India continues to be violent. Our Ambassador in Kathmandu has spoken to the Prime Minister of Nepal in this regard. We urge that issues on which there are differences should be resolved through dialogue in an atmosphere free from violence and intimidation, and institutionalized in a manner that would enable broad-based ownership and acceptance. This would lay the foundation of harmony, progress and development in Nepal.

We extend our best wishes to the people of Nepal.

New Delhi
September 20, 2015

The next day, India's Ministry of External Affairs issued a similar statement:

Ministry of External Affairs
Government of India

Home | Visits | Media Center / Documents | Overseas Indian Affairs | E-Citizen/Tenders | Useful

Media Center

Home › Media Center / Documents › Press Releases

Statement on the situation in Nepal

September 21, 2015

We are deeply concerned over the incidents of violence resulting in death and injury in regions of Nepal bordering India following the promulgation of Constitution yesterday. Our freight companies and transporters have also voiced complaints about the difficulties they are facing in movement within Nepal and their security concerns, due to the prevailing unrest.

We had repeatedly cautioned the political leadership of Nepal to take urgent steps to defuse the tension in these regions. This, if done in a timely manner, could have avoided these serious developments.

We have consistently argued that all sections of Nepal must reach a consensus on the political challenges confronting them. The issues facing Nepal are political in nature and cannot be resolved through force. We still hope that initiatives will be taken by Nepal's leadership to effectively and credibly address the causes underlying the present state of confrontation.

New Delhi
September 21, 2015

On December 21, 2015, India made another statement condemning the killings in Terai:

Ministry of External Affairs
Government of India

Home | Visits | Media Center / Documents | Overseas Indian Affairs | E-Citizen/Tenders | Use

Media Center

Home › Media Center / Documents › Press Releases

Statement on Nepal

December 21, 2015

1. External Affairs Minister was informed by Nepal's Deputy PM and Foreign Minister Kamal Thapa today that the Nepalese Cabinet has taken some important decisions to address and resolve demands regarding the Constitution raised by agitating Madhes-based parties.
2. These decisions include amendments to the Constitution on participation in the state organs on the basis of proportionate inclusiveness and delineation of electoral constituencies on the basis of population. The demarcation of provinces is also to be addressed through an appropriate arrangement in the Constitution on the basis of political consensus. Similarly, others demands including citizenship are to be resolved through negotiations and consensus.
3. Government of India welcomes these developments as positive steps that help create the basis for a resolution of the current impasse in Nepal. As a neighbour and well-wisher, India was deeply concerned at the unrest stemming from internal differences in Nepal on the Constitution. We urge all Nepali political forces to now demonstrate the necessary maturity and flexibility to find a satisfactory solution to the Constitutional issues through constructive dialogue in an agreed timeframe.
4. We are confident that a return to normalcy in Nepal would create a more secure and predictable climate for unimpeded commerce between our two countries.

New Delhi,
December 21, 2015

Nepalese Foreign Minister Kamal Thapa went to Delhi and handed over a four-Point roadmap to Indian External Affairs Minister Sushma Swaraj, which outlined the possibility of constitutional amendments regarding proportional inclusion, an electoral system based on population and the formation of a high-level political committee giving three months to revise the federal boundaries. After his return from Delhi, I had a chance to see the original text of the four-point roadmap. I made some corrections to the language of the roadmap, which were conveyed to the Madhesi party leaders that same evening.

Ministry of External Affairs
Government of India

Search | English

Home | Visits | Media Center / Documents | Overseas Indian Affairs | E-Citizen/Tenders | Useful Links | What's New

Media Center

Home › Media Center / Documents › Press Releases

Statement by Official Spokesperson on developments in Nepal (January 24, 2016)

January 24, 2016

We regard the two amendments passed yesterday by the Nepali Parliament as positive developments. We hope that other outstanding issues are similarly addressed in a constructive spirit.

Media Center / Documents
- Spokesperson's Office
- Speeches & Statements
- Press Releases
- Bilateral/Multilateral Documents
- Media Briefings
- Photo Gallery

UPR Statement on India

During the November 2015, Universal Periodic Review (UPR) in Geneva for the first time in its history, India raised the issues of the Madhesi not only at the bilateral level but at a multilateral platform like the United Nations. See the original statement in the box:

Universal Periodic Review (UPR) Working Group

23rd Session (2–13 November 2015)

2nd UPR of Nepal–Interactive Dialogue

Wednesday, 4 November 2015, 14:30–18:00 hrs

Statement of India

Mr. President,

1. India welcomes the delegation of Nepal led by H.E. Mr. Kamal Thapa, Deputy Prime Minister and Minister of Foreign Affairs.

Mr. President,

2. The people of Nepal, having endured a devastating earthquake in April 2015, are facing another tough challenge during the ongoing political transition. Violence and instability in parts of Nepal has worsened in the

run-up to and after the adoption of Nepal's Constitution in September 2015. Over 45 persons died, mostly civilians, and hundreds injured. Firings, which had ceased just after the adoption of the constitution, have recurred. We are concerned over the lack of political progress.

3. We note the concerns expressed by UN human rights bodies, UN Country Team and Nepal's own Human Rights Commission over continuing incidents of violence, extra-judicial killings and ethnic discrimination in the country. We urge the government of Nepal to investigate and take credible measures to prevent their recurrence. Problems facing Nepal are political in nature and cannot be resolved through force or a security-based approach.
4. As a close and friendly neighbour, India has consistently appealed to the government of Nepal to address all challenges in a spirit of dialogue and reconciliation. We recommend the government of Nepal to,
   (i) consolidate the constitution building and democratization process by accommodating all sections of Nepal to enable broad-based ownership and participation;
   (ii) ensure effective functioning of Truth and Reconciliation Commission and full implementation of its recommendations, including prosecution of those responsible for violent insurgency;
   (iii) ensure the independence and financial autonomy of the National Human Rights Commission, and
   (iv) set up an independent Commission for children and women.

Mr. President,

5. Obstruction referred in the Hon'ble Minister's Statement is on Nepalese side caused by Nepalese protesters.
6. India, with deep-rooted historic and cultural ties, will continue to extend all assistance to Nepal, for peace, stability and socio-economic development of the country.

Thank you Mr. President.

This historic statement surprised many. India had never addressed the UN on human rights issues, including transitional justice. This time India not only highlighted the issue of Madhes and Madhesis on an international platform, but it also indicated that it could no longer protect the interests of the elite. India raised further concerns over the Nepali State's accountability on human rights violations by The army/security forces and Maoists.

India raised three points concerning Madhesis in Nepal. First, that the constitution had deprived Madhesis of their rights and failed to reflect their aspirations. Second, that there is ethnic discrimination in Nepal. And third, that the killings of people during protests in the Terai were brutal as most of them sustained bullet injuries on chest, head or other parts of the body above the knee.

I believe that the Indian Ambassador to Nepal, Ranjit Rai, who was closely following the constitution-making process in Nepal, put those lines in India's Statement for the UPR, risking his career. The Indian UPR statement concerning the issues in Nepal irritated the Kathmandu establishment.

Acknowledging the Indian Ambassador's courageous role, I sometimes joke among my colleagues that the Madhes should name a road in his honour. He has played a praiseworthy role in ensuring social justice for marginalized communities and other issues that are crucial for the marginalized communities' empowerment. The amendment has incorporated proportional inclusion and an electoral system based on population. These efforts will prove to be milestone efforts in building stability and peace in Nepal.

I was in the hall of the UPR session in Geneva when the statement appeared. Before the UPR session started, Sadbhavana party leader Devendra Yadav had protested by burning copies of the new constitution in front of the

UN building in Geneva. This was another surprise for the PEON.

I was not much familiar with leader Yadav. I met him on the flight to Geneva, which included a Nepali delegation led by Foreign Minister Kamal Thapa. I was surprised that he was going to be in attendance, but later came to learn much from him in Geneva, when he showed pictures of police brutality in front of the UN OHCHR building and the burnt copies of the constitution.

During the six-month-long protest, fifty-two people were killed by security personnel in the Terai, under the pretext of bringing the demonstrations under control. Through circulations, updates and reports, the Supreme Court of Nepal, National Human Rights Commission, UN bodies, Human Rights Watchdog, Asian Human Rights Commission, and the governments of the United States, and India repeatedly expressed concerns over the excessive use of force by law enforcement bodies and urged the Nepal Government to use the minimum force necessary to maintain peace. 89 per cent of those who received bullets got hit either in the head or the chest, suggesting that the gunfire from security personnel was deliberate and professional in nature. In fact, the killings stopped only after the Indian intervention.

A week before the second session of Universal Periodic Review, UN High Commissioner for Human Rights Zeid Ra'ad Al Hussein asked the Nepal Government to conduct a full and independent investigation into the Terai killings.

EU–India Statement

On March 30, 2016, the European Union (EU) and Government of India issued a joint statement on the need for a time-bound settlement of the remaining constitutional issues. It came against a backdrop of the six-month-long

Madhes movement and the four-month-long border blockade. Clause 17 of the joint Statement reads as follows:

> 17. The EU and India pledged continued support to Nepal in its reconstruction efforts following the devastating eqrthquakes in 2015, including capacity building and long term development. They also agreed on the need for a lasting and inclusive Constitutional settlement in Nepal that will address the remaining Constitutional issues in a timebound manner, and promote political stability and economic growth. They encouraged an inclusive dialogue between all political parties in the Maldives and reform that ensures respect for democracy, human rights and the rule of law.

The very next day, Nepal's Ministry of Foreign Affairs condemned the EU–India remarks about the new constitution. Foreign Minister Kamal Thapa asserted that the new statute fully reflected the aspirations of Nepalis.

If that were so, why did the Madhesis agitate for six months resulting in the deaths of 55 people, including ten policemen? Why did the government have to make two amendments soon after the constitution was promulgated? Prime Minister Pushpa Kamal Dahal has publicly said that the outstanding constitutional issues, including the demarcation of provinces, would be addressed through constitutional amendments.

The joint EU–India Statement is not the first time that the international community has expressed concern about social inclusion in Nepal. India, the UK, the US and the UN issued similar messages after the constitution was promulgated.

Can such references to the constitution be termed as interference in Nepal's domestic affairs? The EU is one of the world's major regional blocs that supports democracy, human rights and social inclusion. When Nepal's democratic forces fought against the monarchy, the global community

Government of Nepal

MINISTRY OF FOREIGN AFFAIRS

Kathmandu, Nepal

Press Release

Serious attention of the Government of Nepal has been drawn to the reference to Nepal made in the Joint Statement of the 13th EU-India Summit held in Brussels on 30 March 2016.

As is known to all that Nepal has promulgated the constitution through a democratically elected Constituent Assembly. The constitution fully accommodates the aspirations of the people of Nepal. The promulgation of the constitution formally concludes the nationally-driven peace process initiated in 2006 and institutionalizes significant democratic gains including federal and republican system. The constitution making and its promulgation are essentially internal matters of a country. Nepal has now moved ahead along the path of political stability and economic development.

Against this backdrop, the EU-India Joint Statement not only hurts the sentiments of the people of Nepal but also defies the fundamental principle of non-interference in internal affairs of a country in breach of UN Charter and norms of international law. The Government of Nepal calls on all to fully respect the sovereign and democratic rights of the people of Nepal and refrain from making uncalled for statements. The Government and people of Nepal are fully capable of resolving their issues themselves within the framework of the constitution.

Ministry of Foreign Affairs
Government of Nepal
31 March 2016

sided with them. In 2006, the EU called upon Nepal's civil society members to continue their quest for democracy, and issued a statement supporting the democratic movement.

India too, being a democratic country, supports democracy and social inclusion, and there is nothing new in its attempt to back the policy of social inclusion in Nepal. India has always supported democratic forces in Nepal, whether the movement was against the Rana administrators, panchayat system or Gyanendra monarchy. In today's world countries have absolute sovereignty but they cannot avoid external pressures. The well-being of human beings is a matter of concern for everybody in the international community. Sovereignty cannot grant a country the power to commit injustice against its minorities.

No state in the world can escape criticism for denying democracy and social justice to its own people. Had the global community not spoken out against such injudges, we would never have seen so many dictatorships around the world change into democracies. Neither would we have seen the socio-economic rights of human beings, particularly of the marginalized communities, expanded and championed around the world. In these modern times, traditional principles of sovereignty and non-interference are undergoing changes.

Nepal's new constitution has granted one community, the Khas-Arya, status as a constitutional community, thus creating fear in the minds of other communities and leading them to disown the statute. The ruling parties have been saying that the constitution was framed with the support of an overwhelming majority and that therefore no one should question it. My questions are these:

- Can a 90 per cent majority allow injustice to be done against the remaining 10 percent?
- Are there not people like Bimalendra Nidhi and Amresh Kumar Singh among the 90 per cent of the constituent assembly members who endorsed the constitution but wanted amendments made to it?
- If there was no need for any constitutional amendments, why did Prime Minister Sushil Koirala table amendment bills in the Parliament?
- Why did Deputy Prime Minister and Foreign Minister Kamal Thapa give a four-point roadmap to India, outlining the need for constitutional amendments?

When there are constitutional issues in Nepal, it is natural for India or other foreign countries to express concern about them. This does not amount to interference in Nepal's affairs because no country in the world commits injustice against its own people in the name of sovereignty and non-interference. We should not forget that when veteran Indian leader Chandra Shekhar boosted the morale of the democratic fighters at Chaksibari on the eve of the 1990 People's Movement, Nepali leaders were all praise for his speech.

Where did India Fail?

Given the fact that India has long supported the framing of a new constitution in Nepal, it ultimately failed at the time of its promulgation.

By the end of Nepal's constitution-making process, India had lost its clout in Nepal. India pushed for issues of social inclusion in the constitution but it could not convince the members of European Union and the United States of America that its concern for those issues was legitimate and that it had no hidden agenda of declaring Nepal a Hindu State. Instead, EU member states and the US felt that India's advocacy for social inclusion was just a pretext to mask its real agenda in Nepal. Rastriya Swayamsevak Sangh (RSS), a hardline Hindu organization, was also active in Nepal, and the ruling class discreetly used different channels to communicate with the Indian power centres.

Another reason why India failed in Nepal is that it took its traditional allies for granted. It sincerely believed that the Nepali Congress Party, including NC influential leaders such as Krishna Prasad Sitaula, would listen to its advice and recommendations. What India failed to understand was that all the Khas-Arya forces, including the Nepali Congress and the CPN-UML, stood together on constitutional issues particularly vis-à-vis the Madhes. This was also why India did not have any say in the 16-Point

Deal that the four forces—the Nepali Congress, the CPN-UML, the CPN-MC-Maoist and the Madhesi Janadhikar Forum-Democratic—signed on June 8, 2015.

India was unaware until the last minute that the major forces were going to have a provision in the constitution that would give equal seats to each province in the Upper House of the Parliament.

Furthermore, India's Minister of External Affairs, Sushma Swaraj, had a problematic personal link with the Hindu State proponent and Rastriya Prajatantra Party-Nepal Chair Kamal Thapa, who was also Deputy Prime Minister and the Minister of Foreign Affairs in the Oli-led government. Although the Embassy of India in Kathmandu gave their own assessment of the situation, Swaraj often relied on Thapa to verify information that she received from her staff.

Madhesis also failed to convince Indian leaders of the cause they were championing. Instead, Madhesi leaders, at the behest of Indian leaders, went to the Parliament and voted in favour of NC President Sushil Koirala, who contested for premiership against CPN-UML Chair K.P. Sharma Oli. This move by Madhesi leaders, who had agitated against the constitution, was shocking to the people in Madhes, who then protested against the action.

India lent direct and indirect support to the Madhes movement. India supported the blockade imposed on the border entry points, which in a way helped to stop killings of protesters. Prior to the imposition of blockade, a number of protesters, who had gathered in the district headquarters or on the highway to protest against the constitution, died due to the use of lethal force by the police. But India's overt support ultimately proved to be a disadvantage for the Madhes movement. People in Kathmandu and other parts of the country believed that Madhesi forces were instigated by India to protest against the constitution.

India used multiple channels to deal with Nepali power centres and stakeholders. PM Oli was aware of this fact and used it to his advantage. He used industrialist Binod Chaudhary to talk to Indian power centres through Mahindra and Maruti business groups, by asking them to talk to Indian power centres and moderate India's stance vis-à-vis constitutional issues of Nepal. The Oli government also used religious leader Ravi Shankar to exert pressure on the BJP Government, by influencing religious leaders such as the BJP advocates of Sanatan Dharma in India.

India seemed to be interested in settling with Nepali rulers for bilateral concessions. But it failed to wield its influence in the final stages of the constitution-making process in Nepal, even after signing bilateral agreements with the Nepali state, which has led to increased political instability in Nepal.

10

Human Rights Politics in Nepal

Visit to Geneva

Every human rights defender or activist always wishes to visit Geneva, Switzerland some day. Geneva is the second-largest site of the United Nations (UN), second only to the UN Headquarters in New York City.

As someone who closely follows human rights issues in Nepal, the situation that unfolded in the two months leading up to the promulgation of the constitution of Nepal on September 20, 2015, and its aftermath, prompted me to plan a visit to the UN Office in Geneva.

Dissatisfaction among people on some of the contents of the new constitution, particularly among Madhesis and Tharus across the Terai region, triggered protests in Nepal since mid-July of 2015. On these same issues and with the same demands, they had already launched two movements in the years 2007 and 2008.

By October 2015, the third Madhes movement was at its peak in Nepal. Over three dozen people in Madhes were killed in a police crackdown while they were exercising their fundamental rights to protest in a peaceful manner. The blatant actions of law enforcement agencies to crack down on protests against some discriminatory provisions of the country's new constitution also led to the deprivation of the demonstrators' right to life as guaranteed by Nepal's Constitution. This upset me.

Coincidentaly, the review of Nepal's human rights record during the UN Universal Periodic Review (UPR) was scheduled in Geneva for November 4, 2015. As an independent human rights observer, I thought it would be a good opportunity to present the serious human rights violations on the UN platform. I went to Geneva with the motive to lobby with the UN delegations and stakeholders for action against the excessive use of force by law enforcement agencies of Nepal, so that they might raise these issues with the delegation from the Nepal Government.

My visit to Geneva for the first time brought back memories of my first visit to Kathmandu back in 2003.

I still recall Kathmandu was very cold when I first stepped into the capital city that year. Madhes had just finished its greatest festival 'Chhath', and it was the onset of the cold season in Kathmandu. Early one morning, I got off the night bus when it stopped at Balkhu in Kathmandu after almost 12 hours of travel from the Campus Chowk in Janakpur.

Undeterred by the weather, I, a 22-year-old boy of dark complexion and good height, carrying a sack of 20 kilos of rice on my head, and a bagful of my clothes in my hand, walked towards the Balkhu Kumari Club.

At that time, I was in the final year of my Bachelor of Arts degree, and I wanted to pursue legal studies. Mahesh Baba, one of the respected personalities in my village of Mahottari, used to tell me that I had skills to present logic, and suggested to me that I should study law. Since there was no lawyer from my community, he motivated me to become one. His words and belief inspired me further to become the advocate that I am today.

When I shared my plan to study law in Kathmandu my father refused, saying that he could not afford the high cost of my studies and living in the capital. But my mother, who never went to school, intervened. She said that she could send me some money every month after selling rice. Finally, my father agreed to send me a thousand rupees per month. Though my mother was completely illiterate, and could not even write her name, she encouraged me to study law.

The day before I left for Kathmandu from Janakpur, my father handed me a thousand rupee note. And I made the journey to Kathmandu, where I completed my studies and worked for the National Human Rights Commission before I moved on to study for my Master's in Human Rights from Mahidol University in Thailand, and another Master's degree in Conflict and Peace Studies from Bradford University in the UK under the Chevening Scholarship programme.

The circumstances were like going for higher studies when I made the plan to visit Geneva. I wrote an email to Ingrid Massage, who always offered support to any Nepali who stands in favour of human rights and justice. She contacted Amnesty International officials, who were willing to cover my travel costs to Geneva.

Thanks to Ingrid, I flew to Geneva on the evening of October 31, 2015. After 16 hours of flights, I landed in Switzerland's second most populous city.

For two days (November 2 and 3, 2015) before the Universal Periodic Review (UPR) session for Nepal scheduled in Geneva (November 4, 2015), I held informal discussions with representatives of different international human rights agencies and UN member State delegations. In my meetings, I presented the documented evidence proving excessive use of force by law enforcement agencies during protests against Nepal's new constitution.

I attended a meeting with the Human Rights Committee (HRC) members about the implementation of the HRC recommendations in Nepal. All the members of the committee agreed that Nepal always says that it has delivered justice to the victims of human rights violations but, in fact, that rhetoric does not reflect what victims have experienced in real life. I spoke about the Nepal Government's failure to implement the Supreme Court stay order to not use excessive force in the ongoing protests in Terai. The trend of implementing the NHRC recommendations, I said, particularly vis-à-vis the prosecution of human rights violators, was minimal.

I am glad that my lobbying efforts and discussions were able to influence the submission to the Human Rights Council's Universal Periodic Review concerning human rights in Nepal, which covered excessive use of force by security forces, impunity enjoyed by security forces, freedom of expression and caste-based discrimination among others.

Nepal's Second Universal Periodic Review: A Missed Opportunity for Nepal

The human rights records of 14 states, including Nepal, were reviewed by the UPR Working Group during the 23rd UPR session, which took place from November 2 to 13, 2015. This was the second time that Nepal's human rights record were reviewed at this level; Nepal's first UPR took place on January 25, 2011.

A delegation led by Deputy Prime Minister and Minister for Foreign Affairs Kamal Thapa was in attendance representing the Nepal government.

Many countries, including Belgium, the Czech Republic, Germany, Switzerland, Norway, Slovenia, Sweden and the United Kingdom, questioned the serious human rights violations in Nepal.

In response to the questions in advance and recommendations made by UN member states during the Nepal's UPR session, Deputy Prime Minister and Foreign Minister Kamal Thapa delivered a 20-minute speech, speaking about the disruption of supplies resulting from the unofficial blockade imposed by India. Due to the transit disruption, Nepal incurred a loss of $5bn over the past two months, he said. Disruption of transit was not acceptable under any pretext because it infringed the rights of a landlocked country. In response, Indian delegates later informed Mr Thapa that the obstruction was on the Nepali side caused by the protesters, and not by the Indian State. Throughout his speech, DPM Thapa looked emotional, and at the end, he apologized to the chair for becoming emotional, and pleaded for help to reopen transit facilities. He utilized the forum to bring the issue of the blockade to the world's attention.

Instead of acknowledging the issue of human rights violations, he seemed to defend them. He told the session that Nepal was competent enough to handle its own internal issues. He mentioned Madhes many times in his speech, but had no regret for the deaths of the people including security personnel during the protests. He missed an opportunity to win the confidence of the agitating parties and boost the Nepal government's commitment towards its UN obligations.

The Nepal delegation did not recognize the report of its own constitutional body, the National Human Rights Commission (NHRC), which had included details on the deaths of 49 people. This was absolutely regrettable. Instead, the delegation of Nepal utilized the forum to obfuscate the human rights issues. They could have acknowledged the issues of human rights raised during the UPR session, and expressed Nepal's commitments to institutional and policy reforms.

Nonetheless, many countries including Sweden, Switzerland, Belgium, Czech Republic and India raised the Madhesi issue. Despite the government's effort to whitewash the problem, the UPR session mainstreamed the issues of Madhes, and the killings of Madhesis by the security forces. The raising of the Madhesi issue by the UN member states in a big international forum like the UN is a key achievement of the movement. I also take it as the international community's recognition of the movement.

Human Rights Watch, the National Human Rights Commission, Amnesty International, the Asian Human Rights Commission and the Terai Human Rights Defenders Alliance reported on police excesses, extrajudicial killings and discrimination against the local people in the Terai.

Be it a political or genuine human rights concern, a huge shift in India's position on transitional justice is another reason to highlight the Madhes issue. It was a matter of surprise that India, for the first time ever in her history, took a new stance on transitional justice. Earlier, India had facilitated the 12-Point Deal, the peace process and put the rebels in power. For the first time since the peace process started 10 years ago, India raised the issue of transitional justice mechanisms, its independence, and prosecution of the rights violators. India seems to now recognize that its traditional allies are no longer reliable, marking a huge shift in the Indian foreign policy.

False Projection as Traitor and Armed Group Legal Advisor

While I was coming out of the UPR session hall, I saw all the Nepali bureaucrats, human rights activists, media and civil society members together, taking selfies with DPM Thapa. For them, Thapa was a hero for speaking against the blockade, rebutting the Indian statement of killing of 55 Madhesis by the state, and presenting the constitution as the world's best constitution. The real hill fraternity domination was reflected on everyone's face. They even forgot that Thapa was named in the Rayamajhi Commission for suppressing the democratic movement in the past.

I felt frustrated to see the true face of the human rights activists and civil society members. That night, everyone was invited to the Nepali Embassy and they celebrated Thapa's speech. To my surprise, I was seen as a traitor who exposed the state's responsibility for killings of Madhesis.

I did not join them at the embassy but returned to my room alone. Before I fell asleep, I recalled Gramsci, who once said that the power holders and ruling class created their own opposition in the name of civil society because at the crucial time when the issue of power sharing comes, they can bargain with their own class, caste and ethnicity. That is why he proposed a counter-hegemonic struggle to recover the original philosophical and ideological significance of civil society, reconnecting them to truly participatory approaches that challenge dominant power structures.

While I was still in Geneva, a human rights activist mentioned me in a Facebook post, suggesting that I was responsible for taking Debendra Yadav to Geneva. I immediately replied that it was a false accusation. But the rumour had spread that I had participated with Yadav in burning the constitution outside the UN building.

One of my friends who visited Geneva from Nepal told me that I had defamed the country by burning the constitution.

I responded:

"It is not me. But he (Debendra), as a politician, did it. Also as a lawyer, I would never dream of burning the constitution in Geneva or anywhere else."

These accusations from my longtime friend reflected the high social and political polarization that affects even normal people.

In fact, I did not participate in any protest in Geneva. But the photos of other human rights activists from the hill community appeared in the news when they protested against the Indian blockade.

What was more shocking for me was that when I returned to Kathmandu from Geneva, I suspect some of the Kathmandu-based human rights activists circulated a fake document of some armed groups, that contained my forged signature and I was mentioned as a legal advisor to these armed groups. This was beyond my imagination. A number of messages asking for clarification swamped me. I was shocked to later discover that a group of human rights activists from Kathmandu backed by a few gatekeepers in diplomatic agencies in support of locals from Sunsari and high profile leaders of ruling parties were involved in fabricating and circulating the false statement.

I believe that non-violent peaceful methods are the best ways to bring about changes. This is the core principle of my life. They perhaps forgot that I studied non-violence during my master's degree at Bradford University. It does not matter who carries the gun, be it Maoists or Terai armed groups, I could never think of providing advice or support to them.

I know defamation is a tool of the Nepali ruling class. Educated members from marginalized communities are either defamed or coopted. If you refuse to be coopted then they can easily brand you as corrupt, characterless, involved in criminal activities, or uncivilized. The Nepali ruling class has been saying: *Ki hamra ki naramra* ("Either you should be by their side or be ready to be bad"), with no alternative. I was fully aware of this strategy. I asked the police to investigate and take action against those who had made the fake letter and were involved in its circulation. I was also unhappy with the international community who funded this type of anti-human rights activism. I was punished for visiting Geneva and at a reception of the Swiss Embassy, Sudip Pathak, one of NHRC members told me that he had received a letter that I was a legal advisor to the armed groups. A week later, *Hulaki News* published the fake letter and its original, making clear it was someone involved in defaming my character to silence my voice for social justice. These efforts of the Kathmandu-based ruling class Hindu, who also wear the cap of civil society redoubled my conviction to continue my work among the population of the marginalized community. If you fight for people, their blessings and support will always carry you through all kinds of conspiracy.

I only truly felt the benefits of my work in Geneva once I got back to the Terai. On the street, people came up to thank me for challenging the lies of the Nepali state. Most of them had heard my BBC interview. So for more than half of the population, I was a hero. I was relieved and felt justified in my purpose. I received many phone calls for interviews from various radio stations in the Terai. Even in the rural areas people said to me: "Geneva Bala Okil Karara Jawab diya Kamal Thapa ko" (You gave a bold response to Kamal Thapa in Geneva). I was surprised and in fact crying when I travelled to Janakpur remembering the accusations made against me in Kathmandu. It gave me a new sense of how polarized our society has become that one section wants to defame and eliminate me while another called me heroic for my actions. What is my fault? Is being a Madhesi my fault? Does someone with a dark face like me not have the right to engage in human rights activism? Are the legal and human rights sectors just a control centre of one community? These questions often haunt my mind since this experience.

PM Oli Summons NHRC Member Mohna Ansari over her Speech during the 2nd Cycle of UPR

In the morning of April 7, 2016, I learned that Prime Minister K.P. Sharma Oli had summoned NHRC Chair Anup Raj Sharma and Commissioner Mohna Ansari, among others, to a meeting in which PM Oli questioned Ansari over her statement during the second cycle of the UN Universal Periodic Review (UPR) session of Nepal in Geneva.

At the UPR session, NHRC Commissioner Ansari had presented the real situation of human rights in Nepal. In her two-minute speech, she urged the government of Nepal to accept the UPR recommendations. More specifically, she had raised her concerns over the issues, including gender discrimination on citizenship provisions in the new constitution, proper investigation into the Terai's killings during the six months of protests, and delayed rehabilitation of earthquake victims.

All the issues she raised during the March session of Nepal's UPR in Geneva were based on different periodic reports and recommendations made by the constitutional body. Various countries such as the USA, UK, Switzerland, India and other stakeholders, including the United Nations, Human Rights Watch, International Crisis Group, Amnesty

International, and the Asian Human Rights Commission, had presented the same through their circulations.

I was surprised to learn that PM Oli had sought a clarification from Mohna Ansari, and that other members of NHRC remained largely silent while she was being questioned by the PM.

The NHRC is a constitutional body. The constitution has guaranteed its autonomy and independence to oversee human rights issues in the country and draw the attention of the government through recommendations to improve and abide by the rule of law.

The NHRC members were called to the PM's Office for questioning and clarifications over its independent activities. This constituted an absolute breach of the jurisdiction as provided by the constitution, and this also acted against the Paris Principles on National Human Rights Institutions.

However, most of the human rights organizations based in Kathmandu maintained silence as the interference was from the high-level members of the UML, to whom they are close.

Some media outlets (including *Jan Astha*) criticized the NHRC for the UPR Statement. It seemed as if the media, which is regarded as the fourth organ of the state, also favoured the government to put pressure on the constitutional body.

The interfering steps of the PM's Office revealed their anger with NHRC Commissioner Ansari, not with the NHRC itself, but her individually. She is a woman, a Muslim and a Madhesi. Media reports presented the news that the PM's questions were targeted at no other members than her. It seems the media forgot that she made her speech in the capacity of an NHRC Commissioner, not as an individual.

Immediate intervention by international human rights communities, and the opposition from different communities against the PM's move, led him to take a step back. A joint statement of ICJ, HRW and Amnesty criticized the PM's interference in the independence of NHRC. They warned the PM to fulfil the state's constitutional obligations.

NHRC member Mohna Ansari once again proved herself 'the Iron Lady' by making a bold statement for human rights and justice in Nepal during the UPR session.

Politics and Human Rights

One other achievement of the three different Madhes movements, which took place in a span of less than a decade, is that they have significantly boosted the human rights movement in Nepal. During the first and second Madhes movements, the contradictory roles of long-established human rights watchdogs had only created divisions among the people, particularly Pahadi (hill origin) vs. Madhesi. Similarly, even in the hill areas, rights holders and stakeholders perceived their roles in terms of the dichotomy between Bahaun (higher caste) vs. indigenous people and Dalit (the lower castes).

The majority of human rights organizations in Nepal have political affiliates. The political parties tend to use their human rights affiliate to cause problems for competing parties. This makes the roles of human rights bodies contradictory. Concerns over the violation of human rights are determined by the parties or ideologies they carry. As a result, many human rights organizations in Nepal remained silent when state agencies cracked down on the recent Madhes movement.

Some human rights bodies cooperate with the government whilst others remain in opposition. The cooperation and the opposition roles of human rights activists are always influenced by the position of the political parties they are closer to. This influences the nominations for posts or members of different constitutional bodies, commissions or short-term committees. The political nomination of human rights activists on some commissions and constitutional bodies has a high chance of influencing the political parties in dealing with human rights issues.

The practice of manipulating issues of human rights has gained public legitimacy, as civil society usually draws power from political society rather than from their social bases. This trend has devalued both the concept and the actual movement. Krishna Hachhethu calls this political division as "civil in name but political in purpose." The formation of five open forums—the Democratic National Unity Forum, National People's Forum, Civic Rights Forum, People's Right Protection Forum and Human Rights Protection Forum—in 1985 by the Communist Party of Nepal (ML later renamed as UML) is an example of the overlap between human rights and political society

Most of the human rights activists are limited to attendance at and organization of seminars, workshops and meetings. People outside the human rights arena often perceive them as aliens who do not take into account the social reality, and its members as working for high salaries and luxurious standards of living.

Similarly, the lack of internal democratic structure has further created a sense of doubt among common people to question the credibility of the human rights organizations. People have started questioning the source of funding before taking part in their programmes and activities. Based on my experience, what I claim is that the human rights movement in Nepal is merely based on the elite theory of democracy that favours the wealthy and the higher classes, who do not believe in the classical model of participatory democracy.

In the context of Nepal, the human rights movement is totally controlled by hill Brahmin males, mostly affiliated with CPN-UML. And like the UML, these human rights activists have a jaundiced view of social justice. They have a monopoly over the human rights sector, be it INGOs or human rights desks at embassies and diplomatic missions. During their employment, they feed one-sided information into official reports and establish their linkage with international actors. The privileged class dismisses the genuine agenda of justice by terming it as bogus political campaigns backed by external forces with vested interests in Nepal.

Prosecution of human rights violators is rare when they are members of major political parties or government. The closeness of human rights activists to the power centers of political parties and security agencies is therefore problematic. There has hardly been any occasion when human rights bodies in Nepal have stood together and worked together for the justice of human rights violations.

If the human rights movement is to succeed in Nepal, social justice must be an integral part of this movement. As it stands, there is a psychological barrier between the rights activists representing two sections: the privileged class and the marginalized sections. This barrier is at the root of why high caste hill Brahmin human rights activists do not get support from the human rights activists from marginalized communities and vice versa. The current status quo discourages other actors in the marginalized communities to become involved in rights advocacy. They want their staff to appear inclusive, but not take on leadership roles. Those who try to come forward in a leadership role asserting the voice of social justice and equality are either coopted or defamed. The ruling activists say they are by birth free from corruption, well-behaved and follow the principles of human rights, whereas the marginalized community is by birth corrupt (it does not matter how honest the members of marginalized communities are). I simply call it racism, which is more deeply rooted in civil society in Nepal.

Human Rights and the Media

On August 24, 2015, a mob of demonstrators killed eight security personnel, including the Senior Superintendent of Police (SSP) Laxman Neupane.

Soon after the incident, I condemned violence in Tikapur on social media, urging both sides to demonstrate immediate restraint and asking for an independent investigation.

The Nepali media reports about the Tikapur killings were highly provocative. The sentiment on social media was as if all Madhesi and Tharus were "terrorists." I was mentioned in many tweets questioning the responsibility for the incident, as though I were responsible for the violence. That night I could not sleep due to threats and intimidation on social media. Later on, I changed the security setting of my twitter so that I could not be tagged.

It was difficult for me to travel publicly in Kathmandu during this time. I would hide myself in public places because I used to be questioned about the incident. Even at my workplace in the premises of the Supreme Court, I was intimidated on one occasion. I was then compelled to complain to Sunil Pokharel, the then Secretary of Nepal Bar Association, about my being ill treated.

Ironically, when Madhesis were killed in Birgunj, Mahottari, Janakpur, Rajbiraj and Rupandehi, the lives of Madhesis did not matter much to Nepali mainstream media. The killing of Madhesis during protests lacked in-depth reporting. Rather, it looked like incident reporting.

Less coverage about the death of demonstrators and innocent people could not be justified under the pretext of violent protests and consequences of the Tikapur incident. Readers from Madhes were irate at the biased media coverage. They burnt copies of national newspapers in Birgunj, Janakpur and Rajbiraj and vandalized vehicles belonging to the media houses.

Through this experience I came to realize the lack of diversity in Nepali mainstream media. There is very little representation of Madhesi and Tharu communities in the newsroom. The newsrooms are mostly controlled by the hill Brahmins, who only constitute around 12 per cent of the total population. But they have complete control over the media.

In the Unites States, at least the media stand against killings when a black man is killed by a white policeman. However, I found the reverse to be the case in Nepal. The media in Nepal follow the culture of blame game to victimize the victim further.

However, international media and some alternative online media sources like *Setopati* and *Online Khabar*, countered with the other side of the story to reveal the truth. Even when the media was polarized on the incident, *Setopati* and *Kathmandu Post* provided me with space to publish my opinion pieces. They trusted me and did not edit my views to promote particular values, and upheld ethical standards with regard to human rights, rule of law, and non-violent approach in a democratic society.

In August and September 2015, Human Rights Watch (HRW) released a report on human rights violations entitled "Like We Are Not Nepali: Protest and Police Crackdown in the Terai Region of Nepal". The report sparked a public debate in Nepal. It said that during the protests leading up to the adoption of a new constitution, eight policemen and 36 civilians were killed.

Immediately after the release of the report, some Nepali human rights activists and journalists challenged HRW with allegations such as biased and one-sided reporting. Then, social media enthusiast Robert Penner, a Canadian national, who the government of Nepal deported without any substantial proof, wrote an article[1] debunking this misinformation about the HRW report, and has generated another public debate and discussion. Mr. Penner's write-up affirmed that all the allegations by the commentators were baseless themselves.

In the human rights sector, the gap in the United Nations' capacity to monitor human rights is filled by a burgeoning number of non-governmental organizations such as Amnesty International, the International Commission of Jurists, and Human Rights Watch. They have developed a fact-finding capacity that has far outstripped that of the governments or the UN itself. Most aspired to emulate the impartiality and assiduous fact-finding pioneered by Amnesty International and HRW.[2]

The findings of these pioneering human rights organizations provide stark contrasts to Nepal-based human rights organizations that do not practise impartial reporting. Had they followed the practice of writing such a professional report, Nepali public figures could not have raised questions over HRW's report being biased. Actually, the report, which is based on eyewitness testimony and evidence collected during monitoring on ground, is a fine document.

In many cases, journalists have not been adequately trained and sensitized on the issue of human rights. Consequently, media reports incorporate emotion, prejudice and misinformation rather than reporting human rights issues in an objective and professional manner.

Human rights and media are the eyes and ears of a society. They are indispensable elements for the consolidation of democracy. Both of them play an important role in collecting, verifying, producing and distributing information to the general public.

If they turn out to be emotional, ignoring any fact-checking and evidence-based analysis, the society may not only be divided, but will be inclined toward a deep level of discrimination. They may be unable to pressurize the duty bearers to ensure justice for all the victims, and change their attitudes and tactics to prevent these abuses of power from recurring.

Excessive Use of Force in the Terai

A special report on Nepal Protest and Repression, jointly published by the Asian Human Rights Commission (AHRC) and the Terai Human Rights Defenders Alliance (THRDA) in May 2016, holds the state responsible for the use of force in the Terai, which is governed by the constitution of Nepal and by applicable international norms. During my visit to victims' families across the Terai, one of the most frequently asked questions was whether the families would ever receive justice. They also asked how they could prosecute the police who killed their loved ones. Learning about my profession, they inquired if the victims could take the case to the International Criminal Court if justice was denied in their homeland.

Although it was difficult for me to answer their questions, I managed to respond to them as part of the process of reconciliation. I pledged to support and always stand by them for justice. While my answer may have comforted the bereaved families in some small way, I wonder if they will ever get justice. I fear it is impossible in a country like ours where deep-rooted impunity from criminal acts is available to those in power. At the same time, I tell myself that time is the great answer and I hope for the day when violators of human rights will be punished for their actions.

I believe that the killing of security forces in Tikapur and Mahottari is condemnable. But how fair is it to form an investigation commission for the killing of security personnel in Tikapur, and leave other cases uninvestigated? The killing of Assistant Sub-inspector Thaman Singh BK and dozens of Madhesis deserves investigation and prosecution if we want to restore and rebuild the trust of the Madhesi populace towards the Nepali State. In the aftermath of the Tikapur killings, some Tharu-owned houses were set on fire and false charges were filed against some Tharus. These issues are also a subject of investigation.

I took stock of the losses and aspirations of the victims' families during my visits. On a week-long visit to the Terai (Bara, Parsa and Morang) in February 2016, I met Federal Socialist Forum Nepal (FSFN) Parsa Chair Pradeep Yadav, an emerging leader, who coordinated the recent Madhes movement.

On February 28, 2016, Pradeep called an informal gathering of UDMF leaders where I spoke for almost two hours to boost the spirits of those who felt defeated in this movement. The next morning, I was surprised to find that the talk was featured on the front page of *Prateek Dainik*, a popular newspaper of Birgunj.

Following the talk, I visited more victims' families. My childhood friend Dilip accompanied me to the home of Sohan Shah Kalwar. It was a single-room house made of mud walls. Sohan's mother was sitting outside. Whenever we asked how she was, she could not contain the tears in her eyes. She started crying and kept asking us why her son was killed.

Sohan's mother later explained to us that all the family members and two cows had to live together in the same room. Sohan was the only breadwinner of the family. Her story made me wonder at why the poor always sacrifice their lives in these movements.

She told us that Sohan's wife, after his death, started running a hotel near Ghantaghar chowk. When we reached her hotel, she was serving rice in a plate to a rickshaw puller. The rickshaw puller was helping her to serve the other customers. She ran a hotel in a mud hut, which was ill furnished.

We did not reveal our identity, although she might have recognized that we looked different from regular customers. We sat on the chairs and asked for tea. While we were having tea, we asked many questions related to the needs of her family. We also came to learn that some kind-hearted people had pledged to support her by donating a fridge. We also supported her with some cash so that she could purchase goods for her business.

I was sad to learn that a woman lost her husband in the Madhes movement at a young age. I then felt happy to find her running a small business to keep herself busy and earn the livelihood for the family. I appreciated the self-reconciliation process.

Then, I went to Kalaiya, district headquarters of Bara to meet another victim's family. Pinky Yadav, a local woman leader, joined us to visit Hifajat Miya's home. She always remained at the forefront of the movement. The young and courageous lady played a vital role in getting women to take part in the movement.

It was my second visit to Hifajat Miya's home. I first visited the family when Hifajat's dead body was still in the hospital. On the same day when police shot him dead, his wife had delivered a baby.

On my second visit, I saw a newborn boy who looked healthy. I came to learn the name of the baby is 'Imtehan', which means examination or struggle. I carried the boy in my lap while we spent a few hours discussing the family's situation and whether they had received any support.

Hifjat's wife looked healthier than when I saw her during my first visit. According to the family, they had voted for the Nepali Congress, and yet the government led by the same party killed their innocent son. He just wanted his rights to be ensured in the new constitution.

Mohammad Sams Tabrej's grandfather, who I met during my visit to Tejapakad in Rautahat, is a teacher. He told me that his grandson was just 16 when police shot him dead during the Madhes movement while he was on his way back to his rented room in Gaur from Trijudhha Higher Secondary School.

According to his grandfather, Tabrej's sister frequently asked him when her brother would come. The two-year-old sister is still awaiting the return of her brother. She does not know that he will never come back. Hearing this, left me speechless at that time. He asked me how he could get justice.

With THRD Alliance's and our legal aid, the family of Tabrej filed a case in the Hetauda Appellate Court. I could feel the family's high level of commitment. They said that they would fight for justice. The government's compensation provided to them could not return their son. I had pledged my support to help the family get justice.

Another victim, Ram Bibek Yadav, who was just 18, was from Mahottari, the village my sister lives in and in which

I spent my childhood. The newly-married boy was the only son of his father. Ram Bibek's mother recalled that she had stopped her son from going to Jaleshwor on that day. He rode his motorbike to the district headquarters where the demonstrators were staging protests. When police opened fire at demonstrators, Ram Bibek, who was a bystander, got hit and succumbed to bullet injuries.

Ram Bibek's wife gave birth to a baby. I am sure the baby will grow up some day and ask about the whereabouts of his father. To the child, the state cannot compensate the loss of his father.

Priyanka Pandey, whose aim is to get higher education, is now taking care of her two young sisters and running a shop. Her mother was about to close the shutters in Bethari of Rupandehi one evening. A bullet hit her in her head and died.

On my visit to Bhairahwa, Priyanka offered me a cup of tea. I asked her about her studies and the family business. When I asked her if she missed her mother, she was unable to speak.

I could not help myself crying when I learnt that Mahadev Rishidev's five-year-old son from Daniya in Morang always went to the place where his father was cremated. The boy slept there for two hours to feel the warmth of his father's love. Now, the purpose of this young boy's life is to avenge the killing of his father by the Nepali State.

Birendra Ram's wife from Saptari complained that her father-in-law does not want to give her money or compensation, and beats her when she asks for money. The 17-year-old lady, who lost her husband, now had a one-year-old boy in her lap.

Dilip Shah was on his roof playing with his five-year-old daughter when he was hit by a bullet. Can we imagine the level of trauma his young daughter faced? She saw her father's death right in front of her.

The most disturbed I felt was when I visited Bajari of Mahottari, next to my village. Both grandfather and the 15-year-old grandson were killed within a week. The grandson was killed while he was returning from tuition classes and the grandfather was killed while he was in the market to purchase a 'kafan' for his loving grandson.

On September 15, 2015, the 12-year-old Ranjana Singh Kshetri, a resident of Bethari in Rupandehi district, received a bullet in the neck when she stuck her head out of the kitchen to see what was happening outside. On the same day, Binod Lakaul, 48, a resident of Gonaha-6, Bethari, who owned a liquor shop in the market, was shot in the forehead by the police while he was standing behind the counter in his shop.

Such killings and state repression have fuelled the sentiments of the Madhesi and Tharu communities. Like Ranjana, 41 people were killed by the police in the Terai during the Madhes movement and data analysis proves that 22 of them were innocent bystanders like Ranjana and Binod; and 19 others were protesters who did not constitute any immediate risk to the security forces and, therefore, under international standards, should not have been targeted by lethal force.

Politics of Transitional Justice

In a conversation with the former Attorney General Hari Phuyal, a long-time friend, I was told that CPN-MC Chair Pushpa Kamal Dahal 'Prachanda' and senior officials of the Nepali Army had agreed that there would be no amnesty for those involved in four types of cases—killing somebody after taking them under one's control, torture, enforced disappearance, and rape and sexual assaults.

There are about 250 conflict-era cases filed against Maoist leaders by the police, of which 17 cases were filed against CPN-MC Chair Pushpa Kamal Dahal, and 11 cases were filed against top leaders of the party, including former Maoist leader Baburam Bhattarai.

Eight cases were filed by the conflict victims. The major stakeholders have agreed to remove the statute of limitation in serious crimes and criminalize torture and enforced disappearance.

The former Attorney General Hari Phuyal suggested transferring the 250 conflict era cases to a Truth and Reconciliation Commission. He also suggested transferring the eight cases filed by the victims to special court with the consent of the victims and civil society members.

Nepal's peace process is a result of a compromise between the erstwhile CPN-Maoist (now CPN-MC) and the state. Neither the Nepali Army nor CPN-MC have vanquished each other. These two sides are still major power holders. While the Nepali Army (NA) is enjoying state power, the CPN-MC, though reduced to the third largest force in the Parliament, is still in a position to form the government. While the NA enjoys a certain amount of support from India and the United States of America, the CPN-MC enjoys popular support in the country.

This means large scale prosecution will not be possible in Nepal against the Maoist cadres or officials of security agencies. Large scale prosecution will be protested by all three major stakeholders: the security agencies, the CPN-MC and the Nepali Congress, which ruled the country during most part of the 10-year Maoist insurgency. But prosecution in serious human rights violations such as the Doramba incident, Madi carnage, killing of Muktinath Adhikari in Lamjung, killing of Krishna Prasad Adhikari in Chitwan and the killing of Maina Sunuwar of Kavre, is necessary to give a message to the public that serious human rights violations cannot be tolerated under any circumstances. Nepal's Supreme Court has also said that there should be no amnesty in serious cases of human rights violations.

Therefore, there must be prosecution in emblematic cases of human rights violations. One good thing is that both the NA and the CPN-MC have said that they are ready to face 15 to 20 cases of serious human rights violation in the wake of the Madhes movement. Stakeholders need to adopt a strategy to convince both the security agencies and the CPN-MC to face emblematic cases even if the number is slightly higher.

CPN-UML, which controls most of the human rights organizations in Nepal, seems to have adopted dual strategies. On the one hand, the UML consoles the CPN-MC that it does not want to send CPN-MC leaders to jail and rather wants to conclude the issues of peace process to the party's satisfaction. At the same time, however, the UML tells the international community that prosecution in all the cases of rights violation must take place.

The number of cases filed at the TRC and the CIEDP is unexpectedly high. Sources said both the CPN-MC and the Nepali Congress supporters have filed complaints accusing each other. The lack of evidence would be the major challenge in cases filed against leaders and cadres.

Most probably, there will be amnesty for most of the conflict-era rights violations, yet there should be conscious efforts to ensure that Nepal's peace process does not violate universal laws and norms of transitional justice, and that it can bring some semblance of justice to the families of victims.

References

[1] Nepal Public Figures Challenge Human Rights Watch: Madhesi Youth http://www.madhesiyouth.com/human-rights/nepal-public-figures-challenge-human-rights-watch.

[2] Journalism, media and the challenge of human rights reporting http://papers.ssrn.com/sol3/papers.cfm?abstract_id=1551233.

11

Problems with the First Amendment

One of the major reasons behind the agitating forces' resentment against the new constitution was because the new constitution provisioned to treat geography as basis for creating electoral districts besides population. Article 84 (1) stipulated: The House of Representatives shall consist of a total of two hundred and seventy five members, as follows:

(a) 165 members to be elected through the first-past-the-post electoral system, with one being elected from each election constituency of 165 elections constituencies delimited in the country on the basis of geography and population.

Article 285 (5) of the constitution stipulated: While determining election constituencies pursuant to this article, the Election Constituency Delimitation Commission shall so determine the constituencies, having regard to population and geography as the basis of representation, and as to ensure that the ratio between the geography, population and number of members of such election constituencies is equal, so far as practicable.

The three major parties agreed to amend this provision of the constitution immediately after the promulgation of the constitution to address the demands of the agitating forces particularly the Madhesi forces who were demanding that representation should be based on population and not geography. Some lawmakers registered their proposals at the Parliament seeking to amend the provisions.

Nepali Congress' Amendment Proposal

On January 7, 2016, three leaders of the Nepali Congress party (NC)—Bimalendra Nidhi, Minendra Rijal and Dr Farmullha Mansur—submitted three separate amendment proposals to the Parliament.

The content and language used in NC leader Nidhi's amendment proposal were in accordance with the Interim Constitution. It also carried the spirit of the agitating Madhesi parties, who demanded retention of the provisions of the Interim Constitution. NC leader Nidhi's proposal, that consisted of amendment bills to Article 84 (1) (a) and 286 (5), was relatively better when compared with the two others and passing of his amendment proposal will address the issues to some extent.

NC leader Bimalendra Nidhi's proposal for the Amendment of Articles 84 (1) (a) and 286 (5)

> Based on the First-past-the-post electoral system, the House of Representatives shall be composed of 165 members elected on the basis of similar population range, geographical convenience and special characteristics, and, in the case of Madhes on the basis of percentage of population in accordance with mixed electoral system as provided for in the law.

Provisions of Interim Constitution, 2007

> Article 63(3): The constituent assembly shall be composed of the members elected on the basis of similar population

range, geographical convenience and special characteristics, and, in the case of Madhes on the basis of percentage of population in accordance with mixed electoral system as provided for in the law.

Nidhi's Amendment proposal with regard to Article 286 (5)

The Constituency Delimitation Commission, while delimiting the constituencies in accordance with this Article, shall, maintain as far as practicable the ratio between population and number of members keeping population-based representation as main basis in accordance with Article 84.1(a).

Interim Constitution, 2007

Article 154(A)(6): The Constituency Delimitation Commission, while delimiting the constituencies in accordance with this Article, shall, determine the number of members to be elected on the basis of the population of each district in accordance with Clauses (3) and (3a) of Article 63, maintaining as far as practicable the proportionality between the number of members and the population of the districts, and fix the number of constituencies for election of members of the constituent assembly accordingly.

After the words "while delimiting the constituencies", the following words are "equal population and geographic conveniences".

NC Leader Minendra Rijal's Proposal for the Amendment of Article 286 (5)

The Constituency Delimitation Commission shall delimit the constituencies in every Province treating population-based representation as the main basis and geography as the secondary basis in accordance with the Article 84.1(a). Every district in the Provinces shall have at least one constituency.

The amendment bill proposed by NC leader Rijal did not address the aspirations of the Interim Constitution and the agitating Madhesi parties. In the proposal, the use of a phrase delimiting constituencies, and treating geography as the secondary basis, was contradictory. Similarly, determining a constituency based on a district meant continuing the old practice of the constitution of the Kingdom of Nepal, 1990. Maintaining both Province and district as the basis for delineating constituencies is illogical. The constituency delineation based on district will not be applicable at the provincial level once the complete federal set-up is achieved.

NC Leader Dr. Farmullha Mansur's Amendment Proposal

> *Economically, socially and educationally backward women, Dalits, Adibasi Janajati, Madhesi, Tharu, Muslim, differently-abled people, backward classes, gender and sexually minority groups and citizens of backward regions shall have the right to participate in state structures on the basis of the principle of proportional inclusion.*

Ansari's amendment proposal does include the issue of proportional inclusion but leaves the clusters for already empowered communities. Neither does it address the issues raised by agitating Madhesi parties. (see the Chapter on Proportional Inclusion).

Other Problems with the First Amendment

The agitating United Democratic Madhesi Front (UDMF) did not take part in the constitutional amendment process. The major parties and the government also failed to bring the UDMF on board during the constitutional amendment process. Hence, the first amendment made to the new constitution—related to delineation of electoral constituency and proportional inclusion—lacks the ownership of the UDMF.

Amendment on Delineation of Electoral Constituency

Further Amendments need to be made to the constitution to address the issues of citizenship, representation in the Upper House, and the provincial boundaries. On the issue of revision of the provincial boundaries, the United Democratic Madhesi Front, which spearheaded Madhes movement, demands that the issue be settled in furtherance of the recommendations of the former State Restructuring Commission.

The amendment for delineation of electoral constituencies has left room for controversial interpretations. It has yet to answer the question of what the ratio between population and geography will be. The interpretation of this provision could be narrowed down by interpretation of the laws related to delineation of FPTP constituencies to be enacted in the future. On the other hand, treating population as the main basis for delimiting electoral districts is a step forward. The issues of Provinces 5 and 7 are the major issues that need to be addressed because these two provinces have taken 7 districts of Terai into the hill region. The hill and mountain areas have more districts but less population, while Terai districts have fewer districts and greater population. The endorsing of Rijal's proposal means that both districts and provinces would have to be taken into account while delimiting the constituencies. If the province is taken as a parameter, why should each district be ensured at least one constituency?

Media reports have claimed that the constitutional amendment ensure 80 FPTP seats to Madhes, which has more than 50 per cent population. Now the questions arise: Which Madhes will get 80 seats? Which areas will be considered as Madhes? Does Madhes mean only the eight districts included in Province 2 of the new constitution? On what basis do these media outlets interpret that Madhes will get 80 seats? 12 districts of Madhes have been split into five hill provinces. The delineation of electoral constituencies in Provinces 1, 3, 4, 5 and 7 will be done on the basis of provinces and these provinces are linked with hill districts. Therefore, without revising the boundaries of the provinces to ensure two Provinces in Madhes, the region cannot have 80 FPTP seats.

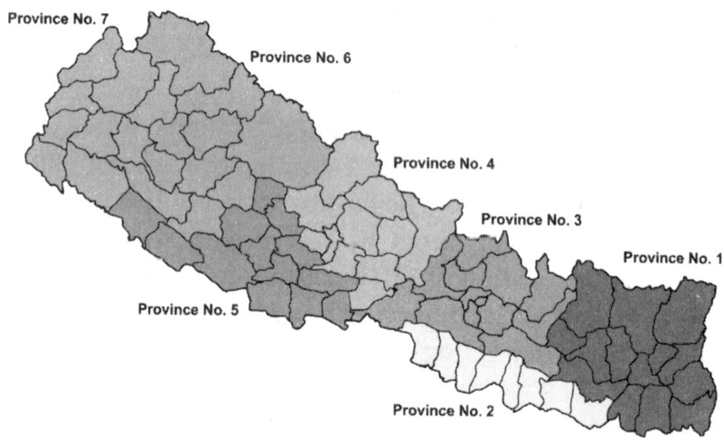

https://en.wikipedia.org/wiki/Nepalese_Federal_States

Despite claims, Terai will, in fact, get just 71 seats under first-past-the-post, not 80. Let's take a look at Table 11.1 for the calculations:

Whether Madhes representatives receive 65 or 71 or 79 seats is subject to interpretation, and can be manipulated in the Acts or by the Constituency Delimitation Commission.

Thus, the new constitution will not address the agendas of the Madhesi parties because they are demanding the implementation of the past deals such as 22-Point and 8-Point Agreements. Both of these agreements mention the

TABLE 11.1

Provinces	*Population* [in figure & percent of total population]	*Number of districts included*	*Electoral constituency provision* for Terai districts*		(A-B) *Remaining seats* [total seats minus one seat per district]	*Per cent of population in Terai districts included in Provinces*	*Seats in Terai Districts* [one seat per district plus seats based on population]
			(A) *Total seats calculated based on population* [Seats in Province = total seats 165*% of total population]	(B) *One seat mandatory for each district* [see above constitutional provision in italicized]			
No. 1	45, 34, 943 (17.1)	14	28	14	14	56% in 3 Terai districts (Jhapa, Morang & Sunsari)	3 + 8 = 11
No. 2	54, 04, 145 (20.4)	8	33	Not Applicable (All Madhes districts)	NA-hill	NA	33
No. 3	55, 29, 452 (20.9)	13	35	13	22	10% (Chitwan)	1 + 2 = 3
No. 4	24, 13, 907 (9.1)	No Terai land	NA	NA	NA	NA	

(*Contd*)

TABLE 11.1 (*Contd.*)

Provinces	*Population* [in figure & percent of total population]	*Number of districts included*	*Electoral constituency provision* for Terai districts*		(A-B) *Remaining seats* [total seats minus one seat per district]	*Per cent of population in Terai districts included in Provinces*	*Seats in Terai Districts* [one seat per district plus seats based on population]
			(A) *Total seats calculated based on population* [Seats in Province = total seats 165*% of total population]	(B) *One seat mandatory for each district* [see above constitutional provision in italicized]			
No. 5	45, 40, 222 (17.1)	12	28	12	16	79% in 6 Terai districts (Rupendhi, Kapilbastu, Nawalparasi, Bnake and Bardiya & Dang)	6 + 13 = 19
No. 6	15, 19, 399 (5.7)	No terai land					
No. 7	25, 52, 517 (9.7)	9	16	9	7	48% in two Terai districts (Kailali & Kanchanpur)	2 + 3 = 5
Total 71 seats in Terai is 41% of total 165 seats despite having 50.27% of population						*Total seats*	71

This data was prepared on the basis of author's Conversations with Prof. Krishna Hachhethu.

delineation of election constituencies based on population in the Terai. This issue had already been addressed in Article 63(3) of the Interim Constitution. Initially, there were two criteria for the delineation of election constituencies in the Interim Constitution: geography and population. But after the Madhes Movement, it was added that Madhes would have constituencies in proportion to its population. The amendment to the Interim Constitution ensured that more than half of the first-past-the-post election constituencies will be in the Terai, consistent with its population base. But Article 84(1)(A) of the new constitution just mentions 'population' and 'geography', omitting the specific term "on the basis of population in Madhes."

Amendment on Proportional Inclusion

NC leader Farmullah Mansur's proposal passed by the Parliament on January 23, only incorporates the word 'proportional' in Article 42(1) of the constitution. In fact, clusters for reservation have not been reduced as demanded by the UDMF, and other marginalized communities.

Incorporation of 'proportional' in front of the word 'inclusion' is a small achievement. However, adding "farmers", "labourers" and "economically-deprived Khas-Arya" is illogical, because farmers and labourers exist in all ethnic and social groups. As far as the economically-deprived Khas-Arya group is concerned, the state should address their concerns through poverty alleviation programmes and not through affirmative action. Thus, the amendment does not fully address the principle of affirmative action.

Reservation should be ensured for the economically, socially and educationally deprived communities. The new amendment states that, any group should be economically, socially and educationally backward in order to be eligible for reservation. But in the case of the Khas-Arya, the constitutional provision only explains 'economically deprived Khas-Arya.' The Khas-Arya group has almost 80 per cent representation in almost all the state organs.

There are poor people who comprise a portion of all communities. What should be the parameters for measuring poverty in a poor country like Nepal? How appropriate is it to reserve seats for Khas-Arya, which has been overly representing in all sectors of the government for centuries? The new amendments have left space for judicial interpretation on these questions.

To address the demands of the agitating UDMF and other marginalized communities, the ratio of proportional representation in the Parliament should be increased from 40 per cent to 60 per cent (under the Interim Constitution this ratio was 58 per cent) and the number of clusters for reservation should be reduced.

Three-Point Agreement and Promise of Constitutional Amendment

On the morning of August 1, 2016, Terai Madhesi Democratic Party leader Hridayesh Tripathi called me and said he was attending a task force meeting that was discussing the contents of the draft of the tri-party agreement. I told him that I had already drafted the agreement roughly, and I sent him a copy. The next day I met him and another party leader, Brikhesh Chandra Lal. He showed me a draft of the agreement which was mostly prepared by the UDMF leaders collectively. It was quite a good draft that covered issues of constitutional amendment such as revision in the provincial boundary, representation in the Upper House, citizenship, language and judiciary. Moreover, it also clearly recommended that a high-level commission be formed to investigate the killings that took place during the Madhes movement. I was quite happy to see the draft, because its language could have given a sense of victory to people in the Terai.

However, late that evening I got a call from Hridayesh Tripathi. He told me that Upendra Yadav did not agree to the draft and the Seven-Point Draft was reduced to three points. Tripathi read the draft of Three-Point Agreement which I found quite logical as it covered almost all issues.

The following morning, on August 3, Nepali Congress leader Bimlendra Nidhi informed me that the draft Three-Point Agreement covered constitutional amendment issues such as demarcation (provincial boundaries), citizenship, Upper House and proportional inclusion. I was happy enough to realize that the constitutional amendment on four issues was moderate and the first step for the Madhesis to accept the constitution.

It was around 1pm and I was at the Supreme Court. I had just finished my pleading in the newly appointed Justice Anil Kumar Sinha's bench and was hurrying to watch ABC television for the live talk on the Prime Minister's election in the Parliament. When I reached the Nepal Bar Association building, I saw the Three-Point Agreement outlined on Keshav Jha's Facebook post. I was very worried when I read the agreement. I realized that it was a missed opportunity for Madhesi forces because in the first point of the agreement there was nothing substantial on the constitutional amendment.

In the agreement, all issues of constitutional amendment were very vague, unclear and subject to interpretation. I took the agreement as a trick to hoodwink Madhesi forces. Madhesi forces launched a movement and over four dozen Madhesi youths lost their lives during the protests. There are no specific constitutional issues mentioned in the document. There had been a broader understanding about clearly mentioning the revision of provincial boundaries, representation in the upper house, amendment in citizenship and proportional representation related provisions of the constitution. Even during my Delhi visit, the Indian foreign secretary had assured us that India would support the constitutional amendment of these four issues. Bimlendra Nidhi had also agreed to mention these four issues in the agreement, which I came to know when he called me that morning.

Many people asked me for my opinion on the Three-Point Agreement. I thought Point No. 2 was perfect and Point No. 3 was just a procedural matter as the UDMF was committed to vote for Pushpa Kamal Dahal's premiership bid. What I was not happy with was Point No. 1, which had nothing substantive in it. I think Madhesi groups missed an opportunity to mention the specific constitutional issues such as revision of provincial boundaries, representation in the upper house, citizenship, language, judiciary and proportional inclusion.

The way in which the Three-Point Agreement was drafted and signed, it gives the NC and the Maoists reason to argue that the constitutional amendment on the subject of revision of provincial boundaries would be adequate. So the main political demand of Madhes still remains unresolved. Even assuming that the new government would bring in good constitutional amendment proposals that will be acceptable to all stakeholders and which could address aspirations of the people, we must wait and watch what the action of the new government will ultimately be.

I don't know who took a rigid position while discussing the Three-Point Agreement. Did the CPN-MC-Maoists (Centre) and the Nepali Congress take a rigid position, or was it a collective mistake of the UDMF or any particular leaders? Why were the Madhesi leaders in such a hurry to vote for CPN-MC Chair Pushpa Kamal Dahal, 'Prachanda'? Is it just because Upendra Yadav is close to Prachanda and he got assurance from Prachanda that all the constitutional issues would be addressed and the constitution would be amended? Is it that Prachanda told Yadav that they should not mention any specific term in the written document or else CPN-UML might link it to its nationalist agenda and polarize the society on there issues?

Flexibility on Constitutional Amendment

What is the value in signing the Three-Point Agreement if UML does not vote in support of constitutional amendment? In fact, the constitution is too rigid on constitutional amendment matters, particularly making it almost impossible to change provincial boundaries in the Parliament that will be formed after a new election. Article 274 requires a two-thirds majority of the federal Parliament, and a majority of the provincial assemblies to change provincial boundaries. This will make any amendment in the constitution almost impossible on boundary questions. So it is ridiculous when our leaders say that the constitution is flexible and it could be amended in due course. Greater flexibility for amendments could have given the constitution a longer life, and its rigidity has shortened its durability.

So for Madhesis, Tharus and people of other indigenous nationalities, this is the final chance to push for constitutional amendments before having a provincial assembly election. In transition, they can do it through political negotiation. So for them it is a do or die battle.

It is also equally important for Madhesis to get support of the UML in order to amend the constitution with a two-thirds majority. However, the UML was involved in keeping six districts such as Banke, Bardiya, Dang, Rupandehi,

Kapilvastu and Nawalparasi out of Terai Province; will they be ready to show flexibility to keep these six districts out of the Hill Province? It is likely that UML will not support an amendment until they get an equal position of power in the government. This may invite more constitutional crises in the near future.

12

The Electoral System

An electoral system plays a crucial role in how the population is represented in a government, and electoral politics in Nepal have always favoured the Khas-Arya group. During the panchayat phase and after the restoration of democracy in 1990, the Madhesi and Tharus of the plains protested against Nepal's biased electoral system, which had left many communities disproportionately underrepresented in the Parliament.

The electoral system adopted in Nepal's new constitution is a mixed one, comprising 60% first-past-the-post (FPTP) seats and 40% proportional representation (PR)seats. Compared to the First CA, where the ratio was 58% PR seats to 42% FPTP, the existing electoral system reduces the rate of inclusion of marginalized communities.

Take a glance over the data from the 'Politics of Representation in Nepal,' by Krishna Hachhethu, Tula Narayan Shah and Ram Kumar Kamat.

Table 1 shows that Nepal has historically had an asymmetric distribution of political power among ethnic groups in its national legislature elections. Hill people, also referred to as Pahadis, constitute 67% of the total population of Nepal. Yet their political representation has been between 79% and 87%. Within that group Brahmin and Chhetri accounted for only 31% of the overall population, but managed to win 50% to 62% of seats in the national legislature. By contrast, Janajatis have been underrepresented, filling 18% to 27% of seats while accounting for 29% of the population. And while Madhesis account for 33% of the population, their political representation has been between 12% and 21%. Even more excluded are the Dalits, both from the Hill regions and the Terai: while constituting over 12% of the population, they almost completely lacked any representatives in the legislature from 1959 to 2008. These data represent the epitome of social inequality.

The book 'The Politics of Representation in Nepal', states: The privileged position of the higher hill castes corresponds to their relatively higher Human Development Index (HDI: 552). Similarly, the higher hill castes have a relatively lower Poverty Index (PI: 18%) compared to the national average (30%). The Governance Index (GI) is particularly telling where the higher hill castes account for 71% of the total. By contrast, the Janajati and Madhesi (except Newar and plains high castes) figure lower on the HDI (494 and 448 respectively) and the GI (19% and 8% respectively). While data on the Poverty Index for Janajatis and Madhesis are not available, seeing the relatively low PI of the higher hill castes (18%) and relatively high (31%) national average, one can infer that to make up for this discrepancy, the non-high hill castes must have a relatively higher PI to offset the balance.

These numbers are in line with the previous analysis, in which it was asserted that due to the socio-politico-economic cycle of power and the phenomenon of rigid path-dependency, the social, political and economic power is entrenched with the high hill castes. This phenomenon is also well explained by Robert Putnam's theory of elite formation, which states that "education, wealth and social status" ought to be viewed as "political resources", underlying the formation of political leadership (Putnam 1976).

Exclusion of Madhesis

Apart from vertical inequality, there is also persistent horizontal inequality in Nepal, both in society and in political representation. Madhesis have long been excluded from the political elite circles of Nepal for a number of reasons. First, the old civil code placed the Madhesi castes horizontally in an inferior position to the hill castes. Second, the economy of the Madhesi is largely influenced, owned and controlled by the hill elites. Third, the Madhesis are generally seen not to be strictly Nepalese, seeing that some are allegedly descendants of 19th century Indian migrant workers. Their cultural proximity with the people living across the border in India induces people to view them as foreigners, outsiders and 'others.'

The Interim Constitution of 2007 saw the election of 601 members of Parliament: 240 elected by first-past-the-post, 335 by proportional representation, and 26 nominated by the cabinet. As indicated in Table 6, the demographic composition of the First CA was substantially different from past national legislatures[1]. The dominance of Brahmin and Chhetris dropped significantly from 56-62% representation to 33%, a percentage which is remarkably close to their proportion of the general population (31%). Janajati Hill people represented by 27% of elected members, only slightly lower than their actual population size. Lastly, perhaps the most significant changes are confined to the results of the Dalits and Muslims, the former of which gained 8% of the seats and the latter received 3%. While these numbers are still short of their population size (11.8% and 4.3% respectively), they are headed in the right direction,

Table 12.1 Representation in CA, 2008 and 2013: Pahadi/Madheshi and Caste/Ethnic

Caste/Ethnicity	*Population (%)*	*FPTP*		*PR*		*Nominated*	*Total*
		2008	*2013*	*2008*	*2013*	*2008*	*2008*
Pahadis							
1. High caste	30.9	99 (41%)	133 (55%)	89 (27%)	103 (31%)	5 (19%)	193 (32%)
2. Janajati	28.5	66 (28%)	46 (19%)	89 (27%)	87 (26%)	9 (35%)	164 (27%)
3. Dalit	7.1	6 (3%)	1 (0%)	30 (9%)	26 (8%)	— (0%)	36 (6%)
Sub total	66.5	171 (71%)	180 (75%)	208 (62%)	216 (64%)	14 (54%)	393 (65%)
Madheshis							
1. Castes	14.8	48 (20%)	36 (15%)	76 (23%)	64 (19%)	4 (15%)	128 (21%)
2. Janajati	8.7	13 (5%)	18 (8%)	30 (9%)	30 (9%)	7 (27%)	50 (8%)
3. Dalit	4.7	1 (0%)	1 (0%)	12 (4%)	13 (4%)	— (0%)	13 (2%)
4. Muslim	4.3	7 (3%)	5 (2%)	9 (3%)	12 (4%)	1 (4%)	17 (3%)
Sub total	32.5	69 (29%)	60 (25%)	127 (38%)	119 (36%)	12 (46%)	208 (35%)
Total	99	240 (100%)	240 (100%)	335 (100%)	335 (100%)	26 100	601 (100%)

Source: NEMAF, Shah and Hachhethu

especially relative to their historical near-absence in the political sphere.

The Second CA of 2013 saw the higher hill castes improve their political representation to 415 elected members (69%), while the Janajatis' position decreased to 23%. Despite the fact that the Second CA saw a regression in the inclusiveness of political representation, relative to the previous elections, 2008, Second CA elections saw a remarkable improvement in ethnic/caste representation in politics.

Electoral Representation from Madhes Angle

Sadbhavana Party Co-chair Laxman Lal Karna headed a task force in the Second CA, whose mandate was to decide the electoral system for the constitution. Below is an excerpt of an interview with him on the subject:

> The ratio for the FPTP and PR constituencies was almost 50/50. But things changed dramatically after UCPN-M Chair Pushpa Kamal Dahal and Madhesi Janadhikar Forum-Democratic Chair Bijay Kumar Gachhedar joined the Nepali Congress and CPN-UML to sign the 16-Point Agreement.

The Bhattarai-led committee later formed a task force, which consisted of Purna Bahadur Khadka from Nepali Congress and Jitendra Narayan Dev from MJF-D. The UDMF boycotted the task force. Subsequent to the signing of the 16-Point Agreement, the Parliamentary form of government and a mixed electoral system (with 40% PR seats and 60% FPTP seats) were adopted mainly on the basis of compromise reached between the four forces through the 16-Point Agreement.

Although they signed the Agreement together, the major parties and Madhes-based parties differed over representation in the House of Representatives and the upper house. The NC and the CPN-UML were in favour of ensuring equal representation from the provinces in the upper house, whereas Madhesi forces wanted representation in the upper house to be based on population of the provinces. NC leader Ram Chandra Poudel proposed to have 205 members in the House of Representatives; I believe that all leaders were prepared to accept this proposal.

The task force agreed to divide the FPTP and PR election system on a 50/50 ratio. They also agreed to count the votes of the losing candidates to ensure representation of those parties who had not secured their representation. The task force even discussed alternatives so that PR candidates could have their constituencies and end political parties' monopolies over the selection of PR representatives. However, the task force's efforts were in vain and its recommendations were not implemented.

How Fair is the Current Electoral System?

The Constituency Delimitation Commission which is going to be formed ahead of the general elections to be held before January 2021 is responsible for delineating first-past-the-post constituencies. The commission will use population as the main criteria, and geography as the second criteria to demarcate constituencies in the provinces. The commission will also have to ensure that each district within a province has at least one constituency.

Article 286(12) of the constitution stipulates that constituencies will be reevaluated every 20 years, which is double the 10-year period recommended in the Interim Constitution. The 10-year time period was a logical and practical provision because the census is also conducted every 10 years. Instead, a gap of 20 years could allow for four general elections to be held between evaluations of a constituency demographics. And although geography is the second criteria for delimiting first-past-the-post constituencies, the constitution contains no explanation of how it defines the term 'geography', so now it depends on the interpretation of the concerned bodies.

For the seats decided by proportional representation, Article 84(2) has divided the 110 PR seats among 10 clusters, which is double the number of clusters that were outlined in the Interim Constitution. This scheme may only give one seat to Madhesi Dalit, but what one needs to understand is that the PR system is a compensatory provision for those communities whose representation cannot be ensured through a FPTP system. In previous elections other than the First CA election, Khas-Arya group won 55 to 70 per cent of seats under the FPTP system. If the current ratio remains unchanged for future elections, the representation of Khas-Arya would be around 42 per cent. Given that, how fair would it be to have an additional cluster of the Khas-Arya group represented through the PR system? Had the cluster for Khas-Arya women been created instead of just Khas-Arya, it would have made much more sense.

Similarly, there is a provision for having 59 members in the upper house of the Parliament, whereby each province elects an equal number (8) seats to the upper house, plus an additional three members nominated by the cabinet. The irony is that one province with half a million population and another province with 2 million population will be able to elect equal number of representatives (which is 8) for the upper house. How fair is this?

At present almost a dozen Madhes districts have been mixed with Hill districts. If the representation by population principle is not followed and if there are only two provinces in Madhes, they could only send a total of 16 representatives to the upper house, compared to 40 representatives of the hill provinces in the upper house. Consequently, Madhes, which has more population than the hills, will always remain a minority in the upper house. Furthermore, although an equal number of representatives from each province is sent to the upper house, no autonomy has been given to the provinces in Nepal. Contrast this with America, where all states enjoy full autonomy with residuary powers remaining with the states. Representation by population principle is followed in the lower house of the American Parliament and perhaps this is the reason why equal representation of states in the U.S. Senate, the upper house of the Parliament does not make big difference there. American system is unique in the sense that the framers of the American Constitution thought that arrangement could tempt other states to be part of the American federation.

Nepal has adopted a system akin to that of the United States, but it should have tried to emulate the Indian system, where at least one seat is ensured for all states and the rest of the seats are determined in proportion to the population of the province. Uttar Pradesh of India sends 31 members to the upper house. Similarly, Bihar and Maharashtra, have 16 and 19 seats respectively in the upper house. Small states like Goa and Sikkim have just one seat each (see Table 12.2).

Nepal's Constitution has adopted the quasi-federal model in other structures of the state as practised in India, but it follows the American model on the issue of representation in the upper house. With this system, the framers of the constitution have created a double standard. Representation in the upper house does not ensure inclusion as those seats can be controlled by the big parties. The constitution proposes direct election for local bodies, but these might never be inclusive as the parties themselves are not inclusive in their own executive bodies. The rationale behind having a mixed election system for two levels of federal bodies—the centre and the provinces

TABLE 12.2: Representation of States in Rajya Sabha in India

Number of states and Union Territory	*No. of Seats*	*Number of states and Union Territory*	*No. of Seats*
Andhra Pradesh	11	Manipur	1
Arunachal Pradesh	1	National Capital Territory (Delhi)	3
Assam	7	Nominated	12
Bihar	16	Odisha	10
Chhattisgarh	5	Pondicherry	1
Goa	1	Punjab	7
Gujarat	11	Rajasthan	10
Haryana	5	Sikkim	1
Himachal Pradesh	3	Tamil Nadu	18
Jammu & Kashmir	4	Telangana	7
Jharkhand	6	Tripura	1
Karnataka	12	Uttar Pradesh	31
Kerala	9	Uttarakhand	3
Madhya Pradesh	11	West Bengal	16
Maharashtra	19	Total	245

and direct election system for the local bodies is illogical and impractical.

As Nepal's Constitution has given most of the powers to the federal Parliament, individual provinces will have less power to leverage under the current system. If population size is not considered for allocating seats in the upper house, it will contribute to the consolidation of power at the Centre. Nepal's major political parties have deliberately gerrymandered the electoral constituencies in the Terai. This has left Madhesi and Tharus politically underrepresented.

Tiers	*No. of Seats*
House of Representatives	275 (165 FTP + 110 PR)
Upper house	59 (56 elected from provinces + 3 nominated)

Women in Parliament

The current electoral system has ensured one-third representation of women in the Parliament, which should result in a minimum of 36.67 representatives under proportional representation.

The results of past polls show that women have not been able to win more than 20 seats under the FPTP system. As per the new constitution, at least three women will come to the upper house from each province. This means, there will be 21 women representatives in the upper house and more women will have to be elected under the PR system. The elected women will have to carry two identities—such as Madhesi-Muslim women, Madhesi-Dalit women and so on. Similarly, Janajati women who could be elected under the PR system will also have to carry two identities. This clearly shows discrimination against Khas-Arya women and their under representation. Even the government might not be able to implement the election system effectively.

Fortunately, Article 215(4) of the constitution says that members of the village executive shall include four women members elected from among the village assembly and two members elected by the village assembly from the Dalit or minority communities after the local election results are released.

Upper House

Although the First Amendment sought to increase first-past-the-post electoral constituencies in the Terai, it is still not guaranteed that the region, which comprises more than 50 per cent of Nepal's population, will get electoral constituencies in proportion to its population. The First Amendment did not alter anything as far as representation in the upper house is concerned. Under the existing provision, all provinces will send an equal number of representatives (eight) to the upper house. This means Province-2 which has 5.4 million population will send eight representatives and province 6 which has 1.5 million population, will also send eight representatives to the upper house. How can this be fair?

The basis of the election to the upper house is first-past-the-post (FPTP), and not proportional. The electoral college includes the chief and deputy chiefs of the local bodies, which is complicated. Similarly, the mixed system will reduce the inclusion of excluded groups including Dalits in the house of representatives until a priority list and some special provisions of inclusiveness are adopted. Only one or two parties will control the local bodies since elections will be held according to the FPTP system as stated in the new constitution.

Take a glance at Table 12.3.

TABLE 12.3

Provinces	*Population*		*Caste/Ethnic Based Demography*	
	In figure	*Per cent*	*1st largest group (%)*	*2nd largest group (%)*
No. 1	45, 34, 943	17.1	Khas-Arya (28)	Terai IPs (12)
No. 2	54, 04, 145	20.4	Madhesi castes (52)	Madhesi Dalit (16)
No. 3	55, 29, 452	20.9	Khas-Arya (37)	Tamang (20)
No. 4	24, 13, 907	9.1	Khas-Arya (42)	Magar (17)
No. 5	45, 40, 222	17.1	Khas-Arya (30)	Magar (16)
No. 6	15, 19, 399	5.7	Khas-Arya (62)	Hill Dalit (23)
No. 7	25, 52, 517	9.7	Khas-Arya (60)	Tharu (17)

Source: Hachhethu, 2016

Caste Ethnic Demography in Provinces

Another important fact to ponder over is that the amendment fails to ensure representation in the upper house on the basis of population. Article 86 of the new constitution further states that all the provinces will elect eight members to the upper house of Parliament through an electoral college. The government will then nominate three members. As there seems to be a tentative agreement among the politicians to have two provinces in the Madhes, this means there will only be 16 representatives from the region in the upper house as opposed to 40 representatives from the hills.

Kare Volan* Argues

The Madhesi parties have demanded that their districts shall have a number of seats proportional to the share of the population. If one wants to over-represent sparsely populated areas that would mean that one would first have to draw a line separating the Terai from the rest of the country, and let the most populated areas of the hills be the only ones to carry the cost of over-representing some mountainous areas. It seems more reasonable that populous areas across the country could carry the cost on equal terms. In that case one could introduce a rule leaving more flexibility to the over-representation than the "at least one per district" rule would do.

The following table sets out two alternatives. First, the distribution of seats to provinces is based upon population only and of distributing by population to each district, provided no district gets less than one seat.

The first alternative gives the most even population per seat since only population is taken into account. When

* Volan is an election system expert from Norway.

TABLE 12.4: Kare Volan's Analysis of FPTP Seats

Province No	*Population as per 2011 census*	*Distribution to provinces in proportion to population only.*		*Distribution to districts based upon population, but with at least one per district. The accumulated province result.*	
		Number of constituencies	*Population per seat*	*Number of constituencies*	*Population per seat*
1	4,534,943	28	161,962	28	161,962
2	5,404,145	34	158,945	32	168,880
3	5,529,452	35	157,984	33	167,559
4	2,279,601	14	162,829	17	134,094
5	4,674,528	29	161,191	27	173,131
6	1,519,319	9	168,813	12	126,610
7	2,552,517	16	159,532	16	159,532
Total	26,494,504	165	160,573	165	160,573

Source: Kare Volan's analysis of the provisions and implications for the various stakeholders, November 23, 2015

TABLE 12.5: Kare Volan's Analysis of FPTP Seats

Province No	*Distribution to provinces in proportion to population only.*		*Distribution with Factor = 5*		*Distribution with Factor = 10*		*Distribution to districts by population, but with at least one per district.*	
	Number of constituencies	*Population per seat*	*Number of constituencies*	*Population per seat*	*Number of constituencies*	*Population per seat*	*Number of constituencies*	*Population per seat*
1	28	161,962	28	161,962	28	161,962	28	161,962
2	34	158,945	33	163,762	32	168,880	32	168,880
3	35	157,984	34	162,631	34	162,631	33	167,559
4	14	162,829	15	151,973	15	151,973	17	134,094
5	29	161,191	29	161,191	29	161,191	27	173,131
6	9	168,813	10	151,932	11	138,120	12	126,610
7	16	159,532	16	159,532	16	159,532	16	159,532
Total	165	160,573	165	160,573	165	160,573	165	160,573

Source: Kare volans' analysis of the provisions and implications for the various stakeholders, November, 23, 2015

the seats are distributed with at least one seat per district, Province 6 in the north-west and Province 4 in north mid-west, in particular, will have an advantage. The deviation becomes more than 20%. There is some ambiguity to the result.

There are other ways of combining population and geography, and Table 12.4 gives one such suggestion. It will provide a less arbitrary way of over-representing than the one-seat-per-district method, and at the same time, it offers a possibility of negotiating a compromise between the two viewpoints.

The formula offered there involves a factor, which determines the degree of taking the geographical area into account. A factor = 0 means that population only is being used and with higher factor value the over representation increases. The political decision would be to set the factor to be used.

Table 12.5 Examples of using the formula of the Appendix to produce possible distribution of seats to provinces, combining population and area. In this case, the factors are set to 5 and 10, showing that both these factors would give results between the population only alternative and the one-per-district alternative.

Reference

[1] *Politics of Representation in Nepal,* jointly authored by Krishna Hachhethu, Tula Narayan Shah and Ram Kumar Kamat.

13

Proportional Inclusion as a Tool of Social Justice

Social engineering of inclusion in a population is vital to reduce poverty, political exclusion and social injustice, all of which can ultimately become the root of conflicts in a diverse country. Scholar Gunther Baechler argues that "the only way to cope with ethnic outbidding and ethno-politicization is to be as inclusive as possible."

Although Nepal has 103 caste and ethnic groups, 93 languages and 9 religious groups, this diversity has not been effectively reflected in the state structure. Participants in the People's Movement in 2006 argued for 'inclusive democracy', hoping to transform the long monopoly of one caste, one gender, one language and one ethnic identity into a more inclusive and representative state.

During the democratization of the 1990s, the rhetoric of inclusion triggered hopes among marginalized groups; however those benefits were hijacked by middle-class male elites who manipulated identity as a weapon for acquiring economic benefits and political power-sharing, and abused it as an electoral strategy. Ultimately, the movement was unsuccessful at including the really vulnerable and poorest among the marginalized communities in Nepal's political process.

Today, the emphasis has shifted towards realizable, radical restructuring of the state, with a proportional inclusive design. Social exclusion in Nepal is not only the consequence of the economic system or the labour market, but more importantly it is rooted in the social structures based on group identities such as caste, gender and ethnicity.

The discourse of inclusion is more popular among grassroots civil society organizations, who view the end goal of inclusion as a means of responding to the needs and interests of excluded groups. However, their voice is often viewed as biased by Kathmandu-based organizations and civil actors, who have easy access to and have exploited resources for those in political power.

Peace building in exclusionary societies requires a shift from egalitarianism to the inclusionary reform that requires overcoming all the legacies of social discrimination, class domination, ideological hegemony and structural power relationships. Marshall and Bottomore argue that it is an inclusionary project which focuses upon a comprehensive model of citizenship, taking into account the inequalities of gender, race, nationalism and class.

The crisis of inclusion is not just limited to civic advocacy in Nepal, but is even more deeply rooted in the institutional and internal structures based on family ties, ideological bonds and ethnic identity. These constructs are used as a weapon to limit resources and opportunities to a select few civil elites. Similarly, a new fashion of romanticizing inclusion also emerges in the civic arena, especially in the post-movement period. Of late, the civil society organizations have started practising tokenism of the marginalized communities under the pretext of inclusion. The irony is that the decision-making power remains in the hands of the same dominant male elites. It is, simply, a deal between the ruling classes and the ethnic elites, which only gives an illusion of erasing the socio-economic problems faced by the poorest and the most vulnerable among marginalized communities.

Real inclusion depends upon the extent to which ruling elites would be ready to share power with the poorest among marginalized communities, whom they claim to represent. Giving the powerless a proportional stake in political affairs would delegitimize the status quo enjoyed by the civil elites. In the long term, it would build social cohesion for a more peaceful society.

Right to Social Justice in the New Constitution

The Interim Constitution designated seven marginalized groups with protection for the right to participate in the structures of the state on the basis of the principle of 'proportional inclusion.' Under the new constitution Article 42 ('Right to Social Justice'), the number of protected groups was increased to 17.

This number was later decreased to 15 by the first amendment made to the constitution.

Under Article 42, the socially backward "women, Dalits, indigenous people, indigenous nationalities, Madhesi, Tharu, minority groups, persons with disability, marginalized groups, Muslim, backward classes, gender and sexually minority groups, peasants, labourers, the oppressed and the citizens of backward regions, and indigent Khas-Arya, shall have the right to participate in State structures on the basis of the principle of inclusion."

Curiously, the constitution includes protections for the already-powerful community of Khas-Arya (Hill elites), which have over 80 per cent of representation in the state structures. As per the new constitution, the Khas-Arya community will get reservation under four different groups or cluster—backward region, labourers, farmers and women.

The constitutional issue of reservation for the scheduled castes, which has a long history, can be traced to the constitution of India. Article 16 of the Indian Constitution gives reservation to scheduled castes, tribes, and other backward castes (OBCs). The article remains silent on reservations for already empowered classes. But the latest Constitution in Nepal framed under the large influence of hill elites, has added a separate cluster for their community, which is already an empowered community.

Social Inclusion in Federal Structure

The new constitution has ensured inclusion of marginalized groups in the Cabinet, but it has failed to extend the issue of inclusion to the judiciary and some other constitutional bodies (see Chapter 8).

The new constitution states that each province will send eight representatives to the upper house of the Parliament, regardless of the population of the province meaning that a province with a population of 5.4 million population will send the same number of representatives to the upper house as a province with a population of 1.5 million. The Interim Constitution had earlier ensured the Terai region, home to half of the country's population, would receive a number of seats under the first-past-the-post (FPTP) election system proportionate to its population. This provision, has, however, been diluted in the new constitution.

One Constitutional Community

None of the communities other than the Khas-Arya have been explicitly defined under the constitution of Nepal, 2015. The fact that the Khas-Arya are defined in the constitution has made this already empowered group a 'constitutional community'. They are defined twice, under Articles 84 and 176:

Article 84(2): "For the purpose of this provision, Khas-Arya means Chhetri, Brahmin, Thakuri and Sannyasi (Dashnami) community."

Article 176(2): "'Khas-Arya' shall mean Chhettri, Brahmin, Thakuri, Sanyasi (Dashanami) community."

The definition of only one community in the constitution leaves a question over the ownership of the charter: how can Madhesi, Tharu and other marginalized communities and socially backward women firmly establish their protected place in the constitution?

Diluted Language

The preamble of the Interim Constitution included the phrase 'proportionally inclusive State', which was subsequently changed to 'proportionally inclusive society' in the new constitution. Constitutional experts and lawyers interpret and argue that such changes diluted the provision of social inclusion. 'Proportionally inclusive state' carries an implicit obligation for the state to act, whereas 'proportionally inclusive society' does not place any such onus on the state.

Past Experience

The agendas of inclusion and proportional representation are in practice in the civil service, the electoral system, the Nepal Army, the Nepal Police and all other state organs. The Permanent Establishment of Nepal (PEON) a term coined by columnist C.K. Lal to refer to the bureaucracy, on the other hand, has diluted and weakened the agenda of inclusion on technical grounds. They adopt manipulative methods to take away Madhesis' quota seats, for example by arguing that Madhesis or other marginalized groups must achieve a minimum score in a written exam in order to be entitled to their quota seats; if they fail to do so, they are merged with the general category seats. The state bodies only pass a few candidates from Madhesi and marginalized communities under their quota and take away the large percentage of seats and merge those seats under the general category. And the state enables this process to avoid having to abide by the principle of proportional inclusion. Protecting inclusion from such nefarious tactics needs close monitoring by unbiased and objective parties.

Although the Supreme Court mandated inclusion in the Nepal Army, the national army does not pay much attention to the issue. The Nepal Police's recent results of the selection of Police Inspectors show that they have misappropriated thirteen seats meant for Madhesis to give those seats to representatives of Hill Bahun/Chhetri, who already have over-representation in all sectors of governance. The Public Service Commission also seems biased in this regard; this year they published vacancies for account officers, but they did not include three Madhesi seats among these vacancies because last year no Madhesis passed under the three-seat quota. By law, those seats should have been added to Madhesi quota this year.

Conclusion

Insufficient Amendment on Social Inclusion

Four months after its promulgation, the government and major political parties amended the constitution on the issues of proportional inclusion and electoral constituencies based on population. The amendment to the constitution reduced the clusters for reservation, eliminating protections for two of the 17 clusters (youth and Adivasi or indigenous people).

This amendment failed to remove the clusters of Khas-Arya, as had been demanded by the agitating Madhesi, Tharu and other Janajati parties. The new constitution ought to have retained the provisions of the Interim Constitution as far as inclusion is concerned. A major flaw with the constitution of Nepal, 2015, is that Madhesis and Tharus boycotted the constitution-making process, and therefore their interests were not fully reflected in the final outcome. Indigenous nationalities have also opposed the provisions of the new constitution, and this opposition threatens the survival of the new charter.

Implementation of Inclusion Provision Still a Mirage

Although the new constitution guarantees the provision of proportionate inclusion in all state structures, this principle has yet to be successfully implemented across the board. This is evident from the appointment of Supreme Court judges on March 1, 2016, six months after the constitution's promulgation.

Out of 11 Supreme Court judges that the Judicial Council recommended on March 1, 8 are Hill Brahmin/Chhetris (one woman), two Newars (one woman) and one Madhesi. This means there are 15 Hill Brahmin/Chhetri judges in the Supreme Court which accounts for 71.42 per cent of the total number. The percentage of Madhesi judges at the SC is only 9.52 per cent, and women constitute only 14.28 per cent. There are no judges representing Dalit, Tharu and Muslim communities.

The first amendment to the new constitution inserted the phrase 'proportional' in the inclusion clause, yet a body like Judicial Council did not respect the spirit of the constitution while recommending the names of new judges for the Supreme Court.

Reluctance by Responsible Bodies on Social Inclusion

The chair of the Public Service Commission (PSC), in a public event immediately after the promulgation of the new charter, said that the provision of inclusion should be abolished from the constitution. And none of the major leaders and major parties objected to his statement. The PSC is responsible for incorporating social inclusion in the government bodies.

Likewise, the major forces-the Nepali Congress, the CPN-UML and the CPN-MC-Maoist increased clusters for reservation from 7 to 15 and in the new constitution they have also used vague words and contradictory provisions with regard to inclusion.

Conspiracy Against Practice of Social Inclusion

Madhesis, Tharus, Janajatis, women and Dalits, who have suffered discrimination for centuries, are determined to claim their rightful share in the state structures through the process of social inclusion. However, the Khas-Arya ruling class may not dare to broaden the provisions of social inclusion as it could jeopardize their political power. The way the ruling class is acting these days, it appears that this class has deliberately diluted the provisions of social inclusion in order to consolidate their political position.

If the marginalized sections of the society fail to achieve their constitutionally-protected role in the governance of Nepal, then the journey of social inclusion, which started after the signing of the comprehensive peace accord between the government and the CPN-MC in 2006, will be aborted.

14

Impact of Border Blockade on Madhes Movement

On September 22, 2015, I was in Biratnagar when I came to learn that the United Democratic Madhesi Front (UDMF) had decided to change the manner of their protest following a meeting in Rajbiraj. I rang up Terai-Madhes Democratic Party (TMDP) leader Hridayesh Tripathi, and discovered that the UDMF had also decided to file the cases of the killings during protests to the UN. The agitating parties wanted to appoint me as their lawyer.

The next morning, I travelled to Rajbiraj, headquarters of Saptari, where I met the top leaders of UDMF. I asked why they had changed the manner of their protest, because a large number of people were still gathered at the District headquarters to stage the demonstration.

"We don't want anymore bloodshed," Rajendra Mahato said.

"If we don't go to the border, a large number of protesters will be killed," Mahant Thakur added.

Upendra Yadav further explained the reason for the change in the form of their protest: "The state doesn't treat the protesters as equal citizens. Rather, it views this dispute as a war between the Nepali state and the Madhesi".

Needless to say, the blockade at the Nepal–India border was never possible without Indian support. This is an open secret. The protesters were compelled to stage their sit-in protest at the border entry point. Had they not done so, more protesters could have been killed by security forces since the state had already adopted a crackdown approach against the demonstrations.

The border blockade was not an impulsive decision by the UDMF. A month before taking to the border, they had already warned the government that such action could be taken if their demands were not met.

The government ignored their demands, and after 40 days of demonstrations, they started staging blockades at various points along the Nepal–India border in the Terai. The motive behind the border blockade was to cut off the lifeline of Kathmandu, so that the government would feel pressurized to fulfil the UDMF's demands.

"Unless the lifeline of Kathmandu is cut off," said Rajendra Mahato, "they won't listen."

Kathmandu did not paid any serious attention to the UDMF's peaceful protests; however the blockade was the catalyst for the concerns of UDMF leaders to be heard in Kathmandu, causing a shortage of basic essentials in the country by blocking trade routes with India. The blockade, however, could not be justified under the pretext of social justice; it was the last resort for the agitating Madhesi forces.

Unlike previous movements in Nepal, the border blockade failed to achieve the Madhesi parties' goals. The government simply encouraged black marketing to fulfil the need for supplies in Kathmandu. In order to open the border and resume trade, the state used all its apparatuses.

The blockade impacted livelihoods in the Terai, but the effect were felt most in Kathmandu and the hill areas. UNICEF Executive Director Anthony Lake issued a statement that three million Nepali children under five were under direct risk of death and disease due to shortages of fuel, food, medicines and vaccines.

Even Kathmandu-based human rights organizations, led by hill elites, raised the issue of the blockade as a serious human rights violation. They blamed India alone for the blockade. A group of civil society actors submitted a report to the UN special rapporteur on the landlocked countries. The delegation of Nepal, led by the then-Foreign Minister and Deputy Prime Minister Kamal Thapa, raised the issue of the blockade during his address on human rights violations in UN UPR. People suffered by having to pay higher prices for fuel and gas during the blockade resulting in fuel crisis. The black market was backed by the government. Even some of the local Madhesi leaders were reportedly involved in black marketing of fuel.

The Birgunj border crossing, which is the shortest route between India and Kathmandu, is used to import around 70-75 per cent of Nepal's petroleum products from India. Rs 300 million per day in revenue is generated via this customs point alone. However, the border blockade by Madhesi protesters remained in effect for 135 days, resulting in a significant economic loss for Nepal.

Miscalculation by India

India thought that the ultimate weapon of the blockade would force the Nepal government to respond to the agitating Madhesi Front's demands. However, it proved counterproductive. India and the agitating Madhesi parties both failed to predict that the conflict of Hill-vs-Terai would shift to Hill-vs-India. At the same time, nationalist forces in Nepal used the opportunity to protest against India. The Nepal Government encouraged this stand against their neighbour.

The government's reluctance to fulfil the legitimate demands of agitating parties was the reason that ordinary people faced unprecedented difficulties. Yet ironically, people in the hill and mountain regions did not come to the streets in protest against the government, but did so against India. All media, hill communities, civil society, politicians and business communities were united in their stand against India and agitating Madhesi parties. A clear divide became apparent. People in the hill and mountain regions protested against Indian interference, while agitators in the Terai welcomed India's move.

Even those who had earlier shown solidarity to the Madhes movement took a rigid position against it following the blockade. The stance of the people was like an undeclared war between Nepal and India. A common question was on everyone's mind—Should a giant country like India bully a small country like Nepal?

Opinion-makers in Nepal imposed a particular brand of pseudo-nationalism saying the blockade was tantamount to an attack on Nepal's sovereignty. The narrative of nationalism and fear was propagated in the hill areas, where it was rumored that India would help Madhesis to disintegrate Nepal and that naturalized citizens, migrants from India, intended to capture the Nepali state by holding vital posts such as those of President and Prime Minister.

Due to a strategic campaign against India, the USA, European Union, UN and other international organizations approached India with an appeal to end the crisis in Nepal. Even within India itself, the opposition parties like Indian National Congress, strongly protested against the BJP government.

I was in Delhi a few weeks before the blockade was lifted, to meet with top leaders of the Congress. Former Minister Jairam Ramesh told me that the blockade was unnecessary, and had turned a long-friendly country into an enemy. He blamed the RSS and the BJP-led government for forcing Nepal into declaring itself a "Hindu State". "What you want to keep in your Constitution is your own internal issue," he said. "It's none of our business." He asked how many Madhesi, Tharu and Janajati CA members from the NC, UML and Maoists opposed the provisions of the constitution.

"If CA members of your own community don't oppose the constitutional provisions that discriminate against Madhesis and leaves them under-represented, why should India raise its unnecessary concerns in your internal affairs," Jairam Ramesh opined.

I replied that Amresh Singh and Bimalendra Nidhi from the NC, who were initially opposed to the 16-Point Agreement and fast track process, had finally conceded to sign the constitution under the 'undeclared whip' issued by their party. I explained that they still believe that the fast-tracked constitution is full of flaws.

Lifting the Blockade after 135 Days

On February 4, 2015, top leaders of United Democratic Madhesi Front (UDMF) informed the media about an informal agreement among the four constituents (Madhes-based parties) of the UDMF to lift its five-month-long blockade at Nepal–India border checkpoints, which would be agreed upon at a meeting in Kathmandu on February 6.

However, the next day, local smugglers backed by local administrations and customs agents from both Nepal and India, suddenly attacked protesters at the border. The protesters were few in number, and the attack cleared the obstructions at the Friendship Bridge border crossing between Birgunj (Nepal) and Raxaul (India) at around 1:30 pm. To clear the obstruction, they burnt down tents and destroyed temporary shelters that protesters had built on the Friendship Bridge.

Immediately after the incident, local demonstrators from Birgunj and neighbouring areas gathered at the borders and held consultations with the Indian side. But they lacked unity among them. One of them, Terai-Madhes Democratic Party (TMDP) General Secretary Jitendra Sonal, said to the Indian locals and attackers:

"Just provide us two days. Then we will withdraw ourselves from the blockade."

His requests were ignored, and local demonstrators returned to the Nepali side. At border areas on the Nepali side, around 100 security personnel were deployed soon after the incident, but there was no police intervention. By the time around 50 small and big cargo vehicles from India and Nepal arrived on either side of the border, hundreds of people had gathered in the area. As the number of people from Birgunj and surrounding areas increased at the border, the number of security personnel deployed there increased as well.

Federal Socialist Forum Nepal leaders staging the protest at the Birgunj-Raxaul border claimed that some Nepali police in plainclothes were among the Indian locals and smugglers, encouraging them to send their vehicles and move their goods into Nepal. They claimed that Nepali police had assured them that they would provide security to their vehicles once they crossed into Nepal.

When there was a likelihood of violence at the border, agitating Madhesi party leaders requested the attackers for some time so that they could block the border for at least an hour and formally decide about the lifting of the blockade. But those on Indian side refused to accept any such proposals.

Although the demonstrators took the border under their control for half an hour, they couldn't continue the blockade any longer, due to strong objection by local villagers from India and traders who outnumbered the protesters.

Between February 4 and 7, 2015, local demonstrators made three attempts to obstruct the Birgunj–Raxaul border, again with a view to take ownership of the situation and remove the blockade themselves.

Local leaders who had been staging a sit-in protest at the border for the preceding five months—were not informed by top UDMF leaders about their reasons for lifting the blockade. The way in which the border was ultimately reopened left the Madhesi community with the sense that they had "lost", since no formal method was adopted to end the blockade. Local demonstrators burnt effigies of their top leaders throughout the Terai, including in Birgunj and Janakpur. There was anger and frustration amongst the general people and local demonstrators, as their six months of demonstrations had failed to yield any meaningful results.

Travelogue

I decided to visit Terai districts during 2015 Madhes movement against the new constitution. I decided to visit Terai districts because almost every day at least one protester or bystander was killed by the security personnel. There was no presence of any human rights monitoring body. Major Nepali media outlets which are controlled by Khas-Arya community were not covering the protests. Members of civil society and human rights activists in Kathmandu maintained a mysterious silence on the killings of individuals and human rights violations in the Terai.

In July 2015, people spontaneously took to the streets of Madhes region at a time when they came to learn that the preliminary draft of the constitution had come out.

People's Uprising Across Madhes Region of Nepal

During the third Madhes movement I visited a few areas of Terai–Madhes. I spent a few days in Birgunj, Simara, Lalbandi, Bardibas, Janakpur and Rajbiraj. There were a few things that came up as surprises.

In Peaceful Birgunj, it is the Wedding Season

I had been to Birgunj before but during my last visit in November it looked like a battle zone; there was not a single car on the road, and everywhere I went, I saw the Army, police, people and closed shutters. That is why this time around also, I had imagined that I would encounter a similar situation in Birgunj. When I got out of the airport, I got a cab, which offered me a ride to Birgunj Ghantaghar. On my way to Birgunj, I could not see any 'uprising' or *andolan* (movement). None of the shutters were closed. Light vehicles were plying, and everything looked normal.

I ask a protester; he says the *andolan* is Birgunj-centric, but I see that everything is back to normal. The protester said, the protesters are not tired, the people are tired, and that this is the wedding season.

So where is the *andolan*? I went to the border crossing. There I saw people from different political parties sitting down. One woman showed me her bandaged hand, 'Some goons attacked me.'

I only saw 15–20 people picketing the border crossing on Miteri bridge. I saw that people were crossing from under the bridge. I saw tempos, e-rickshaws make their way till the crossing.

I asked them, there are only 15–20 people here, is that it? What was actually happening was that the 20 represented 20,000. A few days ago when people from across the border attacked the protesters, thousands of people showed up in support. When the protesters call for support, I saw that thousands of people show up. It would be suicidal for

Kathmandu, and Baluwatar in particular, to think that there are just 20 people enforcing the blockade. Thousands of people identify themselves with the protesters. This was a surprising sight.

I talked to Federal Socialist Forum, Nepal's leader Pradeep Yadav who was present there, I talked to him at length. He said the people are confused because the Morcha leaders visiting Delhi had sent a message that New Delhi wants the blockade lifted. The leaders went to Kathmandu, they did not come here. This is one of the reasons why the *andolan* has slowed down, he said.

The other important thing (Yadav said) was that the agitators allowed the schools to reopen in the morning. But they could not go to school because of the cold, so we decided at the district-level to allow schools to *run* even during the day.

Business people in Birgunj also have their qualms. All other crossings are open; there is no *andolan* there. Why only us? How long will we have to bear losses?

I left Birgunj, crossed Simara and I saw no signs of the *andolan*. Everything was as usual; vehicles were on the road.

The other thing to be noted is that gas cylinders and fuel jerry cans find their way through the smaller crossings. On night buses, you find more jerry cans and less people.

The people say there are no shortages in Kathmandu, because everything is reaching there. They may have to pay a bit extra, but there is no shortage. The shortage is in the Terai; we cannot afford anything.

Stopping by Churiya

I was in a private vehicle, and there were no signs of any obstruction. What was going on is that if you have a poster on a vehicle saying that the bride and her groom are on board, the protesters let you pass. I was on one of those vehicles.

I was hungry when we reached Lalbandi, and I wanted to have a samosa. My travel companion, a local leader who was wearing a kurta, wanted to get off, but he said, "They will say, oh you are the ones enforcing the bandh." He was afraid. I told him I would go get the samosa, but the driver did not let me go.

That night we stayed in Bardibas. They asked me, 'We are in Churiya area. Would you still spend the night here? 'Yes, I will. I stayed the night there'.

The two questions I faced in Mahottari

The next day I went to Mahottari. This is also my own district. There was a discussion inside the building of FNJ. This was one of the places where police suppressed agitators during the Jaleswhor movement mercilessly.

What was surprising for me there was that the last time I was there, the people were least bothered about politics. But this time, even an 80-year-old was interested in politics.

There I had to face two major questions. One question was, "we had raised the issue of a Madhes Pradesh; they are not giving it to us; so why not talk about a separate desh (country)?"

I asked, what is a country? "It is to have one's own Parliament, executive and judiciary. Federalism gives all these things in the form of the pradesh assembly, high court and ministries. You can even form your own police. I told them to have a look at the annexure of the constitution."

"Now transform this 'Number 2' Pradesh into a state like UP where no one can become the Prime Minister of India without winning. I told them to look at the population of the state. If it is stretched just a little bit, 80 per cent of all business will take place in this state. It has already been proven that when Birgunj is shut, Nepal's lifeline is shut. Now this state's Chief Ministercan tomorrow become the Prime Minister of Nepal. This is the autonomy and self-rule that you want. Create conditions so that the whole country depends on the state," I said.

I gave the example of Sri Lanka. There was war for 30 years and thousands lost their lives. But in the end what happened to the *andolan*? It ended. For this, the path you are talking about is wrong and we should not go for it.

The second question was about resorting to violence. Some youths said they want to rise in arms against the state. I told them politics of violence was bad. Look at Tibet, Dalai Lama's *andolan* is non-violent; that is the reason it is 'legitimate.'

"Because our voices were not reflected in the constitution, India did not welcome it. Because our *andolan* is peaceful, the US, UK, EU and the UN sympathize with us. If you had talked about resorting to arms, no one would have sympathized.

"The other thing is that if you fight the state with 400 guns, the state will fight back with 400,000 guns. For now, this might seem difficult, but in the long run it would be easy. If you take that route there will be encounters; look at the fate of the armed groups in the Terai in the past. That is why our means should be peaceful."

Janakpur Responds to the Army

When I was in Janakpur in the second week of December 2015, preparations were on to welcome the President. Everyone was saying that the President was coming to provoke the agitators. When I reached there, the Army was taking photos of local houses. People were angry. There was unprecedented security in the area.

When people feel they are powerless, that is when they rebel. This was proven on Wednesday December 16, 2015.

The President's visit added fuel to fire. If an incident happens in any part of the Madhes, it spreads like wildfire. After the Janakpur incident, there were protests in areas like Bhardaha.

There is one thing characteristic of the Madhes; people get angry when they see blood. On top of that the sense that it was carried out by the Pahadi state spreads even faster. Personally, I feel that the President should not have gone to Janakpur.

During the clashes between the police and the protestors, even Indian nationals were injured. They were on a pilgrimage to Janakpur. In the past, business worth

Rs. 10 million would take place in Janakpur on Biwaha Panchami. This would look after the local economy for six months. But the people have now seen that the same level of business may not be there next year. People were afraid; they were agitated.

Dissatisfied Policemen in Siraha

I spent some time in Siraha in October. In the past, the Madhes movement would be centred around Lahan. But this time it was so-so. But what was new was that in areas where forces have been deployed under a Madhesi, an extra officer has been sent from Kathmandu. It seemed that the officials did not trust the Madhesis.

For example, the DSP stationed in Lahan is a Madhesi, and another DSP has been sent to the same station to supervise police activities in the area.

Rajbiraj Lies in Wait

After that, I went to Rajbiraj in December. There I talked to Morcha leaders. Sadbhavana's Dipendra Chaudhary, who was at the forefront, said protestors are confused after the leaders' Delhi visit. He said they were waiting for a new programme.

I also met Forum Nepal's Sailendra Shah. "I noted three or four things" he said. "First, the district-level leaders and central leaders are not communicating well, that is why the local leaders are confused. Even if there was communication, it was with Delhi. If the leaders had said okay, that is not acceptable to us, we could have gone ahead. But they are not in a position to answer to the local people".

The other thing I noted was that he said, "The *andolan* is running by the grace of God." It is moving ahead by using local resources. The leaders are also in a fix: if they do not continue, they face an existential crisis, if they do, they have no resources.

Third, they are waiting for new programmes. And, fourth, how long is the *andolan* going to last? "It is cold, and it is the wedding season. That is the reason the *andolan* has slowed down, said Sarbhendraji.

Lest Kathmandu Think the *Andolan* has Subsided

After the border blockade ended in February 2016, many people in Kathmandu thought that the movement or *andolan* had subsided. Kathmandu should not think that the *andolan* in the Madhes has subsided. Under a dense fog, a fire may not be visible; that is the message from Janakpur.

The Madhesi community has a special character: It has always been proving Kathmandu's perspective wrong, and coming up with surprises. Once again, it has proven Kathmandu's hunch that the *andolan* has subsided to be wrong.

When the constitution was being passed, no one would have thought that such an *andolan* would happen in the Madhes. But the *andolan* has gone on for 120 days, and Kathmandu has been proven wrong. Perhaps, if the leaders could see an *andolan* like this happening in the future, they would have addressed the grievances of the Madhes. Perhaps, Girija Prasad Koirala had thought there would not be any protest if the Interim Constitution remained silent on federalism. But protests happened.

That is why my wish is that Kathmandu does not fall into a delusion, and it acts in a rational and logical manner to accommodate the demands of the Madhes.

15

Madhes Politics

Then and Now

About Madhes and Madhesis

Historical documents suggest that Nepal's Terai region, which is also called 'Madhes', used to be known as 'Madhya Desh', meaning 'the country in the middle'.

During the Anglo-Nepalese War, the people of Madhes sided with the British East India Company to fight against Gurkha rulers. After the annexation of Madhesi land into the Gurkha kingdom, following the war with the British East India Company, the language and culture of Gurkha were gradually imposed on the Madhesis. Although Madhesi territory was annexed into Nepal, its people were never treated as equal citizens. Despite many political struggles, it still remains for them to be represented fully and incorporated into the state organs and institutions of Nepal.

Until 2016, representation of Madhesis was around 8 per cent in Nepal's civil service. Even today, their representation in security forces is at least 6 to 15 times less than what it should be based on the principle of proportionate inclusion. Their representation figures in Nepal Police, Armed Police Force, and Nepal Army are just 2 per cent, 5 per cent, and 2 per cent respectively. The lack of representation in state structures is due to the long-time discrimination against Madhesis during the unification or expansion bid of Prithvi Narayan Shah and his descendants.

Madhesis have a close kinship with their neighbours on the other side of Nepal–India border. They share common languages and culture, distinct from the people living in the hill and mountain regions of Nepal. As a result, Madhesis are often perceived as Indians by the rest of the country, despite the fact that they have been native to the Terai region since ancient times.

Madhesis were the native inhabitants of the region, while the country's ruling class, particularly the forefathers of hill Brahmins, Chhetris and Newars, and the Shah monarchs of the past, historically migrated to Nepal from Rajasthan, Kumaun, Kannauj, Garhwal and Karnataka of India. However, the ruling class of Nepal later claimed themselves as the true inhabitants of the country, and treated the Madhesis as foreigners. They used 'Muglani or 'Bideshi' as terms for Madhesis, meaning 'outsiders' or 'foreigners', and have continuously adopted policies to favour the hill people and disenfranchise Madhesis as a minority in their own region.

Between 1970 and 1980, the Brahmin/Chhetri-dominated government launched a deforestation campaign along the East-West Highway and settled 2.5 million hill people in the Madhes region. These hill people, who the government termed 'landless people', were encouraged to settle in the Terai.

What a paradox is the identity of Madhesis in Nepal! Until 2006, Madhesis opposed the hill people when they were addressed as 'Madhesi,' 'Marshiya,', 'Madise' or Dhoti. Since then, however, they began reclaiming these terms as their own identity, just as the ruling class now insists that they should not assert themselves as Madhesis, but as

Nepalis instead. There is nothing wrong in this statement, but the fact is that the ruling class wants to deny Madhesis of the rights they could claim on the basis of their cultural and geographical identity and long discrimination. If identity is not established, identity-based federalism will not be instituted and Madhesis will have no hope of autonomy in their own provinces.

The fact that Madhesis are different from the hill people can be traced from the celebration of Holi festival. The Holi festival celebrations in Madhes are different from the way the hill people celebrate this festival. Madhesis and people in India celebrate Holi on the same day. In Nepal, there are two separate dates for Holi—one for the districts in the hills, and one in Madhes.

Hindi was, and still it is, the lingua franca for people in Madhes. Earlier, Hindi language used to be the medium of instruction and education. The government banned it from being the medium of education in 1965 and also prohibited Rastriya panchayat Members (the erstwhile lawmakers) from speaking in the Parliament in Hindi. In the post-1990 democratic era, Hindi is being treated in the same way as it used to be treated in the panchayat regime. From 1950 to 1960, when Nepalis practised democracy for the first time after the end of the Rana regime, both Nepali and Hindi were official languages and lawmakers were free to speak in Hindi in the house; but after the constitution of 1990, Nepali became the sole official language. Discrimination against Hindi continues till today.

Under the panchayat system, the ruling class wanted more representation from the hill districts, and electoral districts were skewed in their favour. Some hill districts had one representative for as few as 2,000 to 3,000 voters, whereas in the Terai this number could go up to 50,000 or more. Post-1990, Parliamentary constituencies were created largely on the basis of population, but still the remnants of panchayat policy are felt. Now in the CA, major parties dominated by hill people are lobbying for Parliamentary constituencies on the basis of both geography and population. This would mean that Madhes would not have equal representation in the Parliament. Madhes contributes 83 per cent tax revenue to the national coffers, while receiving only 20 per cent of the budget.

Although the Madhes Uprising of 2007 and subsequent Madhes movements have helped better the situation of Madhesis in Nepal, there are many problems that need to be solved to ensure equality for Madhesi citizens.

Madhesis want to live a dignified life, with equal rights and respect, and protection of their language and culture in their country. The problem is that whenever they demand equal rights, they are accused of working at the behest of India. Madhesis have always been at the forefront of democratic movements, whether it was the movement against the Rana regime in the 1940s, or the movement against the monarchy in 1990, or in 2006, and there is no reason for the privileged class and communities to deny Madhesis their rightful share in the state.

Nepal's Constitution of 1990 was framed after a popular movement against the monarchy. Yet, the state continued its suppressive policies against Madhesis. The provisions relating to citizenship illustrate this fact. The Old Citizenship Act, 1964 was incorporated into the Constitution of Nepal in 2015. Thousands of Madhesis remain stateless even after the constitution was promulgated for the first time ever by representatives of the people.

None of the issues that were at the core of Madhesi empowerment were resolved in the 12 years following 1990. The Interim Constitution of Nepal, 2007 succeeded in addressing the Madhes' problem to some extent, but again, the 16-Point Deal signed on June 8, 2015 among the four major political force—the Nepali Congress, the CPN-UML, the CPN-MC-Maoist party and the Madhesi Janadhikar Forum-Democratic—expedited the constitution-making process in the CA and deliberately attempted to postpone federalism, which is an integral issue of the Madhesi platform. The 16-Point Agreement had stated that the constitution would be promulgated and federalism issues would be resolved at a later date by the new Parliament.

In Nepal, one of the key reasons why Madhesis are discriminated against by the state is because of their cultural and linguistic links to India.

Roti-Beti Relations

Madhesi leaders say that Madhesis share a roti-beti (bread and kinship) relationship with India. 'Relations of roti' refers to economic interactions between the two countries. Similarly, 'relations of beti' means marital relations between the two countries in the border areas. Such relations date back to ancient times with Awadh King Ram and his marriage to King Janak's daughter, Sita. Even today, the symbolic marriage between Ram and Sita is solemnized in Janakpur. Every year, a *parikrama* (meaning, "making a round trip") is held in Janakpur from mid-February to mid-March. Pilgrims from Nepal and India take part in this religious procession.

Many of those living in Delhi and Kathmandu are unaware of how interdependent the people residing in border areas of these two countries are. They share linguistic, cultural and religious practices with their neighbours across the border. People often cross the border to buy groceries or even to use open spaces for defecation. Those who have not witnessed the porous flow of people between the two countries in the border areas sometimes talk of building a fence along the border, which would greatly disrupt the everyday lives of those who live there.

Should I always be denied the chance of being recognized as a true Nepali national just because my face is similar to the Indian faces of people of Uttar Pradesh and Bihar? The faces of some of our Pahadi brethren are like the faces of certain other Indians and Chinese, but their nationalism is never questioned. Yet Madhesi nationalism remains suspect. Why is our loyalty to the nation questioned? Is a dark face the yardstick in this country to brand somebody as a foreigner?

Leftist parties, whose ideas of anti-India nationalism victimize Madhesis, influence 70 per cent of votes in the hill areas. In 2013, the bench of Justice Girish Chandra Lal was hearing a case filed against EC's decision to produce citizenship certificates for listing one's name in the voter's list. I recall Justice Girish Chandra Lal, citing the case of Kalapani, stating that this hill area was being encroached upon, yet this has not been the case for even a single inch of the Madhes border with India. When Lal raised this issue, the then Chief Justice Damodar Sharma had difficulty calming the bench. After a long pleading in the court, the interim order that prevented registration of voters' names in the voter's list without citizenship was vacated by Chief Justice Sharma. This marked the first time in my life that I saw a sitting justice argue boldly in favour of the Madhesi community, and even forced the senior advocate Bal Krishna Neupane to correct his statement that "Indians are taking over this country" in the name of Madhesis.

When I was a student, I was admitted in the eighth grade in Rupandehi and that was the first time I had interaction with Pahadi students. It was there that Pahadi classmates called me 'Dhoti,' and 'Deshi,' which were common taunts for many dark-faced Madhesis. It was only after I faced discrimination in Rupandehi that I came to know that Madhesis were being discriminated against in this country because of their colour. I felt that I was discriminated against in my own country just because my appearance, costumes and culture match with those of Indians.

Nepali rulers never accepted Madhesis as genuine citizens of the country in the past, and this sentiment continues even today. People in Kathmandu interact differently with a dark person of the Terai like me compared to a Pahadi face from Darjeeling. The irony is that when Madhesis go to the Indian side of the border, people ridicule them by calling them 'Nepali butcher.' The worst of all this is that we are called 'Dhoti,' Bhaiya' and 'Deshi' in our own country. What is our real identity? Where should we go? What is our nationalism?

Madhes shares multi-faceted relations with India. Kathmandu, however, does not try to understand this. The open border is Madhes' strength, not a weakness. The Embassy of India always pressurizes Madhesis to compromise with the rulers in Nepal. Kathmandu understands that if it wanted to deal with Madhesi parties, then it can seek Embassy of India's blessings. India, too, wants to maintain good relations with the Nepali state because it is the Nepali state with which Delhi signs any bilateral agreement. India does not see it as beneficial to forge bonds with Madhesis at the cost of the Nepali ruling class. There is already a strong anti-India sentiment in the hills. India should remain cautious that such an anti-India feeling does not emerge in Madhes, particularly in the minds of the next generation.

India thinks that Madhesis should fight for their rights on their own, and that it is not India's role to fight for Madhesis. It is natural for India to protect its national interests. Top leaders of India and Indian bureaucracy fear that if any kind of security threat persisted in Madhes or peace is threatened there, it could have spillover effects in border states of India such as Uttar Pradesh, Bihar and West Bengal. West Bengal plays a vital role in shaping India's relations with Bangladesh, as does Tamil Nadu in shaping India's relations with Sri Lanka. But Uttar Pradesh and Bihar have not been able to play any kind of role in shaping India's relations with Madhes because Madhes has not been able to forge diplomatic ties with Lucknow and Patna in this matter. Madhes has always looked to the government in distant Delhi, which does not understand nor does it try to understand Madhes' language, culture, customs and traditions. Many people in Nepal believe one needs to speak against India in order to be a nationalist. This is why those who protest against India become very popular in Nepal, and those who speak positively about India are treated with suspicion. The Madhesi carry the tag of Indian brokers and RAW agents by birth, because of their ethnicity, geographical proximity and cultural similarities.

Madhesi leaders occasionally go to the Indian Embassy seeking assistance, scholarships, medical treatment and funds for development. Madhesi leaders have not been able to build their relations with the Indian Embassy beyond these things. As a consequence, Madhesi leaders have confined themselves to the role of informers and obedient people to carry out the embassy's orders rather than positioning themselves as counterparts and friends.

Ever since the Bharatiya Janata Party came to power in India, some indications of change in Nepal–India relations can be seen. The Indian Prime Minister, Narendra Modi, visited Nepal twice in 2014, which itself was a favorable sign. Kathmandu was very happy when the Indian PM, during his first visit to Nepal, said that three regions of Nepal—Mountains, Hills and the Terai—should live in harmony. During his second trip to Nepal, the Indian PM wanted to visit Janakpur and Lumbini, which the Nepali state did not allow. When he wanted to distribute cycles to the students of Janakpur, the issue was raised in the Parliament. The cabinet did not endorse a civic reception, which was originally planned for the Indian PM at Barhabigha. Government officials rather said that the civic reception for the Indian PM would be held at the Janakpur Temple, and thus on various pretexts they foiled Modi's visit to Janakpur.

Kathmandu's rulers feared that Indian Prime Minister Modi might make a handsome offer of assistance and development for Madhes. When Modi offered 10 quintals of chandan (sandalwood) at Pashupatinath Temple, Kathmandu rulers had no objection. But when they learned that he would distribute cycles to poor students of Madhes, the Kathmandu rulers argued that it would violate nationalism. During his second visit to Nepal, Modi, while addressing the handover of the Trauma Centre, said that Madhesis and Maoists should not be bypassed in the constitution-making process. This statement served as an attack on Kathmandu rulers. Those who appreciated Modi during his first visit became his opponents after his second trip to Nepal, and the number of people who opposed Modi in Kathmandu increased greatly.

Madhes Politics

Madhesis have been discriminated against for centuries, since the time of King Prithvi Narayan Shah. Ever since, rulers have treated Madhesis as second class citizens. According to Madhesi parties, the reason for this is simple: that Madhesis are the victims of internal colonization.

The Madhes region generates big revenue for the nation but it receives an abysmally low budget for the development of its infrastructure. Madhesis constitute 33 per cent of the population but their representation in bureaucracy, the Nepal Army, the Nepal Police and the Armed Police Force is very low. In the Parliament, Madhesi's representation never increased from 20 per cent in the panchayat system, nor in the multiparty system after 1990. It was only after inclusive policies were adopted in the Interim Constitution that the representation of Madhesis in Parliament increased and Madhesis and other marginalized groups began to see opportunities available to them in some government jobs. This provision needs to be expanded to all other state organs and, if possible, also to the private sector.

Madhesis have long raised their voices against discrimination and in favour of equal share of power, ever since the end of Rana rule in the 1950s when youth leaders formed the Nepal Terai Congress under Bedanand Jha. Jha was the first Madhesi to advocate Madhes' autonomy. The Nepal Terai Congress fielded its candidates in the first democratic general elections held in 1959, but failed to win any seats.

Jha was later co-opted by King Mahendra and he became a minister on several occasions during the panchayat rule. Jha also became Nepal's ambassador to India. During panchayat, the issue of Madhesi autonomy was not raised on the political agenda. During this time, the monarchy ruled the country with an iron fist, and followed a "One Language, One Dress" policy to strengthen its rule.

In 1983, a migration report was published by a commission led by Harka Gurung which tried to paint Madhesis as Indians. This report angered Madhesis who were the victims of discriminatory policies on language, culture and citizenship.

Unable to participate in politics, Gajendra Narayan Singh founded a non-governmental organization, called

'Nepal Sadbhavana Parishad' (NSP). The NSP began with the view of making the Madhesi people aware of the state's conspiracy to paint Madhesis as outsiders or Indians. When democracy was restored in 1990, Singh changed Nepal Sadbhavana Parishad into a political organization, renaming it as 'Nepal Sadbhavana Party'.

Madhesi intellectuals were represented in several political parties, including the Nepali Congress, the CPN-UML and the Nepal Sadbhavana Party. In the first general elections in 1991 Madhesi lawmakers won seats in the election. Although they had little representation in the house from 1991 until 2008, Madhesi lawmakers demonstrated a desire to be involved in positions of power. NSP leaders split several times in their attempt to become ministers or to hold government positions. These internal party dynamics detracted from the appeal of the Madhesi cause, and were a major reason why Madhesi issues would not be raised prominently in the Parliament after 1990.

During the People's War, some Madhesi Maoist leaders raised the issue of Madhes autonomy and empowerment. In 2007 and 2008, the Madhes movement strongly raised the issue of proportional representation of Madhesis in state organs, representation by population in the Parliament and an end to discrimination in citizenship provisions strongly. However, the 16-Points Agreement signed on June 8, 2015 retracted from these agendas of the marginalized community. The CPN-MC was happy with any kind of constitution. Baburam Bhattarai in his speech in the Constituent Assembly in the capacity of Chair of the Constitutional Committee said that "Hami lai sanghiyeta, gantantra, dharma nirpeskchta, samabesi bahye ko sambhidhan ko khosto bhye pani huncha" (they want to promulgate any kind of constitution that just need to have federalism, republic form, secularism and proportional inclusion). They thought if they cannot promulgate the constitution from the Second constituent assembly, their ten years armed revolution would be proved wrong.

Assertion of Madhesi Identity—A Review

Madhesis have suffered discrimination for centuries. They fought for their rights after the end of Rana regime, but they have not been successful in winning their share of power in state organs, due in part to disorganized and fractured party leadership, as well as Madhesi people being unaware of their rights.

In recent years, Madhes politics has seen positive reforms, with Madhesi youth becoming well-educated and vocal for their rights. Madhesi youth are willing to fight for inclusion, fair representation and recognition of Madhesi identity. Demonstrations of Madhesis marching for their rights have taken place in the streets of Kathmandu as well as further afield in Delhi, Washington DC and London, when the third Madhes movement launched in 2015 was on the ground.

Madhesi youth are irate that the state has failed to employ them in their own land, and are forced to seek foreign employment, often in Gulf States. This generation has access to internet and its members are well informed about politics and rights, and are active on social media. Once abroad, they come to realize the discrimination they have faced. With education and experience abroad, it is like coming into the light from a dark cave where Madhesi youth can distinguish between right and wrong, as also between equality and inequality. They begin to question the mainstream media's biases and prejudices on social media.

Naturally, every movement gives birth to new leadership. This is true in the case of Madhes politics now. New civil society organizations emerged recently during the 2015 Madhes movement.

Help Madhes

A new organization is 'Help Madhes', a group of Madhesi youth based in Qatar. They voluntarily collected money to help the injured and the families of the deceased during the 2015 movement. This group of youth in the Gulf countries donate a part of their earnings for the cause of Madhes. This is not merely supporting the victims of the movement, but it clearly shows their overwhelming emotions and commitment to fight against the Nepali State.

Madhesi Adhikar Sangharsha Samiti (MASS) in Janakpur

Madhesis in general and Madhesi youths in particular are not happy with the mushrooming of political parties in the Madhes working with the same agenda. They want Madhesi parties to come together and present a united fight. Unfortunately, their aspiration is yet to be realized. MASS was the first group to start protest in Janakpur against the draft of the new constitution in 2015. Janakpur was an epicentre of the Madhes movement. In fact, in 2015 the Madhes movement started from Janakpur when the preliminary draft of the constitution was brought out for the public feedback and suggestions. Ironically, lawmakers of major political parties restricted the participation of people other than their cadres to enter the venue set up for collecting feedback. The police backed these parties to restrict people from participating in the programme. Some youths in Janakpur when they were not allowed to enter inside the venue for public feedback, clashed with the police. Thereafter, they started demonstrating against the constitution-making process. They formed an informal and apolitical group called MASS to oppose that process. Later the MASS worked together with Madhes-based political parties with a view to stage demonstrations under the same banner.

Koshish Group

During the movement, the government adopted the 'crackdown' approach to bulldoze the protests in Madhes. The excessive use of force by law enforcement agencies resulted in the death of over three dozen Madhesis, and injuring hundreds of others. Neither the government nor the agitating parties were able to support the injured.

A group of doctors in Dharan, especially from the Madhes, became life-saving God for them. The group, which they later called 'Koshish' started taking care of all injured in the Madhes movement. They paid for food, medicine and travel cost of the injured and their families accompanying them.

Later, the group also extended their support to those affected by the natural disaster. At the same time, the associates of Koshish maintain a close vigilance over Madhes politics and legitimately warn the Madhesi leadership if and when they compromise the cause.

Madhesi Youth Portal

After the promulgation of a faulty constitution which reneged on previous agreements signed with Madhesi forces, the 2015 Madhes movement started. The unanimous consensus across Kathmandu regarding the movement was that it was a weak protest and it would fade out within a week. The Madhesi civil society had read the draft constitution and put out a list of clear demands vis-à-vis Kathmandu. But, either the demands were not conveyed properly or the determination of Madhesis was unclear to Kathmandu, and they went unnoticed. Thus they began to oppose the oppression of security forces, and the atrocities committed from either side.

While the police crackdown on protesters continued, it was frustrating for Madhesi youths to observe the biases shown in the mainstream media which is largely dominated by upper-caste hill people. There was the lack of proper data for proper corroboration. Instead of calling it conscious subversion, I would affirm that there was a visible cognitive bias amongst media outlets while reporting on Madhesi issues. For example, the shooting at protesters didn't find space while even a small incident involving protesters was highlighted with gory details on the front page.

Despite Madhesi youths' appeal to the mainstream media to maintain their objectivity, the media failed on two fronts. Firstly, it failed in understanding the mood of Madhes and conveying the same to the political class and civic society of Kathmandu. Secondly, they failed to report from ground zero. Some of the journalists were sitting in Kathmandu and writing articles with no knowledge of the situation on the ground with an exception of a few like Ms. Subina Shrestha, a journalist with Al Jazeera, who visited the actual locations for reporting.

The casual approach of the Nepali mainstream media not only appalled the Madhesi youths, but also forced them to bring their version of the atrocities to the world. This denial of media space was one of the catalysts of the birth of http://madhesiyouth.com/portal. The Madhesi youth keep all data related to Madhes on their website and are very active on social media and they can check any manipulation of facts related to Madhes.

Delhi-based United Madhesis of Nepal and Terai Madhes Study Group

New Delhi, the capital city of India is the major destination of Madhesi youths to pursue their higher education. While pursuing their education in Jawaharlal Nehru University (JNU) and other educational institutions in New Delhi, Madhesi youths have become more vocal and raise the issues of their communities. For this cause, they had earlier formed an organization called 'United Madhesis of Nepal' (UMN), and they have recently formed another group namely Terai Madhes Study Group (TMSG).

The facebook page of UMN introduces itself as follows:

> This is an NGO in Delhi. Main objective of the organization is to assist Madhesi ,Tharu and Janjati people of Nepal who are discriminated against by Nepali State.

The study group describes its objective as follows:

> Terai Madhes Study Group is an initiative of non-partisan free thinking liberal students group on the issues of Terai and Madhes. This is a modest attempt to engage with constructive academic discourses, dialogues and discussions pertinent to Madhes region.

On February 19, 2016, the Indian police deployed at the New Delhi based Nepali Embassy arrested members of United Madhesis of Nepal for waving black flags at the Nepal's PM K.P. Sharma Oli in front of the embassy. A total of 22 Madhesi students were charged under IPC 107 and IPC 151 for disrupting public tranquility and sent to Tihar jail till 23rd of February.

Right after their detention, some of the Madhesi students closely interacted with the Delhi police to secure their release but to no avail. Finally, they were sent to Special Judicial Magistrate's bench and SJM sent them to judicial custody till 23rd of February.

These students did not disrupt public tranquility; rather they exercised their rights to peaceful protest in a democratic country like India. Under international human rights law binding on India, states are allowed to impose restrictions on the right to peaceful protests on the grounds of 'public order'. However, any such restriction must be demonstrably necessary and proportionate, and must not jeopardize the people's right itself. Filing criminal cases against peaceful protesters was a clear violation of the Indian Constitution and many international treaties such as International Covenant on Civil and Political Rights, especially Articles 18 to 22. Showing a black flag to the Nepali PM against killing of Madhesis did not create any threat to the interests of national security or public order. The constitution of India guarantees the right to protest as a fundamental right. This action of the Delhi police violated fundamental rights including Article 19 (1) of the constitution of India that guarantees the right to freedom of speech and expression. India's Supreme Court has also laid down a precedent that any restrictions relying on the grounds of public order are valid only when there is a close connection between the action and public disorder, and there is an imminent threat of lawlessness. This showed that the rule of law was completely undermined by the Delhi police to arrest Madhesi youths. This was a condemnable act.

USA-based Madhes Human Rights (MADHUR)

The USA-based Madhes Human Rights (MADHUR) has been documenting cases of human rights violations in the Terai by the state and passing them on to the international stakeholders, including the USA and UK Governments.

During the movement, the organization had written a letter to U.S. President Barack Obama and heads of different U.S. government departments, requesting them to demonstrate their concerns on Madhesis' issues in Nepal. They raised the issue with the government of Nepal through various formal and informal channels of communication which was discussed in the chapter of "The Role of International Community in the Constitution Drafting Process".

It was never imagined before, but the Madhes movement led to the emergence of these institutions and groups taking over the legitimacy of the movement. This is clear evidence of the fact that the Madhes politics is changing. Although it is not visible directly, the leadership of the Madhes movement is gradually changing. The legitimacy of Madhes politics is shifting to new leaders and institutions. More educated, committed and professional leaders are invisibly taking over the agendas.

Madhesi Leaders are More Cautious of their Actions

Madhesis who are not in any political parties are much stronger than the parties' men and women. Madhesi leaders are cautious that if they make any mistakes, the civil society members and intellectuals will criticize their actions and that would make their life difficult on the ground. So they think a great deal before getting into any agreement. This movement has not only weakened NC/UML/Maoists Centre in the Terai in the public's eyes but has equally eroded the image of some Madhesi leaders who are not truly committed to the Madhesi agenda. For India, Madhes politics is a weak card not because of a lack of public support but because of its leadership and parties' structure. Madhesi forces unfortunately remain fragmented.

Whither Madhes Movement?

Madhesi people at the ground level feel that these Madhesi leaders have failed to achieve the agenda set by the Madhes uprising.

Madhesi identity has already been institutionalized through the constitution. The death of around 150 Madhesi youth during the first, second and third Madhes uprisings within 10 years, has redefined nationalism.

The Madhes uprising gave a new assertion capacity to Madhesis to resist the derogatory term 'dhoti' that the Pahadis often use to refer to Madhesis. Now, even those who are working in hairdressing salons and selling vegetables on their bicycles in the street corners of Kathmandu have the confidence to protest against any discriminatory and bullying behaviour. Madhesis in Kathmandu have now the courage to give befitting replies to those who dare to call them 'bhaiya' and 'dhoti'. The hill monopoly on culture, language, dress, and state structures faced heavy blows after the uprisings. Those who discriminated against Madhesis to prove that only they (hill people) were nationalists were exposed.

The 2007, 2008 and 2015 Madhes uprisings were different from the previous movements in Nepal. Previous movements in Nepal were limited to the regime change but this movement was for the socio-economic revolution and political restructuring of the unitary Nepali State that had the discriminatory practices built into it. Actually, the change that was brought by the Maoists' movement was incomplete. The Madhes uprising was a complement to the Maoists revolution and People's Movement-II. It contributed to the efforts to bring revolutionary changes in the Nepali society.

Matrika Yadav's efforts to paint the walls of Kathmandu with the slogans "Garba se kahu ham Madhesi chi, bideshi bhagauda nai dhartiputra chi" (We are proud to call ourselves Madhesis, We are not foreigners or refugees, we are the sons and daughters of this land) was a commendable job.

Legendary Madhesi leader Gajendra Narayan Singh's consistent fight for citizenship and Madhes autonomy post

1990 increased Madhesis' awareness of their rightful share in the state.

Federalism, the cornerstone of the 2007 Madhes movement is at the crossroads. The ruling elites and power centers do not want Nepal to be federated. However, they do not want to say this directly. So, they have adopted the strategy either to dilute it or convert it into five administrative regions. The dissolution of the First CA and structural manipulation in the Second CA election formed part of the same game plan to avoid, dilute and deface federalism.

Incapability, division and lust for money and power caused the defeat of the Madhesi parties in the Second CA election. Now the question is, whether they are still capable of carrying the agenda of federalism as envisioned by the Madhes uprising? If they are not, what are the possible ways to push for institutionalizing real federalism?

The new groups in Madhes have emerged as a strong force to counter the Madhesi parties. Sudhir Sharma in his book *Prayogsala* also mentioned this fact as an experience of the First CA dissolution. Mahant Thakur and Bijaya Gachhedar compromised with the power centers and that was totally rejected by Madhesi intellectuals and civil society. The new generation and educated Madhesi groups working for different national and international institutions are closely watching and are ready to counter any kind of dilution of the federalism and other vital aspects of the Madhesi agenda.

Madhesis strongly believe that the sacrifices of 150 youths during the Madhes movements should not go in vain. This is a long fight and change of actors and losses on the electoral front do not make much difference to the issue. Madhesis have the responsibility to keep the flame of the movement burning to achieve the agenda of the

Madhes uprising. The individual character of the Madhesi leaders does not affect the issue. New actors take over when others fail. This is an ongoing process in any movement.

Kathmandu likes the broker institutions and type of leaders who can appease and serve the ruling elites' interests, but the last decade of experience has shown that the model of 'clientilistic politics' does not work anymore especially after three Madhes movements. The new generation of Madhesi is not like those of 1970s, 1980s or 1990s. Today's situation is different. Tharus and Madhesis actively participated in the Maoists armed struggle and contributed to the popular 1990 and 2006 movements. They have awakened. The youths assert their rights and are in no mood to tolerate discrimination on any grounds. The game of playing Madhesi against Madhesi using the face of artificially created nationalist Madhesis to counter genuine agendas of Madhesis seems irrelevant.

Thus, it is a question of how much engagement there is with this new reality, especially the political culture, without which any institutional or legislative change is of no use for Madhesis and Tharus. Kathmandu's approach to isolate and defame educated Madhesis who are vocal about their rights will not work anymore, especially given the political ethnic divisions of society from the top to bottom in Nepal.

In order to better grasp these new dynamics of Madhes politics, one has to stop scratching the surface and gazing at the masquerade of the hill-hegemonic domination that causes conflicts rooted in social injustice. Resolution of Madhes dissatisfaction is not a quick fix to complex and long-term problems; rather it is a systemic transformation of structures and culture that provides legitimacy to inequality and change in general perception that Madhesis are Indian. It is about redefining who are genuine "Nepali" and including Madhesis in that definition.

16

Failure of Second Constitutional Amendment

The Backdrop

Hopes were high that the constitution would be amended for the second time. Before the formation of the government, the ruling parties—Nepali Congress (NC) and CPN-MC (Maoist Centre)—had inked a three-point deal with the Madhes-based political parties that the constitution would be amended to address their demands.

But attempts for the second amendment to the statute have failed under the NC-MC coalition government. The first Prime Minister Pushpa Kamal Dahal 'Prachanda' under the NC-MC coalition government did not put substantial efforts in amending the constitution. His efforts were more in the implementation of the constitution than its amendment.

Holding elections is a part of the implementation of the constitution. The government led by him successfully held the first phase local body elections after a gap of 20 years. On 14 May 2016, the first phase of the local body elections in three provinces were held and Dahal claimed success as a Prime Minister for holding the elections. However, as the Prime Minister, he lost a great opportunity once again to bring the Madhesi parties on board during the elections.

The Rastriya Janata Party Nepal (RJPN) did not take part in the local elections for the first and second phases after their political demand that the constitution bill be passed was not met. However, the Federal Socialist Forum Nepal (FSFN) took part in the first and second phase local body elections.

After NC President Sher Bahadur Deuba took the premiership of the government as a part of the power-sharing deal between NC and CPN-MC, the Deuba-led coalition government put the constitution Amendment Bill to vote on August 21, 2017.

But this time, the RJPN changed its earlier stance. The party agreed to participate in the third round of local body polls, no matter what the outcome of the vote on the constitutional amendment bill. This move was a result of pressure from India, which had earlier supported Madhesi Movement.

Out of 553 Parliamentarians present in the Parliament, 347 lawmakers cast their vote in favour of the amendment bill, which mean that the bill lacked the two-third majority for endorsement. 206 lawmakers including those of CPN-MC and Kamal-Thapa-led Rastriya Prajantantra Party cast their votes against the amendment bill. Eventually, the Second Constitutional Amendment failed.

Following the failure to pass the constitution Amendment Bill, RJPN took part in the third phase of local polls slated for 18 September 2017.

Why Constitutional Amendment Failed

Had the ruling coalition tried its best, it could have succeeded in mustering the required two-third majority in passing the constitutional amendment bill. Here are the clear reasons for the failure.

First, some of the lawmakers from the ruling NC and the CPN-MC, which registered the amendment bill to vote, were also not present in the Parliament. The ruling parties could have asked their lawmakers to vote in favour of the bill. The absence of their lawmakers in the Parliament cannot be an excuse for the parties when a crucial bill is put to vote. This proves that the ruling parties did not put their genuine efforts into passing the bill.

Moreover, there is a big group of leaders within the NC and CPN-MC who seem to be silently supporting the CPN-UML's stands on the constitutional amendment. Even in the CPN-MC leaders like Top Bahadur Raymajhi, who is from Arghakhanchi opposed the constitutional amendment so as to keep almost a dozen districts of Terai in the hill provinces. At a programme organized by the Reporters' Club after the government registered the First Constitutional Amendment Bill on November 29, 2017, Raymajhi threatened to take to the streets if the boundary of Province 5 was changed. This shows the unity of Khas-Arya clan and community in Nepal. Despite belonging to different parties, their stands on constitutional amendment remain the same. Sections of the NC and CPN-MC also believe in what the UML's vocal stance, and some of them are public while others play behind the curtain.

Second, while Pashupati Shamsher JB Rana-led Rastriya Prajatantrik Party (Democratic) lawmakers did not take part in the voting, the Kamal Thapa-led RPP could have voted in favour of the Bill; Rana had always said that he favoured passing the constitutional amendment bill.

Third, the major political parties—NC, CPN-UML and CPN-MC—did not feel intense pressure to pass the bill. This is simply because of the division among those parties that championed the cause of Madhesis and Janajatis. Upendra Yadav-led Federal Socialist Forum Nepal (FSFN) took part in the first and second phase of local body polls without the government addressing any of the key issues raised by the agitating forces. The Bijay Kumar Gachhedar-led Nepal Democratic Forum (NDF) also took part in the election without raising any demands. Such a division was seen within the RJPN. Two members of the RJPN— Mahendra Ray Yadav and Sharat Singh Bhandari were in favour of participating in elections irrespective of the fate of the constitutional amendment bill. The RJPN tried to build pressure on the major parties to pass the constitutional amendment bill, but later it felt let down by India.

Madhesis, however, had expected that Coordinator of RJPN Mahantha Thakur would at least express his reservation about taking part in the polls but that did not happen. Only Anil Kumar Jha spoke against taking part in the election without the key demands of the party being addressed. It seems that the Madhesi forces have lost their battle. It would be very hard to amend the constitution in future.

Fourth, the government of India, which had extended moral and diplomatic support to Madhesi forces to champion their cause eventually, backed down and advised the RJPN to participate in the elections. Neither Indian minister of external affairs or any top leader of the ruling BJP directly pressured the RJPN leaders to take part in the elections but top Indian bureaucrats including diplomats and top government authorities pressured the RJPN to take part in the elections even if their demands are not met.

Last but the most important factor that led to the failure of the Second Constitutional Amendment was the main opposition party of the CPN-UML which has always stood against the demands of Madhesis and voted against the amendment. Had the UML supported the amendment, RPP could have come along.

The fall of the K.P. Sharma Oli-led government in July 2016 complicated the process to amend the constitution.

Oli and his party saw Pushpa Kamal Dahal's move to form a new government under his leadership as a betrayal, and wanted to teach him a lesson.

No matter what the UML leaders say publicly, this party is adamant on not allowing any amendment to the constitution. The UML knows that this is the only card for the party to get into power in the upcoming general elections. The UML was ready to show more flexibility for amending the constitution but before it could do so, the UML-led Government was dislodged in 2016. Since the fall of the UML Government, the party took a rigid position on the issues of the constitutional amendment.

One thing that is true is that the UML always wants to remain in power. Without being in the government, the UML is like a fish out of water because it is a party of bureaucrats, NGOs and construction company networks which enjoy the benefits when the UML is in the government. It is hard for this party to stay out of power for a long time. Arguably, the UML can be flexible on constitutional reform only when it is in the government.

Consultation with Madhesi Parties

Informally, I was asked to give my opinion on the constitutional amendment and before giving my opinion to the government I met UDMF leaders Upendra Yadav, Mahantha Thakur and Rajendra Mahato.

My understanding is that Yadav toes the line of maximalist approach while Mahato, at times, favours the minimalist approach, and avoids a clear stance on certain issues. Thakur believes that without the major stakeholders showing flexibility for constitutional amendment, UDMF cannot show flexibility.

The Chair of Federal Socialist Forum-Nepal, Upendra Yadav told me that over 100 articles of the constitution including the preamble should be amended to ensure, among other things, the rights over indigenous nationalities, particularly indigenous nationalities' rights on local natural resources and the implementation of ILO Convention, 169. He told me that he was preparing the ethnic fronts of his party to expand the current movement as a national movement so that amendments could be made to those articles where they are needed. My impression is that Yadav will not be satisfied with only a few amendments to the constitution.

The Chair of the Sadbhavana Party (seven constituents of the UDMF merged to create a unified party Rastriya Janata Party-Nepal in April, 2017) Rajendra Mahato appeared to be ready to give a federal commission the task of resolving the issues of five Terai districts—Jhapa, Morang, Sunsari, Kailali and Kanchanpur after creating a separate Terai only province from Nawalparasi to Bardiya. On the issue of citizenship, Mahato told me that he favoured retaining the provision of the Interim Constitution.

The Chair of Terai Madhes Democratic Party Mahantha Thakur said the UDMF leaders might be flexible on the constitutional issues but since there is no guarantee that the constitution would be amended and the ruling parties would be flexible on their stance, it would not be wise for the UDMF to show flexibility. But my view is that the agitating forces should demonstrate maximum flexibility and try to get whatever they can from the current Parliament where their number cannot influence anything.

Again on April 28, 2017, I received a phone call from the newly-formed Rastriya Janata Party, Nepal leader Sarvendranath Shukla. He told me to come to his party office where the members of the RJP-N presidium wanted to consult me over the proposals that the government could register on the constitutional amendment bill to satisfy the agitating Madhesi and Janajati forces. I was there almost for three hours in a closed door meeting with the members of RJPN presidium sharing my views with them. The discussion focused on what kind of amendment proposal Madhesi parties should negotiate with Prime Minister Pushpa Kamal Dahal and Nepali Congress President Sher Bahadur Deuba on the constitutional amendment bill.

My advice was that RJPN should register Amendment proposals on the constitutional amendment bill to state that the Parliament could revise the provincial boundaries after consulting the province concerned and not with the consent of the province concerned. I also told the leaders that amending the constitution to address the demands of the agitating forces was neither the agenda of Prime Minister Pushpa Kamal Dahal nor of Nepali Congress President Sher Bahadur Deuba. With these words I left the meeting.

The government withdrew the First Constitutional Amendment Bill that it had registered on November 29, 2016 and registered a new constitutional amendment bill on April 11. The major difference between the two bills was that the First Bill intended to create another Madhes province from Nawalparasi Bardghat-Susta West to Bardiya district whereas the new bill intends to resolve the problem of provincial boundaries through a commission.

The amendment proposal has added that all the mother tongues as stipulated in Article 6 of the constitution would be included in the Schedule (Annex) of the constitution on the recommendation of the Language Commission. In the context when Article 6 of the constitution has recognized all the mother tongues spoken in Nepal as national languages, there was a problem as to where to look for the list of the same. Likewise, even as the country has already adopted a multi-lingual policy, no constitutional provision ensures that other languages except Nepali language could also become official languages. Hence, it is but natural to add them to the schedule in order to increase the ownership of all stakeholders. As a result, this amendment is not new but a proposal for the implementation of Article 6 of the constitution.

I. Language: The following has been added after Clause (2) of Article 7 of the constitution of Nepal as clause Z(a):

> "(2a) On the recommendation of the Language Commission, the government of Nepal would include the languages decided to become the languages of official use in the Schedule of the constitution.

This should have been Clause 1, but has become Clause 2 by mistake. As the provision of only Nepali becoming the language of official use is against the preamble of the constitution which says that Nepal is a multi-lingual country, this amendment was essential in order to make other languages spoken in Nepal as also the languages of official use also. This Amendment is also only for the implementation of Article 7. No new subject/issue has been included. And as it has been mentioned that the languages of official use would be included in the schedule of the constitution on the recommendation of the Language Commission, the issue of amendment for giving completion to the task of the language commission and to include the existing provision in the schedule is correct. To match with the Language Commission TOR Amendment has also been proposed in the Language Commission provision such as: "Amendment to Article 287 of the Constitution: The following (a1) has been added after section (a) of Clause 6 of Article 287 of the constitution of Nepal as 'a1': If need (a1) To prepare a list of all mother tongues spoken in Nepal as per Article 6, and recommend it to the government of Nepal."

The Second Constitutional Amendment Bill talks of listing the languages recommended by the Language Commission in the schedule of the constitution but this provision was proposed for the provinces. My understanding is that such a provision should be applied to the centre so that if the Language Commission recommends Maithili, Awadhi, Bhojpuri or any other language spoken in Nepal to be official languages then those language would be the official languages or languages of communication. This provision is related to the issue of addressing linguistic diversity of the country. For example, Eight Schedule of the Indian Constitution lists Maithili at the 10th number and Nepali at the 14th number.

II. Citizenship: Instead of Clause (6) of Article 11 of the constitution, the following Clause (6) has been proposed:

> (6) A foreign woman who has married a Nepali citizen can, if she wishes so, acquire Nepal's naturalized citizenship by marriage as per the law, provided she acts to abandon the citizenship of her country.

Regarding citizenship, only the language has been changed, and there is nothing in the amendment that has any effect on its substance. Especially, in relation to the citizenship of an office-bearer (holding an official position) in Article 289, a supplementary amendment was needed to be proposed in the case of citizens by birth and naturalized citizens. This would also address the sentiment related to citizenship as demanded by the Madhes-centric parties.

Despite having nothing substantive on citizenship, the main opposition CPN- UML termed the Second Constitutional Amendment Bill anti-national and dangerous than the First Constitutional Amendment Bill. The UML mainly opposed the citizenship provisions. In fact, citizenship provision of the amendment proposal was virtually the same provision that was contained in

Article 9 (5) of the Constitution of the Kingdom of Nepal, 1990. I told the RJPN leaders that UML leader Madhav Kumar Nepal was also one of the framers of that constitution. Does this mean he acted against the interests of the country for allowing such a citizenship provision in that constitution? The provisions related to citizenship in the new constitutional amendment bill just intend to adjust some words of Article 11 (6) of the new constitution of Nepal. This Bill has not done anything that could alter the main spirit of the constitution.

III. Upper House: The following Section (a) was proposed instead of Section (a) of Clause (2) of Article 86 of the constitution of Nepal:

> (a) Fifty-six elected members including 21 consisting of at least three including one woman, one Dalit and one from persons with disabilities or minorities, from each State and the remaining 35 to be elected by provinces in proportion to the population of each province.

The Second Constitutional Amendment Bill proposed that all the provinces will send three representatives to the upper house and the remainder of the representatives would be elected by the provinces on the basis of their population. This means 35 members would be elected to the upper house on the basis of the province's population. Province with more population will have the chance to send more members to the upper house of the Parliament. Province-3 will have more advantage than any other province. Province-2 may only add two to three seats. Therefore, this proposal should not be termed dangerous.

The UML strongly opposed the taking out of local bodies' voting rights to elect the upper house members from the Electoral College of the upper house. However, there is no fundamental difference between the rights of provincial assembly and the rights of the local levels' office bearers to elect the representatives for the upper house of the Parliament. The delinking of the voting rights of the chiefs and deputy chiefs of the local levels would neither benefit nor cause any loss to Madhesis. For example, Ethiopia has 112 representatives in the upper house representing 66 ethnic communities. The upper house is a body, which ensures representation of diversity, communities and provincial geography. This House is also known as the House that provides an opportunity to minority communities and deprived groups to protect their rights through enactment of laws. Members of legislative assembly are virtually controlled by the chiefs of municipalities and village municipalities of their constituencies. It is almost impossible for one to win a legislative assembly seat without the support of those who have won elections in the local levels. This practical aspect can also address the issues related to the control of the local office bearers on the members of local assemblies and reflection of their desire in the votes cast by members of local assemblies to form the upper house. If a provincial assembly chooses representatives of the upper house against the aspirations of the local levels, then the provincial assembly will have a hard time in the next elections. In India too, provincial assemblies choose the representatives for the upper house. Recently Bharatiya Janata Party won provincial elections in Uttar Pradesh. With this win, the Modi Government will be able to easily pass bills in the upper house of the Parliament because UP sends 31 representatives to the upper house. Similarly, Nagaland, Tripura, Goa and Assam, send one representative each to the upper house while West Bengal and Bihar each send 16 representatives to the upper house of the Parliament.

IV. Provincial Boundaries Revision: The Second Constitutional Amendment Bill contains a provision whereby the legislative Parliament could change the boundaries of the provinces. The legislative Parliament has also been given provincial assembly's power for changing boundaries because the argument is that if the provincial assembly's consent would be sought for the revision of provincial boundaries, then that will never be possible because no province would ever agree to carve its areas out of its territory.

On this issue of revision of provincial boundaries the new bill says that such a notification should be sent to all the provincial assemblies concerned. Here the UDMF wants to drop the word 'all the provincial assemblies concerned.' The government has agreed to remove the term "all" now. The amendment proposal that the ruling parties registered on the constitutional amendment bill states that provincial boundaries can be revised after consulting the province concerned. This is a big departure from the existing rigid provision of the constitution which says that consent needs to be taken from the majority of provinces even for changing the boundary of one province.

The new constitutional amendment bill proposed to remove the restrictive clause of Articles 274 & 396. Article 274 says that if provincial boundaries are revised, then the consent of the province concerned and the majority of the provinces must be sought for the same. The new constitutional amendment bill proposes to remove the provision of Article 274 (7) that says revision of provincial boundaries can take place only if the majority of the provinces approve such a proposal. The federal Parliament could revise the provincial boundaries even without the consent of the provincial assembly concerned in case the provincial assemblies have not been formed. This provision is tricky in the sense that the federal Parliament could be formed only after the three types of elections—local, provincial and Parliamentary are held.

This restrictive clause of the constitution has made the constitution very rigid, which makes revision of provincial boundaries almost impossible. It is almost impossible that four out of seven provinces would ever agree to revise provincial boundaries. If this provision is retained, then if a conflict over the provincial boundaries has to be resolved tomorrow, then the constitution will have to be thrown away. It is the flexibility and not rigidity of the constitution that ensures dynamism. On the one hand, the constitution has provisions for a federal commission because it accepts the fact that the provincial boundaries are still disputed, and on the other, the constitution has provisions for seeking the consent of majority of the provinces to revise provincial boundaries. This means that the recommendation of the federal commission may never be implemented. These were contradictory provisions and it was in the interests of our constitution and the country to end this contradiction. So Article 274(7) has to be completely deleted from the constitution. But then there will be a disadvantage as well. If the current provision that mandates the Parliament to seek consent of the province concerned and majority of the provinces is removed from the constitution, then the ruling parties could easily revise the boundaries of the provinces.

The new bill stipulates that the government will form a federal commission to recommend the number and change of boundaries and the terms of reference would be as determined by the government.

Both sides also agreed to form a Federal Structure Review Commission, which could be formed on the basis of the principle of proportional inclusion. The UDMF pressurized the government to accept that the commission should take into account the report of the erstwhile State Restructuring Commission and past agreements signed between the government and the agitating Madhesi and Janajati forces.

The dispute of demarcation is relatively easier before the elections of the provincial assembly, and would not be so easy after the elections because this is a matter associated with the interests of many sides. It is now so difficult to seek a solution to this matter when the interest of three to four political parties are linked to it and therefore one can imagine how difficult the issue would become tomorrow. When there is not much of discontent when the ruling parties are trying to change the borders of village and cities, one can easily assume how difficult it would be to address the dissent when the issue of changes in the borders of the provinces come to the fore tomorrow.

And, in fact it is the UML's roadmap to resolve the issues related to provincial boundaries through a commission. When K.P. Sharma Oli was the Prime Minister, a commission was formed under Kamal Thapa to resolve the question of provincial boundaries. If such a commission is formed tomorrow, it can be acceptable to all if credible people are appointed to it. The terms of reference to be attached to such a commission have not been made thus far. Such terms of reference should be prepared in a way that all the stakeholders agree on them. The provision that says the consent of the provincial assembly concerned is not required is just for one time or till the term of the current Parliament. The term of the Parliament ends on January 21, 2018. If a federal commission to be formed does not make recommendation in time, the relevance of such a commission would end because such a power (power to revise the provincial boundaries) will not be available to the federal Parliament. The UML must be happy because such a power will be available for just one time.

Those who are in a situation to give something to somebody may think that they are giving too much but those who are in a situation to get something from somebody are not getting anything substantial. It was in fact only a face saving proposal for the Madhesi parties as they appeared to be eager to join the local elections due to the pressure from their cadres on the ground. Madhesi parties appear to have compromised on the Second Constitutional Amendment Bill that the government registered in the Parliament after withdrawing the First Bill as the Second Bill has dropped the issues related to the revision of provincial boundaries at least for now.

UML's Opposition to the Amendment

I was surprised when the UML Chair K.P. Sharma Oli, said in the Parliament that the basic structure of the constitution was being destroyed by the amendment proposal. No article of the constitution can claim that it contains the basic structure of the constitution. Article 274 (1) of the constitution stipulates that provisions of the constitution other than the provisions related to sovereignty, territorial integrity and independence can be amended. In other words, republican order, federalism, proportional inclusion, secularism and the rule of law are the basic structures of the constitution and no attempts are being made to destroy these structures. The Supreme Court of India, on April 24, 1973 had, after 66 days of hearing, delivered a verdict in the case of Keshavanand Bharti vs. State of Kerala saying that the Parliament cannot destroy basic structures of the constitution. From that time, a debate is going on as to what are the basic structures of the constitution. In that case, constitutional supremacy, the rule of law, separation of power, judicial review, federalism, secularism, sovereignty, republican order, freedom, directive principles, fair elections, Parliamentary system, judicial freedom, etc. were listed as the basic structures of the constitution. The current constitutional amendment bill does not intend to harm any of these provisions and hence there is no question of basic structures of the constitution being destroyed.

The UML levelled the accusation that the bill was brought at the behest of India. In Nepal, there is a tendency to link Madhesis' issues with India whether it is Madhesis' demands to amend the constitution or address issues related to their representation and identity. India has its own interests, and it forces Madhesis to compromise after its interests are fulfilled. Madhesis and India have their own interests, which rather collide at crucial stages. Therefore, it is not appropriate to link Madhesis' issues with India. Madhes pays a price for sharing roti beti relations with India. This came to be true when popular journalist Prashant Jha wrote a news story on May 16, 2017 in the *Hindustan Times* "India 'shifts' stance, asks Madhesis to drop demand for changes in constitution[1]". India advised the Madhesi leaders to drop the constitutional amendment agendas and contest local elections. Immediately after the news broke, I tweeted "the Madhesi movement did not happen due to any external force nor will it fade due to any external force. India is free to take its decisions. Madhes will stick to its agenda". The UML's accusation of amendment being pushed by India ultimately proved to be false.

The UML appeared to have devoted all its energy to foil the constitutional amendment bill as it revived the old nine-party alliance. One thing is true that the UML does not want to amend the constitution. It does not want to address Madhes problems. It wants to establish singular dominance among the Pahadi electorates and therefore, it raises the issues of Pahadi nationalism. This is at the root of current problems. This is the only reason the UML tries to link everything with India.

What the UML has failed to understand is that the new constitution faces big questions of its justifiability, legality and wider acceptance, therefore, implementation of the new constitution will remain a challenge until and unless the political actors seriously address the disappointments of the different castes, creeds, and gender. Amidst big political upheavals, the first phase of local elections were held on May 14, 2017 and second phase of local elections were held on June 28, 2017. The ruling parties have agreed to increase the number of local bodies in Terai districts to address the concerns of Madhesi forces that want local bodies formed on the basis of population. This will determine future of the constitution ownership by Madhesis and other marginalized communities.

Bimalendra Nidhi's Role to Push Amendment

NC Leader Bimalendra Nidhi who was also the Deputy Prime Minister with the home ministry portfolio had done a lot to broker a deal between the United Democratic Madhesi Front and the ruling parties particularly the NC and the CPN-Maoist Centre. But when the ruling parties were preparing a proposal on the constitutional amendment bill, Nidhi was not involved. NC leader Krishna Prasad Sitaula was given the chance to deal with the issue. His involvement in the matter means there is only a slim chance of the constitution being amended to address the demands of the agitating Madhesi and Janajati forces. When the ruling parties were preparing the amendment proposal, Sitaula was not ready to insert the term 'proportional inclusion' to state that a federal commission would be formed on the basis of proportional inclusion to recommend revision in the provincial boundaries. The ruling parties had already agreed before that they would insert the term 'proportional inclusion' in the amendment proposal so that a federal commission would be formed on the basis of proportional inclusion. Then the leaders who were preparing the draft of the amendment proposal on the constitutional amendment bill called NC President Sher Bahadur Deuba who then told them to insert the word 'proportional inclusion' and he could take a final call on the matter later. Deuba's first priority is to become the next Prime Minister. Nobody from the Nepali Congress wants the multiple language policy ensured at the centre whereas the definition of State and Preamble to the constitution all state that Nepal is a multilingual country.

A few days before the candidates filed the nominations for the first phase of local polls, Bimlendra Nidhi played active role to get two-third majority to pass the amendment bill. And in fact, the ruling parties had already garnered more than a two-thirds majority (almost 400 votes in the Parliament even without the CPN-UML) but the former King Gyanendra suddenly played a game and made 10 RPP lawmakers disappear from its Parliamentary party meeting. After this incident the ruling parties started saying that they would try to amend the constitution after first phase of local polls.

On April 30, 2017, Home Minister Bimalendra Nidhi resigned from the position of Home Minister for not being consulted over the moving of impeachment motion against Chief Justice Sushila Karki in the Parliament. It was believed that there was a major difference of opinion between the NC chairperson Sher Bahadur Deuba and Nidhi from the beginning of the IGP's appointment and on some other issues. Madhesi analysts also speculate that the NC's high command was willing to curtail the growing importance of Nidhi in Nepali politics. Nidhi who played a key role in bringing Madhesi leaders to the negotiating table to discuss constitutional amendment appeared to be disappointed and on May 3, 2017 he discussed with me this matter. However, on the following day he withdrew his resignation.

Europe Visit to Generate Support on Constitutional Amendment Bill

To generate international support on the constitutional amendment bill and to raise international awareness on investigation of excessive use of force in the Terai, I travelled to Germany and UK in the month of April 2017. In Germany I met twelve members of the Parliament and explained to them why the passage of the constitutional amendment bill was important. They were quite convinced on the issue. Moreover, I got a chance to talk to the Secretary of the all party groups on human rights of the British Parliament after which a lawmaker tabled a Terai motion in the UK Parliament on April 20, 2017 signed by eight MPs that called for holding local polls only after amending the constitution. The excerpts of the motion are as follows:

> That this House is concerned that the Madhesis minority from the Southern plains, known as the Terai region, will continue to be marginalised in Nepal unless constitutional amendments are passed before local elections in that country; understands that although the Madhesis represent over 33 per cent of the population of Nepal, they hold only 12 per cent of Government positions; is worried about ongoing human rights violations being committed in the Terai region, including reported killings of protestors by security forces using excessive force, such as an incident on 6 March 2017 when five people are believed to have been killed and many more injured; notes that local elections in Nepal are due to be held for the First time in 20 years on 14 May 2017,

> hopefully paving the way for the consolidation of democracy and allowing for provincial and national elections in the autumn; urges the government of Nepal to investigate the killings, bring those responsible to justice and to amend the constitution to allow for fair representation; further urges political activists and protestors in Nepal to carry out their activities peacefully; and calls on the government to ensure any funding to the Nepalese security forces is carefully assessed for compliance with international human rights criteria.

This motion was covered in all the media outlets of the country and it became a subject of public discourse. For the first time the British Parliament raised the issue of Madhesis. Before the early day motion came, former Attorney General Yubraj Sangraula wrote an article in *Nagarik Daily* on April 13, 2017 attacking me on a personal level. He wrote: in his words:

> Dipendra Jha is one among others, who acts as a puppet of western organizations to destabilize Nepal. Jha is now delivering a speech in Germany that Madhes situated in the east of Gandaki River was not Nepal before. Therefore, the issue of independent Madhes is raised, according to him. He goes to Geneva whose expenses are funded by the western organizations and his , non-Governmental organization has received support from western institutions. Poor people are becoming Christians. Indian media has supported the Madhes movement. Upon the request, India puts a blockade on the border points. Does India know—millions of children, who left school and took to streets due to the blockade saw India to be unfair? Can't Indian intelligence in Nepal notice the western organizations plotting to damage the relationship between Nepal and India? Does India think that the so-called issue of independence in Madhes of Nepali territory, which is creating troubles in Nepal, can help India to maintain stability? If the issue of fragmentation may arise or takes place in Nepal, which has been free and integrated since ages, it will be a great precedent

against India because India has been moving ahead through sequence of integration and disintegration series.

I responded to him in strong words on the same page after three days in the *Nagarik Daily* saying that he was not in Germany, so how can he know what I spoke. And, without having any evidence how can a reputed person and a former attorney general write such a piece. In fact his organization, CELERD itself has received funds for its projects from the western donors from GF, DIHR and British Embassy and many more. And at the time he accused me, THRD Alliance has one project supported by GF but I was neither on the board nor among the staff list of the THRD Alliance. And it is only a project that provides legal aid to torture victims; so how can he call me a puppet of western countries? Then I came to realize that members of all marginalized communities have to go through such a phase of defamation at some point of time. The ruling class makes an attempt to malign the members of the marginalized communities because they think that those who advocate the rights of marginalized communities are a threat to the ruling class. They cannot tolerate anyone from Madhesi community emerging as a human rights lawyer. My recent visit to European countries and my meeting with British Parliamentarians met with the approval of my host and I helped them understand the rights issues of our country. In Germany, there is no debate at all about CK Raut and his political agenda.

And, I also did not write the introduction to Ram Manohar Shah's book and I never said that the southern part of the Gandaki River was a separate country in the past anywhere and yet I faced a false accusation by a renowned jurist. I faced this accusation mainly because I lobbied against human rights violations in Nepal and I am in favour of the constitutional amendment proposal. I believe that it is my right as a citizen to seek equality, and non-discrimination through peaceful and democratic means.

In fact, this is the trial I personally went through while advocating the rights of Madhesis and other marginalized groups. If I have to sum up it in one sentence, then this is the trial of protecting federalism and regional identity.

My personal experience is that any change agent who champions the cause of social justice will cross through four stages. First, the ruling elites will try to dismiss the call for equality. Second, when they do not succeed in their attempt, they will, try to co-opt. Third, they will try to defame using all powers of the state. When their third attempt fails, only then will the dominating class finally start accepting the arguments of the change agents.

Impeachment Drama to Overshadow Amendment

Whenever the Madhesi and marginalized agenda items come to the decisive level, something is created to divert people's attention from them. Whether it is the case of First Constitutional Amendment Bill or the Second Constitutional Amendment Bill. On April 30, 2017, an impeachment motion was registered in the Parliament by 249 lawmakers of the ruling Nepali Congress and the CPN-Maoist Centre against Chief Justice Sushila Karki. It was speculated that the motion was registered to obstruct her possible decision on the IGP appointment case and there was a rumour that had the motion not been moved against CJ Karki, she would have given the verdict in favour of DIG Silwal and would have ordered the government to make Silwal the new IGP.

Some of the Madhes-based parties objected to the impeachment motion against CJ saying it was an attack to independence of the judiciary while others commented that the motion was registered only to divert the public's attention from the constitutional amendment process.

On May 5, 2017, the Supreme Court issued a stay order in response to a case filed challenging the impeachment motion against CJ Karki, and the apex court also reinstated CJ Karki in her post. People argued that it was another extreme step of the Supreme Court against an extreme step of the political leaders. Some also said that the Supreme Court's order was just a sentimental statement, which impinged on the Parliamentary jurisdiction. After the Supreme Court's order, both Parliament and judiciary maintained restraint realizing external and internal pressure from the various power centres.

These examples show the immaturity of political leadership in Nepal on serious issues and other organs like the judiciary are leading the country to a further chaotic situation.

3. Debate and Results of Local Polls

Without giving much importance to the constitutional amendment agenda, major political parties talked of holding local polls as soon as possible. However, agitating Madhesi parties said local polls should be held only after the constitution was amended. This was the reason the agitating Madhesi parties who created a unified party—Rastriya Janata Party-Nepal boycotted the first phase of local polls. In any case they had very limited presence in the 34 hill districts where the first phase of local polls were held on May 14. Only the Upendra Yadav-led Federal Socialist Forum-Nepal, which believes it has some influence in those districts and can win some seats, took part in the first phase of local polls, a decision that created a rift among the constituents of the Federal Alliance. After the FSFN decided to take part in the first phase of elections, constituents of the Federal Alliance held a meeting and expelled Yadav-led party from the FA choosing Mahantha Thakur as the new Coordinator of the FA. Yadav, however, claimed that the meeting that chose Thakur as new Coordinator was not authentic and he (Yadav) was still the Coordinator of the alliance.

As time passes, the new generation in Madhes is losing interest in constitutional amendment issues. They are looking for something broader like structural changes. There is frustration among people of the new generation in the Terai with the state. What Kathmandu fails to understand is that more the time they take to amend the constitution, the state will face higher risks of delegitimization of state institutions in the Terai. Delay and diluting tactics will be self-destructive.

Results of the first phase of local polls show that the NC and the CPN-UML have won most of the local levels out of 281 local levels for which the elections were held on May 14. This will only embolden the UML, which is opposed to constitutional amendment as demanded by the agitating forces. The ruling coalition of NC and the CPN-Maoist Centre which tabled the Second Constitutional Amendment Bill might find an excuse now and say that they tried their best to pass the constitutional amendment bill but could not do so due to continued opposition of the UML.

Conclusion—Social Reconciliation Only Way Out

In the decade since the Maoist war ended, four widespread, peaceful civil protests for basic civil rights and many general strikes took place in the southern belt, Terai. All of them were violently suppressed by the state leaving over 200 dead and injuring scores of people.

Madhesis are around one-third (1/3) of the population of Nepal. They don't feel fully represented in the constitution. The Madhesis, and the Indigenous Community (also 1/3 of the population), untouchables/Dalits and women activists see the constitution as a discriminatory document. And it took over seven years of the constituent assembly to produce the constitution—with a minimum of public discussion and even less consultation.

It is impossible to be confident about social, political and economic stability while Madhesis, Tharus, Dalits and Indigenous People, together accounting for 70 per cent of the population cannot buy into or take ownership of the constitution.

There are double standards, the major parties—NC, CPN-UML and CPN-MC (Maoist Centre) easily addressed the demands of agitating locals of Baglung, Karnali and Surkhet areas within weeks and revised the boundaries of the hill provinces but they did not address the demands of Madhesis and Tharus to revise boundaries of provinces. Ironically, they did not treat Madhesis and Tharus in a similar manner even though they took to the streets agitating for more than a year. Instead, they became victims of excessive use of force by the police. Over three dozen people in the Terai, including bystanders, lost their lives due to police firing during the demonstrations. The plain areas of Madhes, where almost half of Nepal's population lives, remained shut for almost six months. The country suffered a huge loss. The decision makers of the ruling parties were reluctant to resolve the issue due to the mindset that Madhesis are Indian migrants, and not true citizens of Nepal.

Even the law enforcement agencies discriminated them. While the law enforcement agencies used water cannons to disperse a mob of Hindu activists in Kathmandu during protests, they fired live bullets on demonstrators in Madhes. Most of the injured demonstrators and bystanders received bullets in either the head or chest.

The marginalized community just want equal constitutional recognition and power sharing in the state. Merely 10 per cent of hill Brahmin males rule the country and dominate around 80 per cent of state institutions and resources. Demonstrating this phenomenon in Nepal does not require a statistical calculation. It is evident from the last names of CDOs, SPs, LDOs, Chief Judges, heads of government, attorneys and attorney, army heads at district level of 75 districts. As Michel Foucault argues, the powerful communities create their own position. Nepal is a unique example of this argument. The same group of people also dominates civil society arenas.

When children of Hifajat Miya Ansari and Raj Kishor Thakur grow up, they will ask the Nepali state why their fathers were killed. If the state thinks that it can get rid of all the duties and responsibilities after labelling somebody communal or biased, it is wrong.

Kathmandu expressed its concern on the vandalism of Girija Prasad Koirala's statue during the 2015 Madhes movement. But it did not have any sympathy when the security personnel in Birgunj killed five Madhesis. Ironically, some high profile human rights activists issued statements saying that security personnel were facing difficulties in buying foodstuff in the local markets due to the strike. They made no mention of those killed during the protests. The Kathmandu media not only inadequately covered the protests, but it remained insensitive to the pain of the victims' families.

No efforts for the social reconciliation for the affected families in the Madhes movement have so far been made. There is a psychological chasm between the Terai and Kathmandu. The Madhesi society, which had moved ahead with some positive changes, has lost this battle of constitutional reform. But they have not given up their hope to fight a long battle for the changes they are seeking to be ensured in the constitution.

Madhesi demonstrated the best example of social harmony in the aftermath of April, 2015 earthquake. There was a campaign called "Madhes with Pahad". Every village of Madhes sent "rice, lentils, money, clothes and medicine to the earthquake affected hill areas". I still remember the night on which I carried more than 100 packets of rice in Gaurishankar Party Palace in Koteshwor on my head from a truck to bring them next morning to Kavre. We collected more than 100 quintals of rice and I myself visited Kartike of Sindhupal Chowk, the most difficult area for distribution of relief material before the second quake. When there was the natural disaster of an earthquake, Madhes joined hand with Pahad (hill). But when there was a political and constitutional crisis in Madhes, when people were killed in the Terai, there was not much resistance against the government in the hill areas even before blockade. Madhesi Tharu did not know initially that the earthquake for which they collected support would be used as an excuse to enforce a constitution curtailing their rights.

I have personally experienced many incidents of discrimination. In 2013, upon my return from a tour of Lebanon to advocate the rights of Nepali migrant labourers, I landed at the Tribhuvan International Airport and one Nepali woman asked me, "Bhaiya aapka ghar India me kahan hai?" (having a negative connotation) [Where do you come from in India?]. That Nepali lady's remark astonished me. She treated a Nepali national as an Indian national just because of his dark complexion. Likewise, when I visited Chitwan National Park in 2016, a clerk took me to be an Indian visitor. When ex-Justice Girish Chandra Lal delivered verdicts, he was called a 'Madhesi Judge'. But when Justice Sushila Karki, quashed a writ filed against the Nepalese Army, she was merely referred to as 'Judge'. This is the standard that they use here to assess professionalism.

Had my forefathers dared to seek their rights to be accepted and treated as Nepalis, perhaps I would not have been treated as a foreign national today. My grandfather did not have the awareness that I have today. My father was a junior clerk at the National Food Corporation. He used to ask me to deliver fish, rice, lentils, beans and pickles all the time to his bosses or highranking officials. When I was studying law in Kathmandu, he would call me and say, "I have sent some fish on such and such night bus, give it to Pandey Sir." But now I want to make our country a place where my daughter will not have to face any kind of domination and exploitation. I want to broaden the definition of Nepali nationalism. How can we be immune from such allegations when Martin Luther King and Nelson Mandela also had to face such allegations? Everybody, who strives to ensure equality, should be ready to face the accusation of being communal.

However, I still believe that there is a method to remove these kinds of structural discrimination through constitutional reforms. The difficulty of constitutional amendment is striking a balance between various interests of ruling communities while prioritizing legitimate aspirations of people faced with the consequences of exclusion in the Terai. Amending articles of the constitution comprehensively to ensure social justice should be the ultimate goal. Without having ownership of Madhesi and marginalized communities over the constitution, peace cannot be expected in Nepal. Constitutional amendment is a sentimental and symbolic way to include Madhesis in the constitution, who have been excluded on a majoritarian basis.

The fast developing circumstances of majoritarian rule in Nepal pose danger to democracy and social justice. A group of ruling elites in all major political parties and bureaucracy are trying to dilute the progressive policies and values developed for social inclusion. Their exclusivist institutional and internal structures are either based on family ties, ideological bonds or ethnic identity. This is used as a powerful weapon to limit resources and opportunities to a few members of the ruling community who have been exacerbating conflicts rather than seeking to resolve them. Similarly, a new fashion of romanticizing inclusion has also emerged in the post-Madhes movement period. To fashion the inclusiveness, 'a showpiece' symbolic member from the marginalized communities is brought into the system in which decision making power remains in the hands of the same dominant male elites. It is simply a deal between the ruling classes and the ethnic elites, which erases the socio-economic problems faced by the poorest and the most vulnerable among marginalized communities, particularly the triple burden of class, caste and gender women face in their daily lives. This is the new crisis of inclusion.

To change the Nepali conservative society, my own experience is that on the one side, one must find ways not to antagonize the ruling Khas-Arya community and on the other side, to support the marginalized communities to continue struggle for social justice. It is a choice between supporting the status quo and the people's aspirations for transforming Nepali polity towards a progressive direction. This seems very tricky work, however there is no alternative to push for social justice through constitutional reform. Madhesi-Tharu in Nepal can recover their strength and credibility through continuing a street level movement to bring about changes in their identity and social status.

The Crisis Group's recent report "Nepal's Divisive New Constitution: An Existential Crisis" has rightly suggested that dialogue for social reconciliation can be used as a strategy to gradually fracture and decentre the hegemonic ideas and ideology, opening space for all possible opinions to be represented and rearticulated equally. Particularly, at the time of the constitutional amendment debate where all are demanding to address their concerns, it can be mobilized as an opportunity for cooperative actions by appreciating others' viewpoints, modifying them and if necessary, accepting them. To search for a common ground on constitutional amendment issues, an engaging horizontal dialogue is essential that can defuse social polarization designed, provoked and protected by the power centres.

Thus, the end of the constitutional crisis in Nepal depends upon to what extent the ruling community or the Khas-Arya community would be ready to share power with the poorest among marginalized communities whom they claim to represent. It is a de-powering process of decreasing hierarchical relationships and attitudes and empowering the poor and the excluded and marginalized groups. Giving a proportional stake to the powerless can be a cause to delegitimize the status quo; however, in the long-term it will build social cohesion for more peaceful societies.

Expecting broader change through constitutional amendments is almost impossible without transforming political culture. And, changing the political culture is not a 'quick fix' magic. It is a long process. It depends on how political parties re-organize, reorient and redefine this role in the new context of a federal republic. A community level social resistance can be a point of departure to uproot the feudal political culture. Moreover, for the marginalized community, a cultural-specific conscientisation through street struggles can be a powerful weapon to be equal and dignified citizens of Nepal. Without social reconciliation between Pahadi and Madhesi, the implementation of the new charter is almost impossible. Apology campaigns through door-to-door visits by activists to say "sorry" for the past injustice and discrimination including blockade between two groups should be conducted to mitigate further polarization and establish fresh relations based on equality. Otherwise, Madhes would go on the path of the Kashmiri model in which the expansion of C.K. Raut's movement in Terai will be inevitable.

Local Polls Results in Madhes Aspire for Constitutional Amendment

Before the much-awaited local body polls were held in this province, each of the major political parties—NC, CPN-UML and CPN-MC—had claimed that their party would emerge as the largest force in Province 2.

However, the results of the vote counting of all 136 local levels in Province 2 remained unexpected for the major political parties and others.

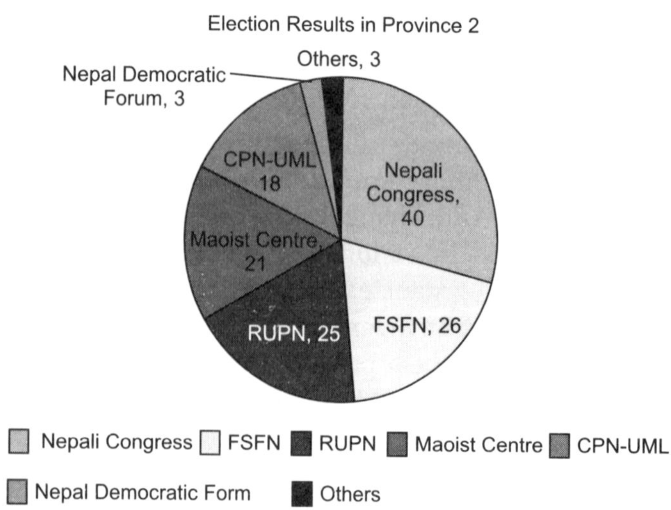

The final results show that Nepali Congress has won 40, FSFN has won 26, RJPN has won 25, CPN-MC (Maoist Centre) has won 21, CPN-UML has won 18, Nepal Democratic Forum has won 3, Nepali Janata Dal has won 2, and Naya Shakti Party has won 1 chief (mayor/chairperson) and deputy chief (deputy major/vice-chairperson) posts.

When analyzing the election results, those political parties pressing for constitutional amendment—mainly RJPN and FSFN—together have emerged as the largest force in Province 2. Since the FSFN has won more seats than the RJPN, which unified six different Madhes-based parties, this can be termed as the biggest achievement for Upendra Yadav and his party FSFN. The RJPN had decided to take part in the local polls at the eleventh hour and the election results have remained unexpected for the party as well. Amid frustration and unfavorable environment, the RJPN had to take decision to participate in the elections. Despite such complexities, the election results are certainly the biggest victory and show a breakthrough for the FSFN and the CPN-MC (Maoist Centre).

UML Stands against Constitutional Amendment and Madhes

The UML, which had emerged as the largest force in the first and second rounds of the local level elections, has become the fifth party in the third round. By electing less number of local representatives from the UML when compared with NC, FSFN, RJPN and Maoist Centre, the voters in Province 2 showed their disapproval of the UML and its stance against the constitutional amendment.

The polls results have also distorted the general perception about the UML strength in Mahendra Highway areas in the north of Province 2 since voters in Bardibas and Hariwan areas elected representatives belonging to the CPN-MC.

Since the UML stands against the agenda of Madhes, its senior leader and former Prime Minister Madhav Nepal could not get any of his party representative elected in his own ward of Rautahat.

Madhes no Longer Belongs to NC

Further it will not be an exaggeration to say that the Province 2 local election results was a loss for the NC. The results have dismissed the narrative that Madhes has always favored the NC because of its long history in the area. The Madhes no longer belongs to the NC.

At a time when the NC claims itself as the largest force in Province 2 as per the election results, the Madhesi parties themselves have emerged as the largest force if the number of elected seats of FSFN and RJPN are combined. Most importantly, the Madhesi parties—FSFN in Birgunj Metropolitan City and RJPN in Janakpur Sub-Metropolitan City—have maintained their strength in the two biggest cities of Province 2. The victory in the headquarters conveys the mood of Madhes and the aspirations of its people. The Madhesi parties have been elected in prominent cities and towns of Madhes, including Birgunj, Janakpur, Gaur, Jaleshwar and Siraha.

In Janakpur, which was the epicenter of the last Madhes Movement, the RJPN Mayoral Candidate Lal Kishor Shah has defeated NC Mayoral Candidate Manoj Kumar Shah with a huge difference, i.e. nearly 9,000 votes. Birgunj, the only metropolitan city of Province 2, got its Mayor Vijay Sarawagi, belonging to FSFN. The strength of Madhesi parties in both the biggest cities of Province 2 proves that the people support the political demand of the parties and the constitutional amendment.

NC senior leader Bimlendra Nidhi failed to get his party's Mayoral Candidate elected in Janakpur Sub-Metropolitan City of his home district.

The NC always use the Madhes as a voter constituency, and when it comes to the rights of Madhesis, the party's action is limited to meetings in Kathmandu. For this, the people have punished the party. While the old generation still votes for the NC, the party is not popular among youths and as time passes, the popularity of NC among the old generation will weaken in Madhes.

Province-2 Wants Constitutional Amendment

The fact that Province 2 stands for the constitutional amendment is evident from the fact that people have elected more representatives from those political parties—Madhesi parties, NC and CPN-MC—that support the constitutional amendment. The local level election results in Province-2 has conveyed a strong message that the constitution must be amended to address the demands of Madhesi and other marginalized communities. All the political parties need to convey this message from Province-2 and act accordingly.

The victory of just three local levels seats by the Bijay Gachhedar-led Nepal Democratic Forum indicates that the party has failed in the eyes of voters to work in the interests of the political agenda of Madhes.

The major political parties and especially the UML need to understand the message given by the poll results in Province 2. The people's mandate shows that there is no alternative to the amendment to the constitution.

The dissatisfaction of Madhesis over the constitution is genuine since the charter has mixed the territory of Madhes, which is seen as their geographical identity, with the territories of hills. This had weakened their political representation. Further, this constitution has not granted the linguistic rights of Madhesis.

The Preamble, which is known as the window of the constitution, mentions all other political movements but not the Madhes movement which ensured federalism in the country. The Madhesis say that all those political movements mentioned in the preamble should be deleted, and if not, the Madhes movement should be mentioned. They argue against accepting the constitution that does not acknowledge the Madhes movement which carries the identity of the Madhesis and was key in establishing Nepal as a federal state.

Why has this constitution put the explanation of the Khas-Arya only? Does this constitution belong to the Khas-Arya community alone? Such explanation could have been mentioned in the legislation. How legitimate is it to write whatever the ruling class can to protect their interests?

Further, there is a reservation quota in the constitution for the the Khas-Arya community, which represents more than 70 per cent in all the state organs. Such a provision in the constitution contradicts the principle of proportionate inclusion. The reservation is a special provision, that remains for a temporary period, in order to facilitate the mainstreaming of marginalized communities.

However, the Khas-Arya community has been provided with 31 per cent of reservation under Proportionate Representation Electoral System, as per Annex 1 under Article 28 of the Election Act 2017, which has been legislated by the Parliament based on the reservation for Khas-Arya as provisioned in the constitution of Nepal 2015. The act has reduced the electoral representation of Madhesis to 15 per cent. The argument for such a decrease in the electoral representation of Madhesis is that the representation of Madhesis has been given to 6 per cent to Tharus and 4.4 per cent to Muslims.

The question arises on the rationale behind the provision of proportional electoral representation of Khas-Arya, whose majority is elected under the first-past-the-post system. The intent, which is crystal clear, is to maintain the majority of Khas-Arya in the Parliament. If the representation of Madhesi cluster are sliced into Muslims and Tharus, why is the representation of Khas-Arya not similarly sliced with the hill Dalits, those from backward region, and Khas-Arya women. This type of maneuvers in the constitution will not ensure its ownership among the marginalized community.

Conclusion

Those aspiring to seek peaceful change should never expect the immediate results. The results of both constituent assembly elections held in 2008 and the last phase of local level elections in 2017 have given a message that the Madhesi parties when united can garner the majority of votes of Madhesis. Had the RJPN not been formed unifying six different Madhesi parties, the party would hardly have won five seats. Even in the local level polls, had the FSFN and RJPN unitedly gone for election, they could have won more seats.

Congratulating Upendra Yadav for the stunning victory of his party in the local polls in Province 2, I suggested that both FSFN and RJPN should go together for the upcoming provincial and Parliamentary elections. The Madhesis should pressure both the parties for electoral alliance in the general elections. If the Madhesi parties are able to garner the majority of seats, their roles will remain as the kingmaker although they will not be able to lead the government. If they use the Parliament and streets in tactful manner and show their sincerity, the constitution can be amended although it may take some time. Here the unity of RJP and Yadav's FSF will be key as they can together win the majority of seats in the southern belt of the Madhes and in the future amend the constitution.

However, the leaders of Madhesi parties need to reflect on the election results. The UML, which stands against Madhes and constitutional amendment, has won the elections in Lahan, which is the origin of Madhes movement. This is a matter to be seriously considered. The victory of Madhesi parties in Lahan matters more for the empowerment of the Madhesi agenda. What Madhesi leaders need to understand is that the majority of votes all over the country is not necessary to get the constitution amended, but what matters is the majority of seats in Madhes alone. This is the aspiration of Madhesi people and for this, the Madheshi leaders must unite.

The people of marginalized communities no longer belong to the 1960s or 1990s. They are knowledgeable in every aspect and have developed expertise in every sector. They have the potential to lead movements for change when needed and are vigilantly watching every political event and incident. The leaders of major political party leaders must understand this.

Reference

[1] http://www.hindustantimes.com/india-news/india-shifts-stance-asks-madhesis-to-drop-demand-for-changes-in-constitution/story-29xYUN0YoCCnRFTSiyOWOP.html

Note: In the course of writing this book, some political parties merged with other parties with similar ideologies and changed their names. Hence, I acknowledge that the names of those political parties are inconsistent in this book. For example, CPN (Maoists) mentioned in the beginning of the book changed its name to CPN–Maoist Centre. Likewise, six Madhes-based parties merged and named the merger as Rastriya Janata Party Nepal.

—Author

Bibliography

I. Primary Sources

A. Constitutions and Conventions

i) Constitutions

1. The Interim Constitution of Nepal, 2007
2. The constitution of Nepal, 2015
3. The constitution of Nepal, 1962
4. The constitution of the Kingdom of Nepal, 1990
5. The constitution of the Kingdom of Nepal, 1959
6. The Interim Government of Nepal Act, 1951
7. The Government of Nepal Act, 1948

II. Conventions

1. Convention on the Elimination of All Forms of Discrimination Against Women, 1979
2. Convention on the Rights of Person with Disabilities
3. Convention Rights of the Child, 1989
4. International Conference on Population and Development and its Declaration, 1994
5. International Covenant on Civil and Political Rights, 1966
6. International Covenant on Economic, Social and Cultural Rights, 1966
7. United Nations Security Council Resolution 1325 (October 2000)
8. Universal Declaration on Human Rights, 1948

II. Secondary Sources

A. Books

Adhikari, Aditya (2014), *The Bullet and the Ballot Box: The Story of Nepal's Maoist Revolution*, New Delhi: Aleph.

Adhikari, Indra (2015), *Military and Democracy in Nepal*, New Delhi: Routledge.

Bhandari, Surendra (2015), *Federalism and Inclusive Nation Building, Himalya Innovative Development.*

Baral, Lok Raj and Krishna Hachhethu, eds. (2013), *Federal Nepal and its Attributes* (in Nepali) Kathmandu: Nepal Centre for Contemporary Studies.

Baral, Lok Raj and Krishna Hachhethu, eds. (2014), *South Asia: Nation Building and Federalism*, New Delhi: Vij Books.

Bhattachan, Krishna Bahadur (2008) *Minorities and Indigenous Peoples of Nepal*, Kathmandu: National Coalition Against Racial Discrimination.

Bennett, Lynn and Dilip Parajuli (2013), *The Nepali Multidimensional Exclusion Index*, Kathmandu: Himal Books.

Bista, Dor Bahadur (1991), *Fatalism and Development: Nepal's Struggle for Modernization*, Calcutta: Orient Longman.

Terai Justice Center, *Nyai Ko Khoji, Samabesi Najir Sangrah* (2013).

Tilouine, Marie Lecomte and Dollfus Pascale, (2013), *Ethnic Revival and Religious Turmoil, Identities and* Representation *in the Himalayas.*

Thapa, Deepak and Bandana Sijapati (2003), *A Kingdom under Seize: Nepal's Maoist Insurgency, 1996 to 2003*, Kathmandu: The Print House.

Vollan, Kare (2015), *Elections in Nepal: Identifying the Politically Excluded Groups: A Study of the Parliamentary Election Results from 1991 to 2013*, Kathmandu, Himal Books.

B. Reports and Articles

CBS (2005), *Poverty Trends in Nepal (1995-96 and 2003-04)*, Kathmandu: Central Bureau of Statistics.

CBS (2011), *Nepal Living Standard Survey 2010/11*, Kathmandu: Central Bureau of Statistics.

Crisis Group (2007), Nepal's Troubled Terai Region.

Crisis Group (2016), Nepal's Divisive New Constitution: An Existential Crisis.

DFID and World Bank (2006), *Unequal Citizens*, Kathmandu: DFID and World Bank.

Gellner, David N., Jonna Pfaff-Czarnecka and John Whelpton, eds. (1997), *Nationalism and Ethnicity in a Hindu Kingdom: The Politics of Culture in Contemporary Nepal*, Amsterdam: Harwood Academic Publishers.

Gellner, David N., ed. (2007), Caste, Ethnicity and Inequality in Nepal. *Economic and Political Weekly* XLII (20): 1823-1827.

Hachhethu, Krishna (2014), Balancing Identity and Viability: Restructuring Nepal into a Viable Federal State. In Budhi Karki and Rohan Edrisinha, eds. *The Federalism Debate in Nepal*, Kathmandu: SPCBN/ UNDP/Nepal, pp. 33-52.

Hachhethu, Krishna, Tula Narayan Shah and Ram Kumar Kamat (2015), *Politics of Representation in Nepal*, Kathmandu: Nepal Madhesh Foundation.

Hachhethu, Krishna (2015), (8 July). Issue of Proportional Inclusive Representation (in Nepali), *Kantipur.*

Hasan, Zoya (2010), *'Politics of Inclusion', Castes, Minorities, and Affirmative Action'.*

Haviland, Charles, BBC News, Why is Nepal's New Constitution Controversial? September 19, 2015.

HRW (2015), "Like we are not Nepali."

NESAC (1998) *Nepal: Human Development Report 1998*, Kathmandu: Nepal South Asia Centre.

Neupane, Govinda (2000), *Ethnic Issue of Nepal* (in Nepali), Kathmandu: Centre for Development Studies.

'No, I Am More Backward Than You Are!': The Discourse on Reservations

Indra Sawhney vs. Union of India (1992).

Phuyal, Hari, "Nepal's New Constitution: 65 Years in the Making", 18 September 2015.

Tamang, Mukta S. (2006), Culture, Caste, Ethnicity in the Maoist Movement. *Studies in Nepali History and Society* 11 (2): 271–301.

UNDP (2009), *Nepal: Human Development Report 2008*, Kathmandu: UNDP/Nepal.

UNDP (2014), *Nepal: Human Development Report 2014: Beyond Geography: Unlocking Human Potential*, Kathmandu: UNDP/Nepal.

Gender Audit Report of IDEA 2016.

The Supreme Court of Nepal's Appointment Guidelines, 2069.

The Civil Service Act of Nepal, 2049.

The Bangalore Principles of Judicial Conduct, 2002.

The Bejing Statement of Principles of the Independence of the Judiciary in the Lawasia Region, 1997.

THRDA and AHRC (2016), Nepal Protest and Repression.

Books

Austin, Granvile (1972), *The Indian Constitution: Cornerstone of a Nation.*

Bhandari, Surendra (2016), *Constitutional Design and Implementation Dyanmics*, Himal Innovative Development and Research Pvt. Ltd., Kathmandu.

Jha, Prashant (2014), *Battles of the New Republic: A Contemporary History of Nepal*, New Delhi: Aleph.

Karki, Budhi and Rohan Edrisinha, eds. (2014), *The Federalism Debate in Nepal*, Kathmandu: SPCBN/UNDP/Nepal.

Lawoti, Mahendra (2005), *Towards a Democratic Nepal: Inclusive Political Institutions for a Multicultural Society*, Kathmandu: Mandala Book Point.

Lawoti, Mahendra (2010), *Federal State Building*. Kathmandu: Bhrikuti.

Manandhar, Mangal Siddhi and Pushpa Sharma (2009), *Bases of Federalism and Demarcation of Provincial Boundary* (in Nepali), Kathmandu: National Coalition against Racial Discrimination.

Malagoali, Mara (2013), *Constitutional Nationalism and Legal Exclusion*, Oxford University Press, New Delhi.

Mishra, Chaitanya and Om Gurung, eds. (2012), *Ethnicity and Federalism in Nepal*, Kathmandu: Central Department of Sociology/Anthropology, Tribhuvan University.

Riaz, Ali and Subho Basu (2007), *Paradise Lost: State Failure in Nepal*. New Delhi: Adarsh Books.

Shrestha, Rajendra (2009), *World Federal States: Constitutional Assembly and Roadmap to Nepal* (in Nepali), Kathmandu: Centre for Federal Studies.

Parliamentary Election Results from 1991 to 2013, Kathmandu: Social Science Baha and Himal Books.